NAZISM
AND WAR

Also by Richard Bessel

Political Violence and the Rise of Nazism
(editor) *Life in the Third Reich*
Germany after the First World War
(editor) *Fascist Italy and Nazi Germany*

NAZISM AND WAR

RICHARD BESSEL

Weidenfeld & Nicolson

LONDON

First published in Great Britain in 2004 by
Weidenfeld & Nicolson

A CIP catalogue record for this book is
available from the British Library.

ISBN 0 297 64696 6

Typeset and printed in Great Britain by
Butler and Tanner Ltd, Frome and London

Weidenfeld & Nicolson

The Orion Publishing Group Ltd
Orion House
5 Upper Saint Martin's Lane
London WC2H 9EA

www.orionbooks.co.uk

CONTENTS

ILLUSTRATIONS

1 Hitler reviews a paramilitary march in Munich, 1923
2 Chancellor Hitler bows to Reich President von Hindenburg, 1933
3 Artillery display at Nuremberg in 1937
4 Military conscription, 1935
5 Jewish humiliation in Vienna, 1938
6 Berliners inspect a damaged shop after 'Crystal Night', 1938
7 Hitler revisits a 1917 battlefield near Vimy in 1940
8 Hitler pays tribute to Germany's volunteers of 1914
9 Ecstatic crowds acclaim Hitler in Berlin in 1940
10 Captured Soviet soldiers in 1941
11 Berliners killed by Allied bombing, 1943
12 Germans fleeing from Soviet forces, 1945
13 Soviet tanks near the Reichstag, 1945
14 German soldiers march into captivity, 1945
15 Bodies bulldozed into a mass grave at Belsen, 1945

Robert Hunt Library: 1
The Imperial War Museum: 5, 10, 11, 15
AKG Images London: 2, 3, 6, 14
Mit Hitler im Westen: 7, 8, 9
Getty Images/Hulton Archive: 4, 12, 13

ACKNOWLEDGEMENTS

This short book is an attempt to examine Nazism by focusing on what lay at its core: racist war. That is what provides its narrative framework, and the criteria for selecting the themes which have been included and the themes which have had to be left out. The bulk of the text was drafted while I was in Germany in the autumn of 2002 and the winter of 2003. During that time I had the great privilege to enjoy the hospitality and resources first of the Universität der Bundeswehr in Hamburg and then the Max-Planck-Institut für Geschichte in Göttingen. I wish to thank my academic colleagues and the support staff of these two fine institutions, without whose help I could not have written this book. In particular, I want to acknowledge my debt of gratitude to two colleagues who made my stays in Hamburg and Göttingen possible, productive and pleasant: Professor Bernd Wegner at the Bundeswehr-Universität and Professor Alf Lüdtke at the Max-Planck-Institut. Both have helped me enormously, not least through discussions over the years, to think my way through the themes discussed here. I would also like to thank the Alexander-von-Humboldt Stiftung for support over the years which made possible earlier periods of research in Germany; that research, on the aftermaths of the two world wars, has found its way into this book both directly and indirectly. At a time when universities and research institutes find themselves under increasing financial pressure, it is all the more important to acknowledge institutions which by their practice continue to affirm that scholarly research is a matter not just of costs but also of values.

ABBREVIATIONS

BDM *Bund deutscher Mädel* (League of German Girls)

DAF *Deutsche Arbeitsfront* (German Labour Front)

DP Displaced Persons

Gestapo *Geheime Staatspolizei* (Secret State Police)

HJ *Hitler Jugend* (Hitler Youth)

KPD *Kommunistische Partei Deutschlands* (Communist Party of Germany)

NSDAP *Nationalsozialistische Deutsche Arbeiterpartei* (National Socialist German Workers Party)

NSF *Nationalsozialistische Frauenschaft* (National Socialist Women's Organization)

OKH *Oberkommando des Heeres* (Supreme Command of the Army)

OKW *Oberkommando der Wehrmacht* (Supreme Command of the Wehrmacht)

RAF Royal Air Force

RSHA *Reichssicherheitshauptamt* (Reich Security Main Office)

SA *Sturmabteilungen* (Storm Sections)

SD *Sicherheitsdienst* (Security Service)

SPD *Sozialdemokratische Partei Deutschlands* (Social Democratic Party of Germany)

SRP *Sozialistische Reichspartei* (Socialist Reich Party)

SS *Schutzstaffel* (Protection Squads)

INTRODUCTION

Nazism was inseparable from war. As a political movement, German National Socialism grew and triumphed in a country deeply scarred by the experience of and defeat in the First World War. Its leader had found meaning for his own life in war, which he described as 'the most memorable period of my life' compared with which 'all the past fell away into oblivion'.[1] As a political ideology, Nazism revolved around war and struggle: to fight was at once the main purpose of a nation and the measure of the health of a 'race'. The ideology of Nazism was an ideology of war, which regarded peace merely as preparation for war, which posited an eternal struggle between supposed races and which was realized in wars launched in order to redraw the racial map of the European continent. The political practice of Nazism was aggressive and bellicose, bringing violence to Germany's streets and glorying in uniformed, military-style formations of political soldiers. The language of war was rarely absent from the propaganda of the Nazi movement and the Nazi regime. Once its leadership had captured state power, they steered a remarkably consistent, if irrational and ultimately self-destructive, course to war. The Nazi leadership sought to militarize the German economy and society, and to indoctrinate the German population into the willing acceptance and even enthusiastic approval of war. It launched a Second World War which proved even more destructive than the First. It changed the nature of war, adding to the horrors of mass conflict in an industrial age the barbarism of a racist war of extermination. It offered the German people participation not in a democratic political process but in violence and war. It brought war to almost every corner of the European continent, and into the lives of almost every German family. It brought to Germany a defeat such as no nation had experienced before, and in its wake left the

Germans to emerge somehow from the political, economic, social and psychological wreckage of the most terrible war which human beings had ever fought and the most terrible killing frenzy in the history of humanity.

Nazism and war form the hinge on which not just Germany's but Europe's twentieth century turned. At the centre of the tumultuous history of Europe during the twentieth century was the spread and then the eventual containment, after enormous bloodshed, of the shock waves created by the First World War.[2] With the First World War, the veneer of civility and, indeed, of civilization was stripped from societies across the European continent. The guns of August 1914 heralded an era in which tens of millions of Europeans met violent deaths and hundreds of millions were subjugated by cruel dictatorships in which the good of the individual was subordinated to what was held to be the collective good. With the destruction of the Third Reich in 1945, the tide was turned, through a savagely destructive world war and at enormous cost. Yet it was not until the end of the twentieth century, with the passing of the post-war epoch, with German unification and the collapse of Communism in the Soviet Union and across Eastern Europe, that the profoundly destructive developments which followed from the catastrophe of the First World War largely were laid to rest on the European continent.

It follows that the origins of Nazism are seen here not to lie primarily in long-established social and economic structures somehow peculiar to Germany but rather in the profoundly destabilizing effects of the First World War and Germany's defeat. Nevertheless, Nazism also was a manifestation and the culmination of a long-running theme in modern European history, namely racism. The belief that human beings can be divided into 'races', and that these 'races' can be ordered in a hierarchy of human worth, took shape and gained widespread support long before the guns began firing in 1914. Nazism needs therefore to be understood as an expression of a system of thought and belief which gained wide currency in nineteenth-century Europe, and which hardly was unique to Germany. What was unique to Germany, however, was that a band of political gangsters, inspired by a crude racist ideology, was able to capture power in one of the world's most developed industrial nations and to use that power to make war on a hitherto unimaginable scale. It is this fact which allowed Nazism to become the most terrible application of racism that has yet surfaced in the history of the world.

The Nazi campaigns of racist genocide – above all, the attempt to wipe out the entire Jewish population of Europe – have, rightly, come to occupy centre stage in recent research on the Third Reich. As interest in class and class consciousness has waned with the retreat of Marxism as an inspiration for historians, as new archival sources have become available, particularly on the activities of the Nazi wartime occupiers in eastern Europe, and as historians have come to take Nazi ideology more seriously, 'race' has been put at the centre of historical investigations. Not just burgeoning research on the murder of Europe's Jews[3] and the impressive and detailed investigations of Nazi occupation and genocide in eastern Poland (Galicia), Belarus and the Baltic countries,[4] but also studies of the leadership corps of the Reich Security Main Office, who formed the executive corps of the campaigns of genocide,[5] of the regulation of marriage and of family policy in Nazi Germany,[6] of the Nazi assault on Europe's Gypsies,[7] of the treatment of people labelled 'asocial',[8] of the criminal investigative police in the Third Reich,[9] of Nazi settlement polities,[10] of the economic empire created by the SS,[11] of medicine and eugenics,[12] just to name a few, have placed 'race' at the centre of their deliberations. To write about Nazism today is to write about Nazi racism and its realization in deliberate, organized, comprehensive campaigns of mass murder. At its most strident, the new paradigm has been presented by Michael Burleigh and Wolfgang Wippermann, who write: 'The main object of [Nazi] social policy remained the creation of a hierarchical racial new order. Everything else was subordinate to this goal, including the regime's conduct of foreign affairs and the war. In the eyes of the regime's racial politicians, the Second World War was above all a racial war, to be pursued with immense brutality until the end'.[13] It is difficult to disagree. Burleigh and Wippermann present an uncompromising argument that interpretations based upon totalitarianism, modernization or global theories of Fascism miss the mark because they fail to address what really mattered about National Socialism: racially inspired war and mass murder.

Yet a narrow concentration on 'race' runs the risk of neglecting important aspects of the history of Nazism – the development of the economy in the Third Reich, the everyday lives of Germans under the

Nazi regime, the attractions of abolishing class differences in a Nazi 'People's Community' (*Volksgemeinschaft*), the military build-up and military campaigns which were, after all, the main preoccupation of Hitler for much of his time as leader of the 'racial state'. Of course, none of these themes can be separated from Nazi racism. The Third Reich may have been one of the great redistributive regimes of modern times, aiming at equality and a classless society among members of the *Volksgemeinschaft*; however, this ultimately rested on the exploitation of other peoples and the systematic looting of the property of Jews who were sent to their deaths.[14] In the Third Reich, the main function of the economy was to provide the resources necessary to fight racial wars; the everyday concerns and opportunities of Germans were affected increasingly by propaganda and policies which had ideas of race at their centre; the *Volksgemeinschaft* was one in which an army officer might marry the daughter of a worker but not a Jew; the welfare of the German people depended increasingly on the enslavement of others; and the German military knowingly and willingly engaged in wars of racial extermination. In a memorable phrase, Götz Aly has described this recently as a 'unity of economic, social, racial, and war policy, which secured support for this state'.[15] The Nazi concept of 'race' and the belief in an essential and eternal struggle between races were about war – war against the political enemy within, war against the Jews, war against the Slavs and war against anyone who stood in the way of plans for racially pure Germans to enslave their neighbours and to settle across the European continent.

This book aims to present a concise discussion of Nazism by focusing upon what lay at its core: racially conceived struggle and war. War was both cause and effect, condition and consequence of Nazism. War was the precondition of the Nazis' success and the essence of the Nazi project; it dominated the activities of the Nazi regime and the lives of people subjugated by Nazi rule; and the consequences of the wars launched by the Third Reich long outlasted Nazism itself. This is what gives this book its structure: four essays which explore the relationship between German National Socialism and war, laid out in chronological sequence: the aftermath of the First World War, without which the rise and triumph of Nazism would have been difficult to imagine; the path to the Second World War, which dominated Nazi policy once Hitler had become head of the German government; the conduct of the Second World War, in which Nazi ideology was made real in a racist war of extermination; and the aftermath of the Second World War, in which the wreckage left behind by Nazism affected the lives of Germans and Europeans far beyond May 1945.

Approaching the history of Nazism in this frame allows, indeed requires, integrating political, economic, social, and military history. It offers a path through some of the immense quantity of specialist literature on the history of the Third Reich which has been generated over the past few decades. It necessarily extends the chronological boundaries of a history of Nazism beyond the dates, 1933 and 1945, which mark the beginning and end of Hitler's rule. That is to say, it means examining Nazism both as the post-history of what preceded it, namely the First World War, and as the pre-history of what occurred after the eradication of the Third Reich in May 1945. Nazism not only left unparalleled misery in its wake; it was also followed by the eventual establishment of a remarkably stable and prosperous (West) Germany and (western) Europe. This post-war success story, if that is what it was, was also a consequence of Nazism and war, but it was realized at enormous cost – on a divided continent and upon the bones of tens of millions of people who died as a consequence of the violence and destruction unleashed by Nazi Germany. The rise and fall of Nazism, and the wars launched by the Third Reich, profoundly affected German and European society, politics and mentalities, and would continue to do so for decades. This makes it all the more necessary to approach the history of Nazism not as some exotic *sui generis* horror show which can be condemned as a singular and unique eruption of evil, but to try to understand it as a terrifying part of the history of the imperfect world in which we live.

CHAPTER ONE

....

THE AFTERMATH OF THE FIRST WORLD WAR AND THE RISE OF NAZISM

Writing in *Mein Kampf*, while in prison after his conviction for leading the failed Munich Beer Hall *Putsch* of November 1923, Adolf Hitler described how his First World War ended:

> During the night of October 13th–14th [1918] the British opened an attack with gas on the front south of Ypres. They used the yellow gas whose effect was unknown to us, at least from personal experience. I was destined to experience it that very night. On a hill south of Werwick [Wervock], in the evening of October 13th, we were subjected for several hours to a heavy bombardment with gas bombs, which continued throughout the night with more or less intensity. About midnight a number of us were put out of action, some for ever. Towards morning I also began to feel pain. It increased with every quarter of an hour; and about seven o'clock my eyes were scorching as I staggered back and delivered the last dispatch I was destined to carry in this war. A few hours later my eyes were like glowing coals, and all was darkness around me.
>
> I was sent into hospital at Pasewalk in Pomerania, and there it was that I had to hear of the Revolution.[1]

In his self-dramatizing account of how, as a blinded corporal, he had learned of the Armistice and Revolution, Hitler claimed:

The more I tried to glean some definite information of the terrible events that had happened, the more my head became afire with rage and shame. What was all the pain I suffered in my eyes compared with this tragedy?

The following days were terrible to bear, and the nights still worse. To depend on the mercy of the enemy was a precept which only fools or criminal liars could recommend. During those nights my hatred increased – hatred for the originators of this dastardly crime.

For Hitler, the lesson was clear:

There was no such thing as coming to an understanding with the Jews. It must be the hard-and-fast 'Either-Or'.

For my part, I then decided that I would take up political work.[2]

This statement tells us a great deal about the origins of Nazism and Nazi politics: as a consequence of a lost world war, expressing blind hatred, and uncompromising in its violent hostility to Germany's supposed enemies and particularly to the Jews. It is difficult to imagine a more revealing end to the First World War than that experienced by Adolf Hitler: lying in a military hospital in provincial Pomerania, temporarily blinded by a mustard-gas attack in Flanders[3] – a helpless invalid – as the German armies collapsed and the hopes and illusions which had sustained support for Germany's war effort evaporated. If there was a single, identifiable moment when Nazism was born, it was in that Pasewalk military hospital in November 1918.

The sudden, catastrophic and, for most Germans, unexpected end of the First World War came as a tremendous shock, and was accompanied and compounded by the shock of political revolution. The apparent unity which had greeted the outbreak of the war in 1914 – itself more a reflection of how the events of August 1914 were reported and subsequently perceived than of the actual reactions of Germans at the time[4] – was overtaken by open, bitter and violent division. Whereas, most Germans believed, the Great War had begun with a people united in their devotion to their country, it ended with the abdication of the Kaiser and the discredit and disintegration of the imperial system amidst social and economic disorder. It was not the military superiority of the Allies, reinforced by hundreds of thousands of fresh American troops in 1918, that framed Germans' memories of the defeat, but their own collapse. Widespread discontent over hardship within Germany during the war; working-class radicalism and strikes; the 'covert military strike' of German soldiers after the failed offensives of early 1918;[5] and finally, in late October and early November, the mutiny of sailors at Kiel and Wilhelmshaven, rebelling at the prospect of being sent on a hopeless suicide mission when the war was as good as lost, helped precipitate the fall of the Kaiser. The Social Democratic politicians into whose laps the German government fell in November 1918 hardly enjoyed universal popular support. Instead, they faced an embittered, suffering population filled with unrealistic expectations about what peace could bring and profoundly divided as to how they viewed the road ahead.

In the months which followed the Armistice and revolution, Germany appeared to sink into economic and political chaos. Although the political transition of November 1918 itself was remarkably peaceful, and although the return and demobilization of Germany's wartime armies proceeded much more smoothly than anyone had predicted, bloodshed soon followed. In what had been the eastern Prussian provinces of Posen and West Prussia, Polish insurgents managed to wrest territories with a majority Polish population from German control. In Berlin, an ill-prepared Communist uprising in January 1919 was easily crushed and the Spartacist leaders Rosa Luxemburg and Karl Liebknecht were murdered. In Germany's industrial areas (in particular, the Ruhr) there were strikes, sharply declining productivity and violence. As the old army withered away, the government aided the formation of, and became dependent upon, freebooter military formations – the *Freikorps*. Consisting of veterans of the war and school-leavers who had missed their opportunity to fight in the trenches, the *Freikorps* units suppressed supposed left-wing threats to the government, often in an extremely brutal and bloody manner, and served as an introduction to politics for many men who later figured large in the Nazi movement. Shortages of coal and food, transport difficulties and raging inflation made Germans' lives a misery. Political uncertainty and economic chaos was reflected in rising crime levels, as property crime soared against a background of inflation and violent confrontations became increasingly common.[6] The

well-ordered society which Germans thought they knew seemed to have
vanished. Shortly before his death in 1990, the great German-Jewish
sociologist Norbert Elias reminisced: 'I still clearly remember the experience that the war suddenly was over. Suddenly order fell apart. Everyone
had to rely on himself. One knew that peace had arrived, Germany had
been defeated, which was sad, and then one tried quite simply to get on
with life.'[7]

The First World War had left Germany a much less civilized, much
rougher place in which 'to get on with life'. Not surprisingly, this
provoked widespread resentment. Faced with the disintegration of
order, Germans looked for somewhere to place blame for the catastrophe which had befallen them. Rather than confront the hard
truths about how their country had got into, fought and had been
impoverished by the war, they looked angrily in two directions:
externally, at the Allies who imposed the allegedly intolerable Versailles
'*Diktat*' upon a prostrate Germany; and internally, at those at home
who supposedly had stabbed Germany in the back. The Versailles
Treaty, which Germany was compelled to sign in July 1919, came as a
terrible shock. For Germans, many of whom at the time of the
Armistice had looked forward in naïve hope to a peace inspired by
the lofty principles enunciated by American President Woodrow
Wilson in the autumn of 1918, the treaty seemed unbearably harsh.
The loss of territories in the west (Alsace-Lorraine, Eupen-Malmedy),
the north (northern Schleswig) and, most importantly, in the east
(Posen, West Prussia, parts of Upper Silesia), the imposition of a huge
reparations bill which would take decades to pay and the 'war-guilt
clause' which ascribed blame for the outbreak of war to the German
government were regarded as intolerable and unfair. Without the
economic resources which the Versailles settlement removed from the
Reich, it appeared to many that the country's future was bleak. Thus
it became easy to ascribe Germany's difficulties during the 1920s not
to the material and social costs of a lost world war, but to an allegedly
unjust peace settlement imposed on a prostrate country by the Allies.
Condemnation of the Versailles settlement was voiced not only on
the right but across the political spectrum; indeed, hostility to the
Versailles '*Diktat*' became perhaps the only point of consensus in the
conflict-ridden world of Weimar politics.

The question of how Germany had landed in this mess was no less damaging to responsible democratic politics. Many Germans came to believe that, after steadfastly defending Germany against a world of enemies for four long years, the armed forces had collapsed because of treason at home. Not the superiority of the Allies but a 'stab in the back' was the alleged cause of the sudden, unexpected defeat. Given the context of Germany's defeat in the First World War – with German armies still on occupied enemy soil, after having knocked Russia out of the conflict and having imposed a punitive peace on the defeated power to the east, and after years of optimistic propaganda and news management by a high command and government which promoted illusions about Germany's prospects – it was easy to believe that German soldiers had not been defeated on the field but instead had been undermined by traitors and revolutionaries at home. Whereas the frontline soldiers allegedly had fought an heroic struggle to the end, it was the faint-hearted population at home, whose morale had been sapped by shortages, hardship and unscrupulous left-wing agitators who knew no Fatherland, who supposedly had failed to sustain Germany's war effort. A myth of heroic struggle was coupled with a myth of betrayal, and the myths proved easier to swallow than the ambiguous, messy and uncomfortable reality of how Germany in fact had lost the war.

The politically corrosive myth-building began the moment Germany gave up the hopeless military struggle. In mid-November 1918, for example, the Prussian War Ministry gave instructions for the 'festive welcome' for 'our field-grey heroes [who] return to the Heimat undefeated, having protected the native soil from the horrors of war for four years'.[8] Friedrich Ebert, the Social Democrat who assumed the leadership of Germany's provisional government after the November Revolution and who himself had lost two sons in the war, spoke in similar terms when he greeted returning German troops in Berlin on 10 December 1918, declaring: 'Your sacrifice and deeds are without parallel. No enemy defeated you!'[9] Although Ebert also observed that 'only once the superiority of the opponents in men and materiel became ever greater did we give up the struggle', a pattern had been set. The assertion was accepted that German forces had been undefeated on the battlefield. But if not on the battlefield, then where? Soon after the armistice was signed, the allegation was heard increasingly in Germany that the Reich had been 'stabbed in the back' at home. This claim was taken up, and amplified in a characteristically disingenuous manner, by Field Marshal Paul von Hindenburg, who testified to a parliamentary committee of investigation in November 1919 that Germany had lost the war not because of a failure on the part of the military leadership or of the fighting troops, but because the *Heimat* had not remained steadfast. In a sentence which would have far-reaching repercussions, Hindenburg repeated the allegation, which had been circulating since December 1918, that, as an 'English general' supposedly had said, 'the German army was stabbed in the back'.[10]

Hindenburg, who together with Erich Ludendorff had been responsible for the conduct of Germany's war from 1916 to 1918, should have known better. But that did not prevent the phrase from becoming fixed in the political vocabulary of Weimar and Nazi Germany, or from being taken up by millions of people who had their own reasons for accepting stab-in-the-back legend rather than facing the messy truth about what had occurred when Germany lost the First World War. Thus the stage was set for the substitution of memories of the war experience by a myth of war experience. Rather than seeing it as senseless slaughter in the service of an autocratic regime, Germans could, in the words of George Mosse, look 'back upon the war as a meaningful and even sacred event. [...] The Myth of the War Experience was designed to mask war and legitimize the war experience; it was meant to displace the reality of war.'[11]

The way in which Germany's First World War ended and was remembered had grave consequences. It meant that the new, democratic republican order which emerged after 1918 and which was a product of defeat, faced division from the outset: a large proportion of the German population – the majority as it turned out – remained either sullenly hostile or violently opposed to the new democratic 'system'. It meant that those who had been responsible for Germany's catastrophic participation in the First World War – which left more than two million Germans dead, millions more scarred for life, former German territories to the west, north and east taken from German control, and an economy in deep trouble – were able to evade their responsibility. It meant that the new republican government faced popular expectations which, in the extraordinarily difficult position in which it found itself diplomatically and economically, it could not hope to fulfil. And it meant that Germans did not really come to terms with their defeat and make the transition from a wartime to a peacetime society after 1918. The hatred so frequently given expression in German political life – against the Versailles 'Diktat', against democratic politicians, against the alleged 'November criminals', against the rich, against Jews and foreigners – was in large measure a legacy of the First World War.

This provided fertile ground for the growth of a political movement built on hatred, committed to liquidating the political system which emerged from military defeat, overcoming political and social divisions through the establishment of a German 'people's community' (*Volksgemeinschaft*) and reversing 'the terrible events', 'the dastardly crime' of November 1918. Adolf Hitler, who quite literally could not see what was happening in Germany when the Armistice was signed, was determined that the stab-in-the-back never should happen again. Never again would there be a betrayal at home of German soldiers at the front; never again would allegedly un-German elements be allowed to spread their poison among the civilian population. The answer to the rhetorical question Hitler asked in the passage of *Mein Kampf* describing his experience of November 1918 – 'Were we still worthy to partake in the glory of the past?'[12] – would become an emphatic 'Yes'. The shame of 1918 would be expunged, through either total victory or total defeat. The traitorous elements would be eliminated; there would be no second armistice.

The German Workers Party, later to become the National Socialist German Workers Party (or Nazi Party), was born in the immediate aftermath of the First World War. It had been founded on 9 January 1919 – one of many small, right-wing political groupings which sprang up in Munich in the chaotic conditions which followed defeat and revolution. Munich, perhaps even more than Berlin, had experienced profound political upheaval after the war. Here the Bavarian Wittelsbach monarchy fell on 7 November, two days before the Kaiser abdicated, and was followed by a succession of radical left-wing regimes, the last of which (the Munich Soviet Republic, which looked to Moscow for its inspiration) was crushed at the beginning of May after a chaotic month in power. Eventually it was succeeded by a conservative Bavarian government which created a congenial home for right-wing opponents of the republican government in Berlin. The future leader of the Nazi Party had returned to Munich from Pasewalk on 21 November, but remained in the army as long as he could; indeed, he was not formally discharged until the end of March 1920. In this, Hitler was quite unlike the great mass of the veterans of the First World War, who wanted nothing more than to leave the military behind and return to civilian life. Hitler found employment in the army as a *V-Mann* (*Vertrauensmann*, an informant) and, after being assigned to an anti-Bolshevik 'instruction course', became one of a squad of army informants charged with the surveillance of the many radical political groups which were springing up in the Bavarian capital. It was in this role that, on 12 September 1919, he attended a meeting of the German Workers Party. A few days later, he became a member.[13]

Hitler's path into politics, joining the small, 'boring' German Workers Party, was a direct consequence of his experience of the end of the First World War and of his continued employment by the army. In this very tangible sense, Nazism was linked with war from its beginnings as a political movement. There were other links as well, including the *Freikorps*, which in many respects functioned as a 'vanguard of Nazism'.[14] The *Freikorps* units, which were led by officers with recent war experience and which numbered roughly 250,000 men in March 1919,[15] served not only to buttress the army and protect the government against real and imagined threats from the left; they also carried war into the post-war period and provided a temporary home for many men who later became prominent in the Nazi movement. Among these were Ernst Röhm, who was Chief of Staff in the *Freikorps Epp*; Rudolf Hess, who had been a member of the *Freikorps Epp*; Martin Bormann, who had served with the *Freikorps Rossbach*; Viktor Lutze, who had joined the *Organisation Heinz* and the *Freischar Schill*; and Reinhard Heydrich, who had served under General Maercker in the *freiwilliges Landesjägerkorps*.

Given that almost all young adult German males had served in the armed forces during the war, it was inevitable that veterans of the trenches would loom large in the unrest and radical politics of the post-war years. However, it was not just the experience of combat during and after the First World War that shaped Nazism and the Third Reich. Many of those who became instrumental in carrying out the most radical Nazi policies, including the policies of genocide, were of the generation which experienced the war and post-war unrest as adolescents (more often than not with their fathers away at the front).[16] Their war had been the experience of the home front, but was no less important for that. Indeed, it was in this generation, more than the 'front generation', that the acute observer Sebastian Haffner discerned the roots of Nazism: 'The truly Nazi generation was formed by those born in the decade from 1900 to 1910, who experienced war as a great game and were untouched by its realities.'[17]

The fledgeling Nazi movement – Hitler changed the name of the German Workers Party, which he quickly came to dominate, to the National Socialist German Workers Party on 7 August 1920 – was characterized by anti-Marxism, antisemitism, opposition to the Versailles settlement and a commitment to violence, domestic and foreign. Each of these attitudes stemmed from the war which had just been fought and lost; each pointed towards the war to which a future Nazi regime would dedicate itself. 'Marxist internationalism' was regarded as a threat which drew German workers away from their national, racial community and undermined the unity of the *Volk*, which had sabotaged Germany's struggle in 1918, and which therefore had to be broken. The Jews were regarded as a bacillus which lay behind the Marxist threat, which sought to pollute, weaken and destroy the German *Volk*, and therefore had to be eliminated. The Versailles settlement was seen as a means by which Germany's enemies aimed to keep the Reich prostrate for ever, and which had to be overturned not merely to restore the *status quo ante* but to allow Germany to expand and seize the 'living space' which it allegedly needed in the east. And violence was viewed as the means by which to achieve a Third Reich and a German-dominated Europe – by smashing the democratic Weimar 'system', destroying Marxism, solving the 'Jewish question', breaking the 'chains of Versailles' and building up the armed forces so that Germany again could go to war. In sum, Nazism was a movement which dedicated itself to waging war both within (against Marxists, Jews and their sympathizers inside Germany) and without, and which was guided by a racist view of the world which posited a hierarchy of human value with the German 'Aryan' at the top of the heap and 'the Jew' at the bottom.

In this the Nazi movement was hardly unique. Numerous radical right-wing fringe movements sprang up in the feverish and violence-soaked atmosphere in Germany after the First World War, drawing into their ranks the resentful, the angry, and the desperate who were deeply antagonistic towards the republican order which had come to power thanks to defeat in war. Violent hostility to the new republic, to the Marxists, to the Jews, and to Versailles attracted considerable support in the immediate post-war period. In place of the bitter divisions which weak Weimar governments appeared to amplify there was to be a united German *Volksgemeinschaft*, which would overcome class and social divisions and from which the racially 'foreign bodies' (*Fremdkörper*) would be removed. The violent rhetoric and practice of the Nazis – who quickly established strong-arm squads, the Storm Sections (*Sturmabteilung*, SA) which from 1921 were used aggressively to protect political meetings and to spread propaganda – fitted in with a climate of latent civil war characterized by *coup* attempts, hundreds of political murders, industrial unrest and rising crime. And the racist, antisemitic message of the Nazis, while it may have been more extreme than that offered by some of their competitors, was in tune with a climate which saw an upsurge in antisemitic incidents and violence.[18]

With Hitler at its helm, and his speeches drawing ever larger crowds from in and around Munich, the young Nazi movement attracted growing attention and support during the early 1920s. Then, with the failed Munich Beer Hall Putsch at the height of the inflation in November 1923, the immediate post-war period of Nazism came to a crashing end. It was one thing to launch rhetorical tirades against the alleged 'November criminals' in Berlin while enjoying the hospitality of the Bavarian government; it was quite another to commit a violent act of treason. With its inept attempt to bounce the Bavarian government into supporting the overthrow of the Berlin administration and challenging the Reich government by force, the Nazi movement met the same fate as the various left-wing groups which had violently confronted the German state in the immediate post-war years: when Hitler, with the former Quartermaster General of the old army Erich Ludendorff at his side, started his march on Berlin (imitating Mussolini's March on Rome the year before), he was stopped by armed force in front of the *Feldherrenhalle* near the centre of Munich. The Reichswehr may not have been able to defend the country against foreign armies, but, when push came to shove, the German army was prepared to defend the German state against violent overthrow from within.

The Beer Hall Putsch attempt was a turning-point in the history of Nazism, and in ways which were not necessarily apparent at the time. It marked the last in a series of attempts to overthrow the Weimar Republic during its early years. What had appeared to be the moment of the greatest instability of the Weimar Republic – with French and Belgian troops occupying the Ruhr to force Germany to pay reparations, with hyperinflation reaching levels of monetary depreciation never before seen in world history, with the German economy in freefall, with violent challenges coming from left and right – turned out to be the moment when the republic turned the corner to the relative stability of the mid-1920s. With the failed Nazi *coup* attempt, the stabilization of the currency soon afterwards, and the efforts of the German government under Gustav Stresemann to reach an accommodation with the French which would allow an end to the ruinous Ruhr occupation, the 'great disorder' of the immediate post-war period came to a close.

The Beer Hall Putsch also turned Hitler into a national figure. Not just the *coup* attempt, which had caused Germans in the north and east of the country to take note of the Nazi agitator in Bavaria, but even more so the subsequent trial (which Hitler turned into a platform for himself) brought the Nazi leader on to the front pages throughout the country. Perhaps most importantly, the failure of the putsch resulted in the Nazi movement breaking with much of its practice in the early post-war years. The involvement of Nazi storm-troopers with other armed paramilitary groups – which had intensified in early 1923 and contributed to the pressure on Hitler to take action in November lest his more radical supporters desert him – had led to disaster, and was reversed once the NSDAP was re-established in the mid-1920s. When the Nazi Party re-formed after Hitler's emergence from a remarkably light prison term for treason, it was no longer a veterans' movement willing to engage in violent extra-parliamentary action. It became a disciplined political party, committed to playing the parliamentary game in order to destroy parliamentary democracy.

When he re-established the Nazi Party in Munich on 27 February 1925, Hitler was determined not to repeat the errors which nearly had ended his political career in November 1923. Henceforth, the campaign against the Weimar system would be carried out within the framework of formal legality. The NSDAP would be a unified and centralized organization, based upon unconditional and undiluted loyalty to the leader. Nazi Party members were not allowed to belong to other political or paramilitary groups; the Nazi leadership was to ensure 'the internal unity of the movement and its organization from the ground up'; the SA was not to admit 'armed groups and formations' into its ranks, and was to be an unarmed squad whose tasks were protecting meetings and 'enlightening' the public. However, the basic goal of the Nazi movement remained the same: to fight 'the most dreadful enemy of the German people . . . Jewry and Marxism'.[19]

The party continued to aim to overcome class divisions among Germans, create a *Volksgemeinschaft* which would exclude the Jews, and destroy the Weimar system. It remained committed to a militant, anti-democratic, racist political programme and was uncompromising in its refusal to accept Germany's defeat in the First World War and the Versailles settlement. Yet times had changed since 1923. The disorder of the immediate post-war years had passed, and public support for political extremes had ebbed. German democracy might not have endeared itself to the German people, but during the mid-1920s it no longer appeared in imminent danger of destruction. In the national Reichstag elections of May 1928, the Nazi Party managed to attract a mere 2.6 per cent of the votes – less than half what the German *Völkisch* Freedom Party had gathered in the Reichstag elections of May 1924.

However, by 1928 the Nazis could boast a number of crucially important achievements. The NSDAP had begun successfully to extend beyond its early strongholds in Bavaria, becoming a national political party; in northern and eastern Germany, the various *völkisch* groups which had fought the 1924 elections under a single banner coalesced increasingly as Nazi Party organizations.[20] This meant that whereas in 1924 the Nazis had had to work alongside other *völkisch* organizations, by 1928 they had established a virtual monopoly of radical right-wing, racist politics in Germany. The NSDAP might still have been small, but it no longer had any major competitors for the racist vote. Although the Nazi Party did not yet attract a significant proportion of Germany's voters, it succeeded in attracting a substantial number of political activists: in late 1928, the NSDAP numbered roughly 100,000 members[21] – an impressive number for a party which had managed to attract a mere 810,000 votes nationally in May of that year. The Nazis also began to bring a younger generation into its ranks; in drawing young men into the storm-troopers organization and attracting remarkable levels of support among university students,[22] it managed to extend its support well beyond the generation of those who had fought in the First World War. And in Adolf Hitler the Nazis had a leader who aroused great public interest and popular support and who held an otherwise extremely fractious membership together in a disciplined political organization. Indeed, without Hitler at the helm, it is possible that the NSDAP would have fallen apart; the dictatorial 'leadership principle', with which Hitler legitimated his position, probably was a key to the survival of the Nazi movement during the relatively stable years of the Weimar Republic.

In effect, the resuscitated Nazi movement of the mid-1920s had to play a waiting game. It may have been 'a numerically insignificant ... radical-revolutionary splinter group incapable of exerting any noticeable influence on the great mass of the population and the course of political events', as a confidential report of the Reich Interior Minister put it in July 1927.[23] However, its achievements during this period – the creation of a disciplined party organization, the quashing of challenges to Hitler's leadership, the establishment of a virtual monopoly of radical-right politics in Germany – put it in a good position to profit from problems embedded in Weimar society and politics once these surfaced, as they did in the late 1920s and early 1930s.

Despite successes during the Stresemann era of the mid-1920s – relative economic stability and a reintegration into the community of nations – Weimar politics never acquired a solid democratic foundation. Political parties which accepted governmental responsibility were almost invariably rewarded at the polls with a drop in support; every party which participated in government coalitions between 1924 and 1928 received fewer votes in 1928 than it had four years previously. Political parties tended to see their role as furthering sectional social and economic interests rather than representing the welfare of the whole nation, and the German electorate cast their votes accordingly. A sizeable proportion of the German population, on both the left and the right, remained hostile not just to this or that government coalition or political party but to the republican system of government as a whole. Many Germans no doubt agreed with the sentiments which the Brandenburg regional association of the *Stahlhelm*, the right-wing veterans organization which numbered some 400,000 to 500,000 men nationwide during the mid-1920s, expressed in September 1928:

> We hate the present-day system with all our soul [...], because it obstructs our view for freeing our enslaved Fatherland and cleansing the German people of the untruthful war guilt, of gaining the necessary living space in the East, of making the German people again fit for military service.[24]

Notwithstanding the fact that in 1925 the First World War hero Paul von Hindenburg – hardly the embodiment of the democratic Weimar 'system' – had been elected Reich President after the death of Friedrich Ebert, hostility to the republican government in Berlin remained virulent. Indeed, the fact that this aged general attracted so broad a coalition of conservative and ring-wing voter support to become head of state of the German Republic was an ominous sign for the future.[25]

As the shrill war-cry of the *Stahlhelm* suggests, the legacy of the First World War poisoned the politics of Weimar Germany. It did so in a number of ways which created a climate in which Nazism would flourish. The first was the injection of violence into domestic politics. Amidst the chaos and bitter divisions of the immediate post-war years, political assassination had claimed the lives of, among others, Hugo Haase (one of the six-member Council of People's Representatives who had assumed

government responsibility in November 1918) in 1919; of Matthias Erz-
berger (the Centre Party politician who had signed the armistice in
1918 and later became Reich Finance Minister) in 1921; and of Walther
Rathenau (Foreign Minister, and wartime head of the Raw Materials War
Office) in 1922. *Freikorps* units had employed deadly violence liberally
as they crushed real and imagined left-wing rebellion. Paramilitary
formations became a pervasive feature of the Weimar political scene;
political rhetoric became extremely violent; and a widespread tacit
acceptance of violence formed one of the most important characteristics
of public life in Weimar Germany.[26] Second, it was accepted across the
German political spectrum that the Versailles Treaty was totally unjust,
that the reparations which arose from it were intolerable. This conviction buttressed the illusion that things would be all right once again
if only the external burdens, imposed by the vindictive Allies, could be
lifted. Rather than face the consequences of having fought and lost a
world war, Germans opted instead for a fundamentally irresponsible
politics, in which so much of their difficulties could be blamed on
external factors, on foreigners, on the Versailles 'Diktat'. Third, the
territorial losses, especially on the eastern side of the 'bleeding frontier'
with Poland, were regarded as an open wound and a constant reminder
of the lost war – and, for many, of the need to fight the next one.
Altogether, German society remained in a state of latent civil war which,
when the moment came, proved more than conducive to the growth of
the Nazi movement.

While war, foreign and domestic, played a huge role in the politics of
Weimar Germany, the number of men in the German military
remained quite small. The terms of the Versailles Treaty had limited
the German Army, the Reichswehr, to 100,000 men, about one-sixth
of the total under arms in Germany on the eve of war in 1913.
Furthermore, those who served in the Reichswehr were volunteers,
who had to sign up for twelve-year terms of duty. This meant that
the armed forces had much less direct interaction with German society
than had been the case before the Versailles Treaty came into force in
1920: there was no conscription; there was no steady stream of young
men emerging from the military into civilian life; a career in the

military was not open to all those who might want it. Yet Weimar Germany was permeated by memories of war, by the effects of the war, by military imagery and militaristic values. It became normal for political parties to have uniformed strong-arm squads. The Nazi Storm Sections of the SA formed the largest and most successful of such formations of 'political soldiers' by the end of the Weimar Republic, but they were hardly unique. The Communists had their Red Front Fighters League (and, when that was banned in 1929, the Fighting League against Fascism); the Social Democrats were supported by the *Reichsbanner Schwarz–Rot–Gold*, which boasted a substantial membership; and even the Catholic Centre Party, hardly renowned for its militancy or militarism, had its *Kreuzschar*. It was almost as if, in the absence of opportunities to sign up for the army, young men in Weimar Germany looked to various paramilitary organizations and uniformed squads to express their admiration for military values and to have an outlet for violence.

Not only was the Reichswehr unable to satisfy the desire of many young men for a military life; it also was unable to defend the country effectively against attack. While the Reichswehr could, if push came to shove, defend the state against internal rebellion, it was in no position to repel an external military threat, outnumbered as it was by the armies of France (750,000 men in 1925), Poland (300,000 men) and even Czechoslovakia (150,000 men).[27] Any illusion that the armed-forces leadership might have had about their ability to defend Germany was destroyed in 1923, when they had to look on powerlessly as French and Belgian forces marched into the Ruhr to extract reparations payments in kind.[28] No less serious was the danger posed by Poland. The Reichswehr regarded Poland as a serious military threat during the Weimar period, and was convinced that the German armed forces lacked the strength to deal with an attack by the new Polish state.[29] The Reichswehr could and did plan for future rearmament and future wars, planning which meant applying the lesson of the 1914–1918 conflict – namely, that war in an industrial age required the economy and society to be harnessed to military goals – and which framed an uneasy relationship with democratic political structures.[30] However, in the meantime it had to seek cooperation among 'patriotic' citizens, particularly along the poorly defended eastern border.

This left the army leadership in a difficult position, which provided a basis for the beginnings of its fateful relationship with the Nazi movement. While the Nazis continued to be regarded by many with suspicion and as perhaps not having given up the idea of violently overthrowing the government, on the ground in eastern Germany a basis for practical cooperation was taking shape in the early 1930s. The failure of the Reichswehr to reach an agreement with the SPD-led Prussian government about the organization of border defence in the east had made it appear all the more necessary to tap into the potential presented by the 'national' paramilitary formations which were a prominent feature of Weimar politics.[31] Particularly after the stunning success of the NSDAP in the Reichstag elections of September 1930, this meant looking to the Nazis. The Reichswehr leadership sought popular support for resistance to a possible Polish incursion, and an increasingly large proportion of patriotically minded (i.e. not Marxist) young men were to be found in Nazi formations (in particular, the SA), which therefore had to be taken into consideration in plans to defend the eastern borders.[32] Even though Hitler reportedly asserted, in Lauenburg (in Pomerania) in April 1932, that the Nazis would 'protect the German borders only after removal of the leaders of the present system',[33] SA members in fact proved quite willing to participate in border-defence formations during the final Weimar years. Nazi supporters were eager for military training and to confront the Poles, and the Reichswehr welcomed the help of those who offered it. This was particularly true in the 'island province' of East Prussia, which was cut off from the rest of the Reich by the Polish corridor and where the regional Reichswehr leadership included men who later would play noteworthy roles in the Third Reich: the commander of *Wehrkreis I* (East Prussia) from October 1929, Werner von Blomberg, who became Hitler's Reichswehr Minister in 1933; Blomberg's chief of staff Walther von Reichenau, who later became *Chef des Wehrmachtsamtes* and a Field Marschal during the Second World War (and who would expect his troops on the eastern front to be 'the bearer of a merciless racial idea');[34] and the divisional chaplain of the *Wehrkreis I*, Ludwig Müller, who became the first (and only) 'Reich Bishop' of the German Protestant Church (the Nazi 'German Christians') for a short period after Hitler achieved power.

Of course, Nazi storm-troopers and party activists were not solely, or primarily, concerned with border defence in the early 1930s. Their main focus was on the increasingly frenetic, and often violent, campaign to capture political power. Towards the end of the 1920s, with the beginnings of a new economic crisis (first felt actutely among agricultural producers) and the crumbling of support for the established middle-class parties, the NSDAP started to attract significant electoral backing. Provincial election results revealed growing support for the Nazis (from 4 per cent in Mecklenburg-Schwerin in June 1929 to nearly 7 per cent in Berlin in October 1929, 8.1 per cent in Lübeck in November, 11.3 per cent in Thuringia in December and 14.4 per cent in Saxony in June 1930), and local Nazi Party groups were forming up and down the country. The early 1930s saw an acceleration of political activity in a succession of election campaigns, which provided the occasion for huge waves of Nazi meetings, marches, propaganda and rallies. One of the most striking characteristics of those who became members of the rapidly expanding NSDAP and SA was the degree of active commitment which they displayed. Unlike membership in the established 'bourgeois' parties, membership of Nazi organizations meant constant activity, not just during the election campaigns which followed so closely on one another (and when a local party or SA group could be beating the Nazi drum every evening) but also during the periods in between. Nazi activists often travelled considerable distances, for example to hear a speech by Hitler or to engage in a major march of storm-troopers, contributed regularly to party funds, attended meeting after meeting and rally after rally. For many young men who joined the NSDAP and the SA during the 'period of struggle' (*Kampfzeit*), their service in the Hitler movement offered activity, adventure and a chance to escape from the boredom and isolation of their own homes and communities, as well as a substitute for military service. This was active politics, which could dominate the lives of those who opted for it.

Nazi politics was also violent politics. Although Hitler publicly and repeatedly committed his movement to 'legality' in its campaign to destroy the Weimar Republic, this essentially meant avoiding a direct and potentially catastrophic confrontation with the armed force of the state. It certainly did not mean avoiding violence. The Nazi movement remained militaristic and violent, and indeed this was among the attractions for the young men drawn to its ranks. Military-style hierarchy, marches and uniforms proved alluring – both to Nazi activists and to many bystanders who looked on approvingly, seeing in the Nazi movement a dynamic young force which would smash Marxism and the Weimar system and rejuvenate Germany in a martial spirit. Even though the Nazi storm-troopers were supposed to remain unarmed, the military-style training of the SA (including self-defence, field exercises and on occasion even practice with grenades and machine-guns) was common in the early 1930s.[35] As one storm-troopers' leader put it in September 1932, military exercises and weapons training formed an 'especially good means for raising the morale and fighting spirit of the SA'.[36] Hitler repeatedly used violent rhetoric, stressing that 'heads will roll' once the Nazis seized power.[37] In the case of the notorious Potempa murder of August 1932, the Nazi leader publicly declared his 'unbounded loyalty' to a band of Nazi thugs convicted of the murder of a Communist sympathizer brutally beaten to death in the Upper Silesian village.[38] Goebbels wrote of the storm-troopers during the *Kampfzeit* that 'the SA man wants to fight, and he also has a right to be led into battle. His existence wins its justification only in battle.'[39] The Nazi leadership conceived of politics as a 'battle', and made no secret of the fact.

This aggressive posturing was paralleled by violence on Germany's streets, and the Nazi movement gloried in it. From the late 1920s through 1933, the growth of the Nazi Party and of its propaganda activities were accompanied by a rise in the number of politically inspired violent incidents. Brawls resulting from political rallies and marches or from chance meetings of groups of differing political persuasions became increasingly common, as did beatings, stabbings and shootings. Rallies and marches became challenges, and challenges could not be left unanswered. The numbers of people injured and killed in violent political confrontations grew, and peaked in the summer of 1932, at the height of the frenetic electioneering which characterized the last year of the Weimar Republic. In one of the worst incidents, the Bloody Sunday of 17 July in Altona (bordering Hamburg), a confrontation between Communists and Nazi demonstrators left eighteen dead and sixty-eight wounded. Altogether, hundreds died and thousands were injured, and the Nazi movement glorified its dead as martyrs to the Nazi 'idea', to its

leader and to Germany. To be sure, the Nazis were not alone in fomenting
the climate of political violence. The Communists, in particular, admon-
ishing their supporters to 'hit the fascist wherever you meet him', gave
as good as they got;[40] and nor did the Social Democratic *Reichsbanner*
shy away from a fight. However, in the early 1930s politics increasingly
were conducted on the Nazis' terms, and their terms were violent.

Nevertheless, the Nazis had to be careful not to go too far. This was
demonstrated clearly in the wake of the Reichstag elections of 31 July
1932, when the NSDAP reached its peak of support in free elections,
capturing 37.4 per cent of the vote and becoming by far the largest
political party in the Reichstag. Yet this success at the ballot box did not
lead directly to power in Berlin. The Nazis had drawn on just about all
their reserves of support, barely increasing their share of the vote over
that in the Prussian and presidential elections of April 1932, and failing
significantly to dent the support of the two Marxist parties, the SPD
and KPD, or the Catholic Centre; and Reich President von Hindenburg
proved disinclined to allow Hitler, as leader of the largest party in the
parliament, to form a government.

Some of the Nazis' more intemperate supporters, particularly in the
eastern Prussian provinces, decided to take matters into their own hands
and engaged in a terrorist campaign of bombings, arson and assassination attempts.[41] However, this uncontrolled Nazi violence proved a
path not to power but to potential disaster. The police cracked down
quickly; the Reich government enacted stiff emergency legislation to
combat political terrorism; and the Nazi terror campaign was stopped
in its tracks. What is more, while limited political violence, particularly
against the Communists, had appeared to bring support to the Nazis –
either from those who liked beating their enemies or from those who
liked the idea of others beating their enemies – uncontrolled violence
alienated support: the terror campaign of early August 1932 clearly
contributed to the downturn in the NSDAP vote in November 1932. The
Nazis could play at bringing civil war to Germany, but they had to back
off before civil war actually came about.

It may seem odd, given what occurred in German-dominated Europe
during the early 1940s, that the main targets of Nazi violence during the
final years of the Weimar Republic were not Jews but Communists
and Social Democrats. Jews did not escape the attention of the storm-

troopers, of course, and no one could have been in any doubt that the NSDAP was a militantly racist and antisemitic party. However, attacks on Jews at this time appear almost an afterthought, an extra outlet for aggression, when viewed alongside attacks on supporters of the left.[42] The targets tended to be defenceless shopkeepers, lawyers or people of supposedly Jewish appearance attacked on the streets in fashionable parts of town (as in the notorious violence of roughly 500 SA men along the Kurfürstendamm in Berlin on 12 September 1932).[43] Jewish shop windows provided inviting targets for bricks and stones. This, of course, was to some extent a reflection of the composition of Germany's Jewish population, which was concentrated in commerce and the professions (with a disproportionally large number earning their living from medicine and the law).[44] In any event, the Jews at the receiving end of Nazi violence generally were not the sort of people accustomed to punch-ups or who easily could fight back. Unlike the more frequent assaults on the Nazis' Marxist political opponents, the attacks on Jewish targets essentially were superfluous to capturing power, yet they provided a constant backdrop to the successful political campaign of the NSDAP in the early 1930s.

It also appears that overt antisemitism may have been of secondary importance in gaining the Nazis popular support. Of course, there can be little doubt that prejudice against Jews, and racist attitudes generally, formed an obsessive motivation for many activists to join the Nazi movement during the 1920s and early 1930s.[45] However, the same cannot be said of the great majority of the millions who cast their votes for the NSDAP between 1930 and 1933. As the leadership of the Cologne chapter of the Central Association of German Citizens of Jewish Belief, the main Jewish organization in Weimar Germany, put it after the shock Nazi success in the September 1930 Reichstag elections, 'it certainly would be wrong to equate these $6\frac{1}{2}$ million [Nazi] voters with $6\frac{1}{2}$ million anti-semites'. The danger, they recognized, was rather different: namely that 'the aversion of the non-antisemitic voters of the Hitler Party against hatred of Jews was not so large as to deny the NSDAP their support'.[46]

Antisemitism, like rage at the Versailles Treaty and the refusal to recognize the 'bleeding frontier' with Poland, formed a general back-drop, a broad world-view about which many if not most Germans could agree. The reluctance of any political party publicly to defend Jewish

interests, the fact that antisemitism was by no means confined to the
Nazi Party and the widespread acts of violence and hostility committed
against Jews throughout the Weimar period all point to a broad culture
of toleration of antisemitism at the very least. Nazi activists made no
secret of their hatred of Jews and, even when the tactical considerations
dictated that other themes be more prominent in their propaganda
during the election campaigns of the early 1930s, antisemitism was never
absent from the Nazi repertoire. Nazi speakers fulminated about the
alleged crimes, malicious and all-pervading influence, depravity and
inherent inferiority of the Jews. Even when other topics were at the top of
the list in Nazi speeches, antisemitism and general racialist assumptions
provided the glue which held the ideology together. However, to assert
that the Nazis came to power primarily because they successfully tapped
into a deep, rabid antisemitic vein in the German body politic, although
this may be understandable given what happened during the Second
World War, probably would be mistaken.

Who, then, was drawn to the Nazi movement during its struggle for
power? What groups of Germans did a militantly anti-democratic,
antisemitic, bellicose, revanchist political party attract? The answer
appears to be: just about everyone, except Germany's Jews. The NSDAP
became, in the phrase of Thomas Childers, 'a unique phenomenon in
German electoral politics, a catchall party of protest',[47] one which by
1932 had managed to attract more support from a broader cross-
section of the German population than any other political party had
ever done before. Hitherto, German political parties essentially had
appealed to particular social and economic groups. The NSDAP was
different. The Nazi Party was more successful in attracting middle-
class voters than working-class voters, Protestants than Catholics, men
than women, Germans who lived in the countryside and small towns
more than those who lived in the big cities, Germans who lived in
the north and east more than those in the south and west, and the
NSDAP had a particular appeal for the young. However, it also
managed to attract workers, Catholics, women, urban dwellers and
the old in greater numbers than any political party had done previously.[48] The only other political party in Weimar Germany which

had been successful in attracting votes from across the social spectrum was the Catholic Centre Party, though it remained firmly rooted in the Catholic milieu and was seen to defend Catholic interests. The Nazi Party did not merely repeat the ideology of the *Volksgemeinschaft*, in which all Germans would unite regardless of social class or (Christian) religious confession; during the last years of the Weimar Republic, it actually seemed to reflect such a 'community' in the support it attracted.

How did memories of the First World War fit into this? Over ten million German veterans of the war survived the conflict and were able to cast their votes in the fateful elections of 1932 and 1933, and at least eight million probably did so.[49] Among the remainder of the electorate, all had been affected deeply by what they had been through between 1914 and 1919 – whether as workers struggling to navigate a path through the war economy, as women compelled to provide an income for households deprived of a male breadwinner, or as children whose early years were scared by wartime privations. All those entitled to vote in 1932 were old enough to remember the war in some form or other; even the youngest German voter in 1932 would have been six years old at the time of the Armistice in 1918. Indeed, it would appear that particularly among the younger electorate – among the men who had been too young to fight in the First World War – the bellicose and radical Nazi message held a special attraction. Certainly talk of recreating the 'Spirit of 1914' or the camaraderie and sacrifice of the trenches, when Germans of all classes and confessions supposedly were united behind the national cause as never before, resonated in a country wracked by bitter political and social divisions. A mythical picture of the 'front spirit' during the war offered a stark and attractive contrast to the divisive, crisis-ridden politics of the Weimar 'system'. Thus the Nazi goal of overcoming supposedly artificial 'class' divisions through the establishment of an egalitarian racial community, a *Volksgemeinschaft*, arose in large measure from the First World War and the memory of the war. The Nazi movement grew as Germany experienced a 'remilitarisation of public opinion from 1929 onwards'[50] and as war literature found a mass audience,[51] and this underlines the resonance of Hitler's own experience as an ordinary soldier who had served at the front between 1914 and 1918.

As the Weimar system crumbled – as Germany's voters lost faith in the established political parties and the economic and political crisis came to a head in the early 1930s – the Nazi message offered a focus for resentments, a promise of revenge, an outlet for aggression and a hope for a better future to a growing number of voters. As the sectional politics of the other political parties offered less and less promise of improvement, the message of the Nazis – who claimed to transcend narrow interests – became increasingly attractive. In the place of material, sectional interest, Nazism offered Germans a transcendent faith in a future egalitarian racial community. That the National Socialist German Workers Party made so public an attempt to win workers to the national cause was important not just because it drew some support away from the Communists and Social Democrats, but also because it demonstrated to the Nazis' other supporters that here was a movement capable of uniting all Germans in a true *Volksgemeinschaft*. This would be not a community based on law, on respect for the individual, on the rational pursuit of economic and social welfare, but a racial community of warriors and producers of warriors. The Nazi movement struck a deep chord in a profoundly disturbed post-war society, a society and country which had never really overcome the legacy of the First World War, and it came to power with a deep ideological commitment to war and racism.

The experiences of the First World War and defeat in 1918 cast a shadow over Germany for more than a quarter of a century. Much of the conduct of the government of the Third Reich, from its domestic social policies to its conduct of the Second World War, were responses to the legacy of 1918.[52] As a result of military collapse and political revolution, democratic politics came to be associated with disorder; however, as a result of the myths which framed its memory, the war came to be associated with the promise of overcoming disorder. The transcendent faith which Germans in their millions placed in Nazism and its leader was, at root, a faith in war. This is not to deny that the wartime and post-war years were years of extreme disorder. However, perhaps even more important than how Germany actually experienced the aftermath of the war was how Germans imagined that they had experienced it – and, as a sort of inverse image, how they came to imagine the war itself in strangely positive terms. Their failure after 1918 to escape from the shadow of the First World War allowed a bellicose, racist political movement, which was run by a band of political gangsters and which came from outside the established political élites, to attain a position where, in January 1933, those who had the keys to the Reich Chancellery invited its leader to form a government – and thus condemned the first German democracy to destruction and Europe to another world war.

CHAPTER TWO

··

THE NAZI REGIME AND
THE PATH TO WAR

On the evening of 3 February, just a few days after being appointed Reich Chancellor and forming his government of 'national concentration', Adolf Hitler met with the commanders of the various Army districts at the home of General Kurt von Hammerstein-Equord, Chief of the Army Command since October 1930. In a two-and-a-half-hour speech after dinner, Hitler sketched out what he regarded as the role of the armed forces in a Nazi regime. According to notes taken at the meeting (apparently by General Hammerstein's daughter),[1] the new head of government laid out his goals. Hitler began with a characteristic statement of his view of life as a struggle between the races: 'As in the life of individuals the stronger and better always prevail, so it is in the life of peoples.' Then, after holding forth on the problems caused by the First World War, on Germany's place in the world economy, and on the 'poisoning of the world by Bolshevism', the Reich Chancellor moved on to his main message:

> How can Germany now be saved? How can one get rid of unemployment? I have been a prophet for 14 years, and I say again and again: all these economic plans, the granting of credit to industry and state subsidies, are nonsense. One can get rid of unemployment in two ways: 1. through exports at any price and by any means. 2. through a large-scale settlement policy that has as its precondition the expansion of the living space of the German people. This latter path would be my proposal. Within a period of 50–60 years one would have a completely new and healthy state. Yet realizing these plans can

only begin if the necessary preconditions are created. The pre-condition is the consolidation of the state. One must no longer be a citizen of the world. Democracy and pacifism are impossible. Every-one knows that democracy is out of the question. It is harmful in the economy as well. Works councils are the same nonsense as soldiers' councils. Why does one therefore think that democracy is possible in the state? [...] Therefore it is our task to capture political power, to suppress any subversive opinion most rigorously, and to educate the people in moral standards. Any attempt at treason must ruthlessly be punished with the death penalty. The suppression of Marxism with all means is my goal.

In my opinion it is senseless if one now supports equal rights in Geneva and then confines oneself to enlarging the army. What good is an army of soldiers infected with Marxism. [...] I set myself the deadline of six to eight years to exterminate Marxism completely. Then the army will be able to conduct an active foreign policy, and the goal of expanding the living space of the German people will be achieved with arms – the objective would probably be in the East. However, germanization of the population of annexed or conquered land is not possible. One can only germanize the soil. Like France and Poland after the [First World] War one must deport a few million people. [...]

We will stand at the side of the army and work for the army. The glorious German Army, in which the same spirit still exists [today] as it did during its heroic time in the World War, will carry out its duty independently.

Now, Herr Generals, I ask you to fight with me for the great goal, to understand me and support me not with weapons but morally. I have created my own weapon for the internal struggle, the army is only here for foreign conflicts. You will not again find a man like me, who with all his power stands up for his goal, for the salvation of Germany.[2]

Much of the Nazi programme which unfolded over the coming years was here: the smashing of political opposition and particularly of Marxism; the destruction of democracy; the education of the German people so that they would be willing to fight and die; the commitment to overturn the Versailles settlement; the determination turn one's back on the world economy; the commitment to build up the armed forces; and to conquer new living space in the east and pursue its ruthless germanization. The one major component of Nazi policy not mentioned specifically was the overall goal of racial war. However, this was implicit in the entire package, and all the other policies of the regime – its economics, its social policy, its propaganda – were framed in that context.

Two days later, the main Nazi Party newspaper, the *Völkischer Beobachter*, succinctly reported that the meeting had taken place, under the headline: 'The Army Shoulder to Shoulder with the New Chancellor'.[3] Hitler's expressed goals were music to the ears of an army leadership which for years had focused on how to overcome the limitations imposed by the Versailles treaty and to rearm, to become capable of effectively defending Germany's borders and engaging in offensive war. As General Walther von Reichenau, the right-hand man of the new Reichswehr Minister General Werner von Blomberg, put it: 'Never were the armed forces more identical with the state than today.'[4]

For an officer corps deeply concerned not to get bogged down in domestic political conflict or, worse still, civil war, Hitler's promise to smash Marxism and destroy democracy was most welcome. In effect, the Nazi leader was offering the army a radical solution to the problem of potential domestic opposition to massive rearmament. The Nazis would see to the enemy within, and the Reichswehr would be given resources to face the enemy without. What is more, Nazism had met with considerable sympathy among army officers, particularly junior army officers, during the late 1920s and early 1930s. Indeed, in early 1933 many junior Reichswehr officers expressed interest in joining the Nazi SA (soon to become the major competitor of the Reichswehr).[5] Altogether, Hitler's overtures and his new government of 'national concentration' offered what the army wanted. Here, it seemed, was a government which was prepared to create the domestic political preconditions for rearmament, and which understood the lessons of the First World War – that the conduct of wars between industrial countries required, even in peacetime, the rigorous and comprehensive organization of the entire nation and its resources for war – and was prepared to act on them.[6] Some officers may have had misgivings, but they kept these largely to themselves, and very quickly the new government set about the business of smashing 'Marxism' within Germany, doing away with democracy, and making the country safe for rearmament. Both the generals and the Nazis regarded the militarization of German society as a necessary precondition for waging future wars of aggression.[7]

National Socialists were only a minority in the coalition government formed under Hitler's leadership on 30 January 1933. Aside from Hitler himself, there were only two other Nazi Party members in the cabinet: Wilhelm Frick, who became Reich Interior Minister, and Hermann Göring, who became Reich Minister without Portfolio as well as Prussian Minister of the Interior. The great majority of the cabinet were either conservatives or supposedly apolitical figures. Franz von Papen, the right-wing Catholic politician whose intrigues had been instrumental in bringing the Hitler government into being, held the post of Vice Chancellor; more importantly, von Papen was convinced that he controlled access to the aged Reich President Paul von Hindenburg, without whose agreement Hitler could not gain the emergency legislation he needed. Alfred Hugenburg, leader of the conservative German National People's Party, received the Economics and Agriculture portfolios, which seemed to put him in a dominant position to determine economic policy. At the Reichswehr Ministry was General Werner von Blomberg, the choice of the Reich President, who took particular interest in the armed forces and regarded the former commander of *Wehrkreis I* (East Prussia) and Nazi sympathizer as 'completely apolitical'.[8] At the Foreign Ministry and the Finance Ministry were men who had held these posts under the two previous Chancellors (von Papen and von Schleicher) and who Hindenberg wanted to keep in their jobs: as Foreign Minister the aristocratic career diplomat Baron Konstantin von Neurath (who had served as ambassador to Italy from 1921 to 1930, and then to the United Kingdom until 1932), and as Finance Minister the career civil servant Count Johann Ludwig (Lutz) Schwerin von Krosigk, who was to remain in this post even after Hitler committed suicide in April 1945. On the surface, it appeared that Hitler had little room for manoeuvre. Alfred Hugenberg cheered himself with the conviction that 'we're boxing him in', and Franz von Papen happily concluded that, far from putting himself at Hitler's mercy, 'we've hired him'.[9] They were profoundly mistaken.

The formation of Hitler's conservative–Nazi coalition government and its rapid transformation into a Nazi dictatorship within a matter of months illustrates two central features of Nazi politics: on the one hand, the willingness when necessary to collaborate with traditional conservative political élites, who in effect gave Hitler the keys to the Reich Chancellery; on the other, the radicalism of the Nazi movement, which broke the opposition on the ground and forced the pace of the Nazi 'revolution' in early 1933. Had Franz von Papen not spent January 1933 in a series of intrigues which finally bore fruit in the form of the Hitler government announced on 30 January; had Kurt von Schleicher been more determined to prevent the Nazi leader from succeeding him; had the aged Reich President Paul von Hindenburg not agreed to appoint as Reich Chancellor the man whom previously he had dismissed as a 'Bohemian corporal' unfit to lead a government; had the established élites not ultimately proved willing to do business with the Nazi leader – then the Third Reich probably would not have come into being. The fact that they agreed with so many aspects of Nazism – the strident nationalism and opposition to Versailles, the determination to rearm, the hostility to 'Marxism', the contempt for democratic government – allowed the conservative establishment, which controlled access to the levers of power as the Weimar Republic crumbled, to go along with the Nazi tide. It is hardly surprising in the circumstances that on 20 February 1933, after having been lectured by the new Reich Chancellor about how 'private industry cannot be maintained in the age of democracy' and how the upcoming elections would be the 'last', assembled industrialists responded generously to requests to finance the NSDAP's upcoming election campaign.[10] The established élites might have preferred to hand the levers of power to one of their own, but the Nazis had something which they lacked in the crisis-ridden atmosphere of the early 1930s: the greatest popular support ever amassed by a political movement in German history. Add to that a good dose of political myopia and a striking lack of moral principle, and the basis of the back-room deal which lifted Hitler into government was complete. As Klaus Mann (the son of Thomas) wrote in his diary on 30 January 1933, after the news came through that Hitler had been named Reich Chancellor, Germany had become 'the land of unlimited possibilities'.[11]

The relationship of Nazism to German political conservatism may explain much of how Hitler got into the Reich Chancellery, but it was the restless, dynamic, aggressive and revolutionary character of the mass movement which enabled it to smash the remnants of democracy. To Nazi activists, Hitler's arrival in government was a signal: now the resources and power of the German state would be at their disposal, and now they would receive their reward; now they could do what they wanted with their enemies in the latent civil war which had raged on Germany's streets. The formation of the Hitler government was greeted with jubilation by the Nazis' followers. In Berlin, thousands of Nazi supporters carrying torches marched past their triumphant leader to salute the New Germany; throughout the country there were triumphalist Nazi demonstrations.[12] Attempts by Communists to mount protest rallies were quashed by police – even before the Prussian Interior Ministry (now under Göring's control) outlawed Communist rallies altogether on 1 February. The refrain of the Nazi anthem, the 'Horst Wessel Song', had come true: the streets indeed had been made 'free for the brown battalions' of the SA.

During the following weeks, the army of Nazi activists – swollen by the hour as thousands of opportunists jumped aboard the bandwagon – took up the campaign for the Reichstag elections which the new government called for 5 March. This time, the Nazis were able to draw on the resources of the state to intimidate and terrorize their opponents. The politics of high-level Nazi-conservative collaboration were overtaken by a politics of Nazi activism and, increasingly, of state-sponsored hooliganism. From mid-February, the police were allied explicitly with Nazi thugs: in his capacity as Prussian Interior Minister, on 15 February Göring ordered an end to the police surveillance of Nazi organizations;[13] on 17 February he stipulated that police were not to interfere with the activities of the SA, SS and Stahlhelm, but instead were to support the storm-troopers 'with all their powers';[14] and on 22 February, he ordered the formation of an 'auxiliary police' (*Hilfspolizei*) to be composed of members of the SA, SS and Stahlhelm.[15] This occurred against a background of emergency legislation issued within days of Hitler's arrival in the Reich Chancellery, beginning with restrictions on freedom

of assembly and of the press in the decree of 4 February 'for the Protection of the German People',[16] and continuing with the emergency
decree 'for the Protection of People and State' of 28 February, following
the Reichstag Fire. The decree of 28 February suspended the articles of
the Weimar Constitution guaranteeing the freedom of expression, of
the press, of assembly and association, the privacy of postal communications and the requirement that warrants be issued for house
searches.[17] The result was a predictable and terrifying escalation of Nazi
violence and a decomposition of the rule of law. Now there was little to
prevent Nazi activists from venting their violent urges, settling old scores
and letting everyone know that they were in the driving seat.

Significantly, the violence did not abate after the elections on 5 March.
Instead, it escalated. The patterns of violence were revealing. Nazi activists became increasingly aggressive against their progressively helpless
left-wing opponents. One after another, the offices of trade unions,
Social-Democratic newspapers and local SPD organizations were
attacked, ransacked, looted and occupied by gangs of brownshirts who
took great delight in raising the swastika flag on buildings which previously had housed their opponents. There does not appear to have
been any central direction to this campaign of violence, but it proved all
the more effective for that: the Socialist labour movement was destroyed
piecemeal in a matter of weeks, and by the time the Nazis officially
banned independent trade unions, orchestrated their take-over by the
'German Labour Front' and declared 1 May a 'Day of German Labour',
there no longer was a functioning trade-union movement left in
Germany. To all practical purposes, the once mighty Social Democratic
labour movement – the movement which had survived years of persecution under Bismarck's Socialist Laws in the 1880s and which had
broken the right-wing Kapp Putsch attempt in 1920 – had ceased to
exist. Before the government in Berlin could formulate a coherent policy
with regard to the trade unions, the storm-troopers had effectively
solved the problem – and made a powerful contribution towards the
rapid destruction of democracy and consolidation of dictatorship. Hitler's promise to the generals that he would 'exterminate Marxism' with
his 'own weapon for the internal struggle' was being kept.

Although their left-wing political opponents formed the main targets
of the Nazis in the weeks after Hitler became Reich Chancellor, the

violence was by no means limited to Communists, Social Democrats and trade unionists. As the weeks passed, and particularly after the March elections, local-government offices were attacked, as Nazi storm-troopers tore the black–red–gold flag of republican Germany from public buildings and replaced it with the swastika banner, and 'undesirable businesses' – department stores and stores owned by foreigners (including Karstadt, Wertheim, Hermann Tietz and Woolworth) – were boycotted and vandalized.[18] While the armed forces looked on and the police happily served the new government, for a short period Nazi activists, it appeared, could do as they wanted.

Germany's Jews, too, came into the firing line. In the weeks after the formation of the Hitler government and with the take-over by Nazi politicians of Germany's police forces, the assault on the Jews was secondary to the assault on the Nazis' political opponents, but the violence escalated alarmingly in mid-March. Göring, who controlled the Prussian police, set the tone on 10 March, when he declared in a speech in Essen that he was 'unwilling to accept the notion that the police are a protection squad for Jewish shops'.[19] Increasingly, customers of Jewish shops were intimidated and individual Jews assaulted while police stood by, as the authorities cited Göring's speech as justification for failing to uphold the law.[20] On 13 March there was a spectacular outburst when storm-troopers attacked Jewish lawyers in Breslau (home to Germany's third largest Jewish community): armed SA men broke into court-rooms and chased Jewish lawyers and judges from the buildings; many were dragged from court-rooms while cases were being heard, and some were beaten.[21] At the same time, storm-troopers appeared on the floor of the Breslau stock exchange, ostensibly to search Jewish stockbrokers for weapons. Such violence was not part of a carefully planned campaign to remove Jews from German life, but rather almost festive acts of sadism by young toughs who were bringing their own brand of warfare into German domestic politics. The same may be said of the boycotts of Jewish shops which were enforced by the SA and which grew more frequent as March progressed – until the Nazi leadership proclaimed a one-day national boycott of Jewish businesses on 1 April.[22] This allowed Nazi activists to let off steam, but the actual removal of Jews from the German economy would be accomplished later, and far more effectively, by administrative means.[23] It was almost as though, after the serious job of capturing political power had been accomplished, Nazi activists were now able to enjoy their new-found power and attack defenceless Jews.

As the new regime began to consolidate its position, however, it became clear that some Nazi activists had gone too far. The politics of hooliganism did not offer a solid basis for a dictatorship. Taking their cue from Hitler, who on 10 March had called for the 'tightest discipline' among the SA and SS and demanded that 'the obstruction or disturbances of businesses must cease',[24] both the Deputy of the Führer Rudolf Hess and the Reich Interior Minister Wilhelm Frick called for the violence, particularly against economic targets, to be brought under control.[25] The desire to curb the violence of the storm-troopers also seems to have played a role in the one-day national boycott of Jewish shops scheduled for Saturday, 1 April. While, as Goebbels wrote in his diary on 27 March, 'one must show them [the Jews] that one is determined to go to any lengths',[26] this national boycott also provided a means by which to rein in a campaign characterized hitherto by independent initiative up and down the country that was threatening to get out of control.

Instead of forcing through a radical, revolutionary transformation of the German state and its institutions, it appeared that the Nazi leader (who on 6 July would proclaim that the Nazi 'revolution' was 'not a permanent condition'[27]) had committed himself and his movement to working within existing structures. This proved an exceedingly effective tactic, for the combination of cooperation with established élites and the pressure from a hungry, violent movement below enabled the Nazis to consolidate their dictatorship more effectively in six months than their Italian Fascist counterparts had been able to do in the six years following Mussolini's March on Rome. Rather than radically restructure the state, the Nazis governed through emergency legislation, replaced rational bureaucratic procedures with increasingly arbitrary decisions and undermined the rule of law. They thus brought about a more radical transformation of the state than could have been dreamed of when Hindenburg handed Hitler the reins of government.

Working with established élites and within existing state structures to consolidate dictatorship led to two striking successes following the Reichstag elections of 5 March, even though the NSDAP had failed to achieve an absolute majority despite the massive intimidation of its opponents. The first was a brilliantly stage-managed propaganda *coup*; the second was the creation of the legal basis for unrestricted dictatorship. First came the propaganda spectacle, replete with symbolism showing how the triumph of Nazism reinforced national values. On 21 March, the first day of spring and sixty-two years to the day since the Reichstag had first convened after the German empire was founded, Hitler formally presented his new government to the aged Reich President in the garrison church in the city of Potsdam. This 'Day of Potsdam' was orchestrated by Goebbels (who had been appointed Reich Minister for Propaganda and Enlightenment the week before, on 13 March) to link the old and the 'new' Germany – the conservative Prussian military tradition and the popular renewal of national values through National Socialism – and thus to assert symbolically that the Nazi government was the legitimate successor to the empire which had been swept away in the revolution of 1918. The city's streets were decorated with the black–white–red flag of imperial Germany and the swastika flag of the Nazis; Hitler respectfully bowed before a Reich President resplendent in the uniform of an imperial field marshal, who then was treated to a march past by members of the Reichswehr, SA, SS and the Stahlhelm; and the entire ceremony was broadcast on radio and given massive coverage in the press.[28] With the Social Democrats refusing to take part and many Communists already languishing in concentration camps, and not one republican black–red–yellow flag to be seen, the Weimar Republic was consigned symbolically to the dustbin of history.

Legislation followed propaganda. Three days after the ceremony at Potsdam, the death blow was delivered to democratic governance, when Hitler received overwhelming parliamentary approval – only the Social Democrats voted against – for the end of parliamentary government. With the Enabling Law of 24 March (officially the Law for the Lifting of Misery from People and Reich), the Hitler government was granted power to legislate on an emergency basis and to deviate from constitutional norms without the need either to refer to parliament or to secure the signature of the Reich President (which hitherto had been required for emergency legislation).[29] Although the Enabling Law was supposed to remain in force only until April 1937 (or until the Hitler government was replaced), in fact it was extended and provided the legal basis for the Nazi dictatorship until the Third Reich came crashing down in May 1945. In the weeks that followed the passing of the Enabling Law, political opponents were removed from the civil service; thousands of Socialists, Communists and Jews were thrown into improvised concentration camps which SA groups set up throughout the country; the press was brought to heel under the control of the new Minister for Propaganda; all Germany's political parties, with the exception of the NSDAP, were dissolved and, with the Law against the Re-Formation of Parties of 14 July 1933 (less than six months after Hitler had become Reich Chancellor), Germany was formally a one-party state.[30] All the while, the armed-forces leadership could feel pleased that, as Reichswehr Minister Werner von Blomberg had put it on 3 February 1933, Germany now possessed a government which was an 'expression of broad national desire and the realization of that which many of the best people had sought for years'.[31]

If there was one thing which did not please the generals, however, it was the thought that the 'brown battalions' of SA leader Ernst Röhm might form the core of a new National Socialist people's army. While this mass organization had grown by hundreds of thousands in the months after January 1933 and vastly outnumbered the Reichswehr, it provided no basis for building an armed force capable of waging modern war. SA leaders – gloating over the spoils of victory as they took over police stations and set up their own concentration camps in 1933 – failed to appreciate that their apparent triumph had set them on a path which would lead to the 'night of long knives' of 30 June 1934.

The winners of the 1934 'blood purge' were the SS – which carried out the killing, with the head of its Security Service, Reinhard Heydrich, playing the key organizing role – and, of course, the Reichswehr. The purge offered the opportunity to settle old scores (e.g. to eliminate Gregor Strasser, who had headed the Nazi Party organization until he broke with Hitler in late 1932 over whether the Nazis should participate in government, and Gustav von Kahr, the Bavarian government head with whom Hitler had hoped to march on Berlin in November 1923), and to get rid of rowdy and ill-disciplined SA leaders (most prominent among them the Silesian SA leader, Edmund Heines). However, its main function was to remove a possible competitor to the army. The Reichswehr remained Germany's army. The Hitler government had committed itself to a substantial rearmament programme, and in 1934 the SA was crushed as a significant force in the Nazi regime. Röhm, who had dreamed of leading a Nazi people's army, instead met death on the orders of his Führer. Not only did the purge remove a potential rival; it also brought Hitler added popularity. Hitler's speech before the Reichstag on 13 July 1934, in which the Nazi leader justified the purge and declared the murder of his erstwhile comrades legal after the fact, was, in the words of one Gestapo report, 'received with great satisfaction by all strata of the population'.[32] According to a police report from Bavaria, the 'purge action and the personal intervention of the Führer against the former Chief of Staff Röhm and the mutinous SA leaders has met with general approval', and 'especially the confidence in the leadership of the state and the personal regard for the Reich Chancellor have risen strongly everywhere'.[33] The purge clearly struck a popular chord among people who had grown impatient with the rowdy behaviour of the storm-troopers and who thought that the killings would herald the re-establishment of order. The murder of troublesome, threatening and in some cases openly homosexual SA leaders, and Hitler's public posturing as a decisive leader who had acted to restore order and morality, proved, in Ian Kershaw's phrase, 'a propaganda coup par excellence'.[34]

While the Army was not involved directly in the murders, it had acquiesced, just as it had acquiesced to the establishment of the concentration camps in 1933. This seemed a small price to pay for Hitler's assurance that 'there is only one bearer of arms in the state: the Wehrmacht'[35] and it cleared the way for the massive expansion of the armed forces which the army leadership desired and for which it had planned. They needed Hitler and, in becoming accessories to murder, had abandoned principles which later might have prevented them from accompanying the Nazi leader down the road to world war and genocide. Not even the brutal murder of General Kurt von Schleicher, Hitler's predecessor as Chancellor and head of the *Ministeramt* in the Reichswehr Ministry during the late 1920s, together with his wife in their own home, caused the army leadership to question their collaboration with the Nazi dictator. Instead, they were prepared to accept Hitler becoming head of state as well as head of government when Reich President Paul von Hindenburg finally died barely a month later, on 2 August 1934. This removed the last constitutional constraint on the Nazi dictator.

Henceforth, German soldiers would take their oath of allegiance to the Führer.

When Hitler came to power, the main focus of public concern was not the state of the armed forces. It was the state of the economy. With over six million people registered as unemployed, and many more in fact without work, Germany had been affected by the world depression more severely than any other industrialized country except perhaps the United States. Economic misery and fear had played a central role in under-mining democratic government and bringing Hitler to power, and it was clear that the new government would be judged by whether it managed to put Germans back to work. Here the Nazi regime appeared stunningly successful. Hundreds of thousands of people were removed from the jobless figures and put to work on the land or on public-works projects – including land reclamation, road-building and road repairs, and improvements in the postal and railway infrastructure. Altogether, at the peak in 1934, nearly one million Germans were employed on various state-sponsored work-creation schemes.[36] Most famously, the government set to work building the *Autobahn* network (for which planning had begun in the 1920s), naming the civil engineer and long-time Nazi Party member Fritz Todt General Inspector for the project in June 1933.[37] The first sites of *Autobahn* construction tended to be in areas of high unemployment, and relatively little machinery was used so that as many people were put to work as possible (some 40,000 on the road-building sites by 1934, with over twice that number employed in supplying and planning the construction).[38] The Nazis made much propaganda of such projects, particularly the building of the *Autobahn* network (although relatively little of the planned network actually was completed under the Nazis). Hitler appeared repeatedly in newsreels digging the first spadefuls of earth or opening new stretches of road, and both Germans and foreign visitors were to marvel at these modern 'Roads of the Führer' which would bind together the nation.[39] It was characteristic Nazi theatre: a powerful impression was conveyed that the Nazi government and its leader really were doing something to overcome the Depression.

This impression was not totally false, and initially work creation rather than rearmament drove down the unemployment figures. During the Nazi regime's first couple of years, the rise in military spending remained fairly modest – at least in comparison with the vast increases in military and arms expenditure which followed the revelation of the existence of the Luftwaffe and the reintroduction of conscription in March 1935. The more than 600,000 jobs created through public work-creation schemes[40] certainly contributed to a rapid decline in the numbers registered as unemployed – from just over six million when Hitler came to power to under four million a year later and to 1.7 million in August 1935.[41] However, there was more to the Nazis' early success in the Battle of Work than highly visible government action; during the first years of Nazi government there also were relatively few young people entering the job market – a consequence of the sharp downturn in births during the First World War.

In the years which followed, steeply rising government expenditure (and the conscription of hundreds of thousands of young men into the armed forces) led to further falls in unemployment, to full employment and then to increasingly severe and widespread labour shortages. By the summer of 1937, only about half a million Germans were registered as unemployed, and from 1938 Germany was experiencing not unemployment but general labour shortage. In agriculture, labour shortages became acute, and in the late 1930s the number of foreign workers in the country rose considerably, from 220,192 in 1936 to 375,078 in 1938 and 435,000 in the spring of 1939.[42] At the same time, the numbers of people employed rose faster than the numbers of unemployed fell, as more and more Germans were drawn into work (while those in work were working longer hours).[43] Increasingly, women were drawn into employment, including the armaments economy (i.e. the chemicals and electrical industries), despite a Nazi ideology which regarded the home as the proper place for women and giving birth as the most important service which (racially acceptable) women could perform for the *Volksgemeinschaft*.

Nevertheless, the purpose of the Nazi economic recovery was not to work miracles or simply to give Germans employment in order to improve their personal standard of living. Nazi economic policies were not some version of Keynesian demand management, which aimed to stimulate economic growth and welfare through deficit spending.

Maintaining taxation at high levels and discriminating against consumer industries and consumer spending, the Nazi regime did not
steer the German economy towards recovery by stimulating consumer
demand. For Hitler, the economy was not primarily an arena for gen-
erating wealth but one for providing the hardware required for military
conquest, and the determination to rearm underlay all the regime's
economic policies. The goal of an egalitarian *Volksgemeinschaft* and of
economic redistribution was taken seriously, but that was to be achieved
through war.[44] The Nazi vision involved a rejection of free-market economics, of integration into the global economy and of economic lib-
eralism (which, in the 1930s, certainly did not appear to be a rousing
success). Instead, it looked to massive state intervention in the economy
and to the maintenance of closed economic blocs.

In practice, this meant the effective suspension of the convertibility
of the Reichsmark, the imposition of government controls over imports
with the introduction in 1934 of the New Plan by Hjalmar Schacht
(Reichsbank President, for the second time, from March 1933 and Economics Minister from August 1934 until November 1937), and massive
direct state involvement in production. The husbanding of Germany's
limited foreign-currency reserves became a critical problem for a regime
which wanted to use precious foreign exchange for rearmament. Huge
government expenditure, particularly after the armament drive accelerated from 1936 onwards, meant that German industry found its richest
pickings when producing for the state. Where private industry was
reluctant, for commercial reasons, to provide investment and production capacity, the state stepped in. It did so most famously with the
creation in 1937 of the Reichswerke Hermann Göring, to produce steel
from low-grade iron ore which could be mined within Germany
(establishing a firm which during the Second World War grew to become
Europe's largest industrial concern),[45] with the development of plants
to produce synthetic oil and rubber, and with the building of a giant
factory to produce a new 'Strength through Joy' car (destined to become
the best-selling car of all time in the form of the Volkswagen Beetle).
This last project, which was intended to produce 150,000 cars in 1940
and 1.5 million two years later,[46] was a revealing Nazi undertaking. The
desire of Hitler, a great car enthusiast, to do for Germany what Henry
Ford had done for America with his Model T and to provide cars for

the German masses, was never quite realized under the Nazis: only a few prototypes were built before war broke out and production switched to military vehicles, and the money (some 275 million Reichsmarks altogether) which Germans paid in advance in weekly instalments to the German Labour Front for their little cars in effect provided further finance for the Nazi war effort.[47]

Nazi Germany remained a capitalist country, in which the means of production were still predominantly privately owned and in which enormous profits were made, particularly by firms which won government contracts. However, this was a capitalist economy characterized by high levels of taxation and a high degree of state control, in which the destruction of independent trade unions in 1933 meant the end of free collective bargaining, in which the proportion of the economy comprised by government expenditure grew enormously, and in which market mechanisms governing prices, wages and investment decisions increasingly were supplanted by state direction. This was a capitalist economy where the capitalists were not in the driving seat. At the core of Nazi economics lay a single-minded determination to rearm and to build up a military establishment capable of waging aggressive war, and a readiness to use the power of the state to make this happen. The aim of Nazi economics was not to make money; it was to make war.

1936 was a decisive turning-point in the economic and military history of the Third Reich as well as in the behaviour of its dictator.[48] By this time, the German economy had recovered from the Depression, and the most important restrictions imposed by the Versailles Treaty on the German military had been removed. The Luftwaffe had been brought out into the open and conscription introduced the year before, and on 7 March 1936 Hitler took what, with hindsight, was perhaps his most significant and risky step towards rearmament: the remilitarization of the Rhineland. With the march of the Wehrmacht into the Rhineland – in which, according to Articles 42 and 43 of the Versailles Treaty (and affirmed in the Locarno treaties of 1925), Germany had been forbidden to station troops – Hitler restored Germany's military sovereignty and removed a major obstacle to waging war (as well as bringing industry in the Rhineland into the rearmament programme). The League of Nations condemned Germany's action, but the protest was without consequences. (In any event, the Hitler government already had taken

Germany out of the League of Nations in October 1933, when it left the Geneva Disarmament Conference and turned its back on a policy of collective security.) Had the French, as the German military leadership feared they might, been able to enforce the treaty provisions, German forces would have had difficulty holding their ground; and without being able to station troops along the western border, the Nazi regime could not have launched a military offensive, for any attack to the east would have left the Reich open to counter-attack from the west.[49] For the Nazi path to war, the importance of the remilitarization of the Rhineland can hardly be overestimated. It was, as Michael Geyer has noted, 'the hinge on which all further steps of rearmament and operational planning depended'.[50] With it, the period of Nazi Germany's defensive rearmament had come to an end, and the period of rearmament to provide for a Wehrmacht capable of offensive war had begun. For Adolf Hitler, this stunning success was confirmation that he was capable of anything. As he told a gathering in Munich on 14 March, one week after the German army had crossed the Rhine, 'I go with the certainty of a sleepwalker along the path laid out for me by Providence'.[51]

The remilitarization of the Rhineland was followed by a massive increase in military expenditure and the introduction of the Four-Year Plan. Set up in October 1936 with an administrative machinery headed by Hermann Göring, the Nazi Four-Year Plan was economic planning of a quite different sort from that of the Soviet Five-Year Plans. It was not aimed at direct state ownership and management of the means of production or the comprehensive state planning of investment and production; its task, as Göring put it, was 'preparing the German economy for total war'.[52] The Memorandum on the Four-Year Plan, which Hitler wrote in the summer of 1936 (against a background of an economy in danger of overheating due to high armaments expenditure and facing critical shortages of foreign exchange), set out the aim with brutal clarity. After opening with a characteristic programmatic statement that 'politics are the conduct and the course of the historical life struggle of the peoples', the Nazi dictator asserted that 'the extent of the military development of our resources can neither be too large nor its pace too swift'. He went on: 'If we do not succeed in developing the German Wehrmacht without delay into the first army of the world in its training, in the drawing up of units, in its armament and above all in its spiritual education, Germany will be lost.' The function of the German economy was to provide the necessary resources to create the 'first army of the world', so that it could conduct successfully the 'historic life struggle of the peoples'; 'therefore all other wishes must be subordinated unconditionally to this task'.

Strictly economic considerations were of secondary importance; autarky was required to free Germany from dependence on foreign imports, regardless of economic rationality. According to Hitler: 'The people do not live for the economy or for economic leaders, or for economic or financial theories; on the contrary, finances and the economy, economic leaders and all theories are to serve exclusively the struggle for the self-assertion of our people.'[53] To prepare for the coming struggle, Hitler demanded nothing less than the total subordination of the economy to the needs of the military, and he concluded with the order:

I. The German Army must be operational within four years.
II. The German Army must be prepared for war within four years.[54]

These demands were, in the words of Wilhelm Deist, 'not mere rhetoric but rather a definite instruction on how to proceed that had already been taken into account by the Army's planners'.[55] They were not imposed on an unwilling military establishment, but were formulated against the background of military planning in 1935 and 1936 which envisaged a quantitative and qualitative transformation in the German armed forces, with all that entailed for the German economy. Armament was pushed ahead on all fronts. In the air, after the existence of the Luftwaffe had been made public in March 1935, with Göring at its head, Germany's new air force was developed as quickly as technical and industrial constraints permitted. On the sea, although Hitler had been critical of the Wilhelmine naval policy, he soon was convinced of the need for expansion and the floodgates were opened: the first goal had been to achieve naval parity with the French; the ship-building programme agreed in mid-1934 then aimed at a fleet half the size of the Royal Navy;[56] and by the late 1930s Germany had a naval building programme which in its intensity 'was the most ambitious that Germany had ever undertaken' (and which meant that in 1938 520,000 tonnes of navy ships were under construction).[57] And, most importantly, on land German military planning looked forward to the development of 'an army capable of waging a decisive offensive war'.[58] This was to be an army almost a third of which would consist of motorized and tank units, for which financial constraints would play no role, and which by 1940 would comprise 102 divisions with more than 2.6 million men (half a million more than the number with which Germany had gone to war in 1914).[59] As Klaus-Jürgen Müller has pointed out, this amounted to an extremely dangerous development: 'The borderline between defensive rearmament and offensive armament had been crossed. Military policy had developed a dynamic which threatened soon to get out of control.'[60]

As a result of this gigantic rearmament, pressures were building up throughout the economy. The achievement of full employment in an overheated economy brought with it dangerous inflationary pressures, as labour became scarce and workers (despite the abolition of independent trade unions) gained a measure of informal bargaining power. Foreign currency reserves were largely exhausted; government expenditure was rising by leaps and bounds; and the expansion of each of the three armed services essentially proceeded independently of one another, making coordinated, integrated armaments planning impossible.[61] In a more rational political context, this would have led to moderation or retreat, and it was precisely this problem which led to major disagreement over economic policy. Economics Minister Hjalmar Schacht, who had organized the financing of the Nazi government's recovery programme in its early years, attempted to keep government finances and the raw-materials requirements for rearmament under control while maintaining Germany's integration in the global economy. He failed. His efforts met with resistance all round – from the Wehrmacht, from armaments industries, from Göring (whose direction of the war economy through the Four-Year Plan undermined the Economics Minister),[62] and from Hitler, whose Memorandum on the Four-Year Plan was an explicit rejection of Schacht's concerns. Instead of integration into the world economy, Hitler sought autarky; instead of moderation in armaments spending in order to maintain sound government finances and to husband foreign exchange, Hitler ordered massive rearmament. Unable to impress his concerns upon Hitler and having lost the struggle with Göring over economic policy, Schacht resigned as

Economics Minister in November 1937. Germany turned away from rational economic and security policy, as its leader charted his course towards an 'historic life struggle of the peoples'. The leadership of the armed forces, together with the leadership of the Nazi regime, had chosen to ignore economic logic and embrace an armaments programme which was unprecedented in peacetime. They had chosen the path to war.

The increase in military spending was truly enormous, and at a time when, as the Supreme Commander of the Wehrmacht, General Werner von Fritsch, admitted (in his 'Order for the Uniform War Preparations of the Wehrmacht' on 24 June 1937), 'the general political situation justifies the assumption that Germany does not have to reckon with an attack from any direction'.[63] This was not just an admission that Germany had no real need to rearm further for her own security; it also points to an important reason why Germany was able to rearm at so furious a pace: no one was prepared to stop her. By 1938–9, over half of government spending went on the military budget, comprising roughly 15 per cent of Germany's entire gross national product.[64] For a country not (yet) at war, these were remarkable figures – with the exception of the Soviet Union in the late 1930s, virtually unmatched in a country at peace with its neighbours. Between 1936 and 1939, two thirds of all industrial investment went into war and war-related sectors of the economy, and by 1939 a quarter of Germany's entire industrial labour force was working on orders for the armed forces – with yet more employed on war-related infrastructural projects, the building of the West Wall fortifications and various raw-materials programmes.[65]

So gigantic a programme of military expenditure was unsustainable in peacetime. The limits of the German economy – whether in terms of industrial capacity, labour supply, foreign-currency reserves or financial resources – meant that such an armaments programme could not continue for very long. That is, unless the armaments were going to be used. Obviously, Hitler was determined to use them, and the Wehrmacht leadership was in little doubt about where things were headed. In August 1936 the army concluded, when assessing the escalating military expenditure projected for the coming years, that 'this situation is unsustainable over the longer term'. 'The Wehrmacht therefore must be used quickly following the rearmament period, or else the situation must be eased by reducing the demands for the level of preparedness for war.'[66] Even more explicit was the conclusion reached by the Head of the Army Weapons Office in October 1936, that the full implementation of the plans for Germany's military build-up made sense only if one had the 'definite intention of engaging the Wehrmacht at a specific, already determined time'.[67]

Where does this leave arguments, once eagerly taken up by historians, about a Nazi Blitzkrieg strategy? Far from planning a series of short wars which would require relatively limited resources, it appears that the Nazi regime armed as much as it could. Hitler accepted that sacrifices would have to be made so that Germany could make war, and in this he had a willing partner in the military leadership. There seems no hard evidence for the idea that in Nazi Germany a coherent economic policy was coordinated with a military strategy of short, sharp wars. It was not a vision of future Blitzkrieg but the memory of the First World War that shaped planning for the conflict to come. Far from preparing for limited war, the Nazi leadership sought as much armament as possible, regardless of the economic consequences and in the knowledge that this would require sacrifice by the civilian population. Nazi war, which aimed at conquest extending (at least) across the European continent, was anything but limited.

At the centre of the Nazi vision of protracted war was the 'historic life struggle of the peoples', which required that 'living space' be secured for the German race. This was neither just a matter of Hitler's ranting in *Mein Kampf* nor some vague metaphor for Nazi war aims; it was a central preoccupation of the Nazi leadership. Germany was over-populated, could not support a large and growing population within its existing borders, and needed to capture land for agricultural settlement in order to secure the future of the 'race'. That land was to be found in the east, in the Slav territories which stretched out beyond Poland and which were in the grip of the supposedly Jewish-dominated Soviet Union. In retrospect, it seems hardly coincidental that Herbert Backe, who as Permanent Secretary in the Agriculture Ministry during the Second World War developed far-reaching plans for the 'reconstitution of the German peasantry in conquered Europe',[68] had written his doctoral thesis in 1926 about agriculture in Russia.[69] The idea that Germany could not support her population on her own territory and therefore needed more agricultural land had been widely accepted in the wake of the First World War. The terrible food shortages suffered by Germany during the 1914–18 conflict, the vulnerability of Germany to naval blockade, and the loss after 1918 of largely agricultural regions in eastern Prussia left Germans with a deeply embedded 'blockade syndrome'.[70] In yet another sphere, the German experience of the First World War fed Nazi visions of the Second, and the resonance of 'blood and soil' ideology needs to be understood within this context.

Furthermore, the rise of the Nazi movement and the establishment of the Nazi dictatorship had occurred against the background of a severe agricultural crisis. The NSDAP had gained overwhelming support among (Protestant) small farmers facing ruin during the early 1930s, and upon taking power the Hitler government moved quickly to protect German farmers from foreign competition and from the threat of foreclosure. Shortages of foreign exchange required for the import of food, sharply rising food prices which provoked popular disquiet during the mid-1930s[71] and renewed labour migration from rural areas into the towns as the armament-fuelled economic recovery took hold[72] kept the problems of German agriculture high on the Nazi agenda. For Hitler, Himmler (who had studied agriculture after the First World War and received his diploma in Munich in 1922) and many of those around them, the perceived need to keep Germans on the farm (and to settle Germans on the lands to be conquered in the east) seemed vital to the survival of the 'race'. As Hitler put it, in a statement repeated approvingly by those preoccupied with 'blood and soil' and the future of the Nordic 'race', 'the Third Reich either will be a realm of farmers [*ein Bauernreich*] or it will perish'.[73]

Nazi visions of 'living space' and 'blood and soil' were linked closely with concerns about the propagation of the 'Aryan' 'race'. The fact that women living in the countryside generally gave birth to more children than did women in the cities was not lost on the Nazis, many of whom regarded urban 'asphalt culture' with scorn. Since ideas of race and of the competitive struggle between the races occupied a central place in Nazi ideology, it is not surprising that the position of women in society and questions of marriage, sex and reproduction should have preoccupied men who were convinced that if German women did not reproduce in sufficient numbers, the German race would succumb in the great battles to come. In the first couple of years after 1933, the Nazis were determined, as one contemporary observer put it, 'to remove German women completely from production and return them exclusively to their tasks [...] as wives and mothers'.[74] A campaign was launched against so-called 'double-earners' (employed women whose husbands also had jobs) who were working in the public sector and who were to make way for unemployed men, and unofficial pressure was applied against the employment of women in the private sector as well. At the same time, marriage was given added encouragement, as legislation designed to combat unemployment, enacted on 1 June 1933, provided financial inducements for women to leave employment, get married and have children. The principal inducement was the provision of marriage loans – which required that employed women give up their jobs and that the prospective partners get an official medical certificate of fitness for marriage, attesting to their mental and physical health, fertility, capability for parenthood and absence of hereditary disease.[75] The immediate problem of reducing the number of registered unemployed combined neatly with a desire to put (racially acceptable) women where they supposedly belonged: in the home, supporting their husbands and producing the next generation.

With the advent of economic recovery and with increasingly acute labour shortages as the rearmament programme stretched Germany's resources to the limit, the attitude towards women's employment changed. In the mid-1930s, the attempt to limit women to their functions as housewives and mothers was set aside. According to the President of the Reich Chamber of Labour in November 1936, as labour shortages were beginning to bite: 'If need be, women will have to perform work in factories in large numbers. They therefore must be prepared for this. Here too the social aspirations of releasing women from the factories must bow to military necessities.'[76] In 1937 the requirement that women in receipt of marriage loans give up their jobs was dropped; during the late 1930s, the numbers of women working outside the home and in factories rose; and two- or three-income households (where married women and pensioners also worked) were positively encouraged.[77]

Nevertheless, the regime did not lose sight of women in their role as producers of babies. This was not a matter of straightforward pro-natalism, however. Some women were to be encouraged to have children while others were to be prevented from doing so. Among those not classified as 'alien' to the *Volkgemeinschaft*, 'child-rich' (*kinderreich*) families were encouraged through propaganda and substantial financial inducements (including the introduction, in September 1935, of one-off grants of 100 Reichsmarks per child to 'hereditarily healthy' parents of four or more children).[78] For those whose reproduction was considered undesirable, it was a very different story. Scarcely had the Nazis captured power then the regime began to change the legal framework of marriage and reproduction. The first major step came with the Law for the Prevention of Offspring with Hereditary Diseases, enacted on 14 July 1933 and coming into force at the beginning of 1934, which stipulated: 'Whoever is inflicted with a hereditary disease can be sterilized by surgical intervention if, according to the experience of medical science, it is to be expected with high probability that the offspring will suffer serious inherited physical or mental defects.'[79] This gave a green light to health authorities, who as a result could sterilize people with allegedly congenital diseases such as schizophrenia, manic depression, epilepsy, Huntingdon's Chorea, congenital blindness or deafness, severe physical deformity or even alcoholism. They actively and avidly took advantage of this new power, and went to work sterilizing patients in psychiatric institutions in particular; in 1934 there were 84,330 applications to sterilize people, 91,299 in 1935, 86,254 in 1936 and roughly 77,000 in 1937.[80] About half those sterilized were women, and altogether about 200,000 women were sterilized as a consequence of the law (180,000 of them in the *Altreich*, i.e. in the Reich within its 1937 borders, comprising about 1 per cent of all the women between the ages of sixteen and fifty).[81] Compulsory sterilization on eugenic grounds was not unique to Nazi Germany. However, the scale on which it would be carried out was, and where the law did not provide sufficient latitude and where there was concern about foreign reactions (as, for example, in the case of the so-called Rhineland-Bastards, the offspring of German women and French occupation troops of African origin after the First World War), sterilization was carried out in secret.[82]

The question of who should be allowed to marry and reproduce attracted particular attention from the regime. In September 1935, the

Nuremberg Racial Laws (about which more below) restricted who was allowed to marry or have sexual relations with whom on racial grounds. 'In order to prevent marriages which are undesirable for health reasons', the Law for the Protection of the Hereditary Health of the German People of October 1935 prohibited unions where the partners suffered from serious contagious disease, mental disorder or hereditary disease.[83] According to one contemporary observer, this law made marriage, 'in contrast to its former character as a private matter, an institution which lies in the public interest' and 'which loses its meaning if, from the outset, reproduction as a biological purpose is impossible'.[84] In July 1938 the law regarding marriage and divorce was revised: following the principle 'that marriage above all serves the preservation and propagation of the *Volk*', a marriage now could be annulled if a partner sought to avoid conception, used means of birth control, was prematurely incapable of conceiving, or suffered from psychic or physical illness which made conception unlikely or undesirable.[85] In practice, these provisions worked to the disadvantage of the woman, who could be left without support when a husband abandoned a childless marriage for another union with greater prospects of reproducing for the *Volk*. The Nazi slogan of 'the common good before the individual good' (*Gemeinnutz vor Eigennutz*) was to be applied to intimate relations; marriage, sexual relations and human reproduction were to be harnessed to serve the *Volksgemeinschaft* in the eternal struggle between the races.

Whether the German people actually were inspired by racist visions of conceiving for the *Volk* or settling on the steppes of Russia was another matter. As elsewhere, in Nazi Germany most people remained preoccupied with day-to-day concerns. For many, if not most, Germans – provided that they were not actively opposed to the regime, were not Jews or members of other persecuted groups – the first six years of Nazi rule, until the outbreak of war, seemed rather positive. The rapid decrease in unemployment allowed millions once again to live what they regarded as normal lives;[86] the increases in the number of marriages and births in the wake of the Nazi capture of power (from 971,174 births in 1933 to 1,261,273 just two years later)[87] suggest not merely the effect of financial inducements but also a confidence that one might enjoy a normal family life in the 'new Germany'. The Nazis themselves boasted of creating conditions in which it was possible once again to lead positive, productive lives, and the seeming possibility of achieving 'normality' after the crisis years of the early 1930s provided an important basis for support for the regime.[88] For many Germans, it seemed for a short period after 1933 that 'good times' had returned.

Yet these 'good times' were hardly normal. Germans may have hoped to get on with their private lives as normally as possible, but the private sphere was under assault. The Nazi regime reached more and more deeply into Germans' everyday lives: membership, whether voluntary, pressured or forced, in various state and party organizations took up a growing proportion of the lives of an increasing number of people. Vast numbers of Germans joined the Nazi Party, which could claim over five million members by the outbreak of the Second World War. The motives for joining were varied: some people were keen to be part of what appeared the wave of the future; for some it appeared a good career move; some feared that they might be disadvantaged in business or the workplace unless they joined; and some genuinely approved of the Nazi message. Whatever their reason for joining, millions did so.

Other Nazi organizations also attracted huge memberships. The storm-troopers organization, the SA, mushroomed in the aftermath of the Nazi capture of power, and numbered some 3.5 million members by the time its leaders were massacred in the summer of 1934. Organizations for Germans with particular interests, such as the National Socialist Motor Vehicle Corps for those with motor vehicles, prospered. German women were organized in the National Socialist Women's Organization (*Nationalsozialistische Frauenschaft*), which numbered almost 2.3 million members in the *Altreich* by the end of 1938 (and roughly six million – or one in five German women over the age of eighteen – in 1941). Millions more were members of or affiliated to the German Women's Enterprise (*Deutsches Frauenwerk*, the umbrella organization which took over the various women's organizations 'co-ordinated' after the Nazis captured power).[89] Young Germans were organized in the Hitler Youth (HJ) for boys and the League of German Girls (BDM), organizations which by 1936 included in their ranks the majority of German youth and membership of which became compulsory in 1939.

The Nazi youth organizations were among the most effective means of cementing the allegiance of the people to the regime, while also serving to dilute and undermine established traditional authority (i.e. of the school, the church, the parental home). In an extremely perceptive report, dating from June 1934, one Social Democratic informant noted:

> The youth remain in favour of the system, [are] for the new: the drill, the uniform, the camp life, [the fact] that school and the parental home take second place behind the community of the young – all this is wonderful. Great times without danger. Many believe that economic paths have opened to them due to the persecution of Jews and Marxists. [...] Young workers participate too: 'Maybe some day socalism will come; one is trying it in a new way; the others certainly did not bring it about; *Volksgemeinschaft* is better than being the lowest class' – that is they way they think. [...]
>
> Parents watch this happening. They cannot prevent a child from doing what all the children are doing, they cannot deny him the uniform that all the other children have. They also cannot prohibit it, that would be dangerous.
>
> At the instigation of the HJ children and young people demand of their parents that they be good Nazis, that they give up Marxism, reaction and contact with Jews.[90]

When they emerged from the HJ or the BDM, young Germans found the next set of organizations awaiting them – the Labour Service and (from 1935, for young men) the armed forces – as well as the largest Nazi organization of them all, the German Labour Front. The Labour Front, which had usurped the role (and the assets) of the trade unions in the spring of 1933, brought together 'all productive Germans of brain and fist' (i.e. employers and the self-employed as well as employees), and came to number more than 14 million members in March 1934 and nearly 20 million in 1938 (each paying monthly dues of 1.50 to 2.00 Reichsmarks).[91] This huge organization had 35,000 full-time employees by the time war broke out in 1939, and involved itself in a dizzying array of activities. It provided occupational training, sports activities, legal advice and medical screening; it operated the Bank for German Labour (one of Nazi Germany's largest banks), and sold roughly 10 per cent of Germany's life-insurance policies by 1938; it did research into labour and wages; it campaigned to improve the appearance of factories and the working environment; and, most famously, it provided 'Strength through Joy'.[92] The 'Strength through Joy' division of the Labour Front offered holidays and leisure-time activities ranging from local outings to trips across the country and, for the lucky few, subsidized cruises to the Canary Islands, Greece or the fjords of Norway. By the time war broke out, some seven million Germans had enjoyed a holiday through the 'Strength through Joy' (with a further 35 million day-trippers).[93] For many, this was the first such holiday they had ever had.

The growth of these organizations, and the pressure on ordinary Germans to join them and participate in their activities, reflected not only the interest of their leaders in building empires within the haphazard administrative structures of the Third Reich. It also reflected a determination to educate the German people, to school them in Nazi ideology and to prepare them for the great tasks ahead. Again and again, Hitler stressed that the purpose of Nazi politics was to ensure that the German people would enthusiastically support the regime's racial and military aims. The enemies of the *Volksgemeinschaft* – political opponents, ideological enemies, pacifists, Jews, and democrats who sought to undermine (or who, due to their 'race', were regarded as likely to undermine) that commitment and the Nazi world-view – had to be suppressed ruthlessly. The German people had to be 'enlightened' as to their true destiny. This was a constant struggle, and although the regime and, particularly, its leader enjoyed tremendous popularity, and although there was substantial popular approval for rearmament and breaking the 'chains of Versailles', the approval was not unconditional. It was mixed with a fair amount of unease about the possibility that Germany might again go to war.

The ambivalent popular reaction towards the military build-up and the degree to which the experience of the First World War coloured that reaction were evident in popular responses to the reintroduction of conscription in March 1935. Reports gathered by the underground network of Social Democratic informants suggest enthusiastic approval alongside widespread fear. After the reintroduction of conscription,

SPD informants wrote that 'the enthusiasm was tremendous, especially among the youth', and comparisons were drawn with the atmosphere of 1 August 1914. However, they also noted that 'there naturally are still relatively sensible people' who 'remember the consequences of 1 August 1914 [and who] warn about the terrible consequences of a war'.[94] While some people believed that it was only right for Germany to conscript young men if other nations did the same and that, as was asserted in Bavaria, 'it does the young fellows no harm if once again they get knocked into shape',[95] the fears also were palpable. According to one informant, reporting from Saxony:

> The veterans whose opinions we could ask about the introduction of general conscription expressed in a very veiled manner that they were not keen to re-live the years 1914–1918. War invalids and war widows spoke to the effect that better the Reich government first should meet its previous obligations and recompense all the victims of the last war before it creates new victims and spends money for armaments.[96]

The Wehrmacht's entry into the Rhineland also attracted enthusiastic approval among those who had supported the Nazi Party and simultaneously provoked widespread fears about possible war, especially in western Germany. From the Palatinate the Social Democratic underground reported that immediately after German troops crossed the Rhine popular morale was 'dominated by fear of war'.[97] From the Rhineland one SPD informant noted: 'There are a lot of people who experienced the World War. They are a strong counterweight to those who are one hundred per cent enthusiastic for war.'[98] The shadow cast by memories of the First World War still hung heavy over the German population, however popular Hitler may have been and however pleased Germans were that their country was a military power once again.

Concern that the Hitler government would plunge Germany into another world war, with all the suffering that might entail, was not the only cause of popular unease. Evidence both from the materials gathered by the SPD in exile and from the regular 'situation reports' made by Gestapo offices across the country reveal many causes of dissatisfaction with the regime. Complaints were voiced about rising prices, low wages, shortages, party interference with religious practice, the unpleasant behaviour of government officials and Nazi Party bosses, and corruption (including, as described in one Gestapo 'situation report' from Potsdam in March 1935, 'the unwelcome phenomenon of "war profits"' which accompanied the rapid growth of the armaments industry).[99] Yet everyday grumbling did not threaten the regime in any serious way, even if it did arouse the attention of the police. Hitler remained exceedingly popular; the broad thrust of Nazi policies, in so far as Germans understood them, met with general approval; the expressed Nazi aim of overcoming class divisions and creating a 'people's community' had considerable popular resonance; and the police apparatus proved extremely effective in suppressing open dissent and preventing rebellion. As one SPD informant from Bavaria was compelled to conclude in the summer of 1936: 'The attitude of the broad masses offers no sign of a weakening of the National Socialist regime.'[100]

Unchallenged at home, enjoying growing prestige abroad and with rearmament well under way, on 5 November 1937 Hitler explicitly presented his programme for war. The occasion was a meeting with War Minister von Blomberg, the Supreme Commanders of the three branches of the armed forces – Werner Freiherr von Fritsch for the Army, Erich Raeder for the Navy and Hermann Göring for the Air Force – and Foreign Minister von Neurath, as well as Colonel Friedrich Hossbach, who took notes (the famous Hossbach Memorandum) of what the Nazi leader said. Once again, Hitler began with his broad ideological vision: 'The aim of German policy', he asserted, was 'the safeguarding and maintenance of the racial group [Volksmasse] and its propagation. It was therefore a problem of space.'[101] Self-sufficiency, he claimed, was impossible within existing borders. 'Germany's future', according to Hitler, was 'wholly conditional upon the solving of the need for space'. Then came the practical consequence: it therefore was necessary to attack Czechoslovakia and Austria by 1943–5 at the latest. While the Hossbach Memorandum was not a blueprint for the world war which actually began with the invasion of Poland two years later – no mention was made of Russia, for example – it was a categorical statement of Hitler's intention to launch a European war inspired by racist ideology.

During 1937 and 1938, Hitler was able to remove a number of obstacles to the risky course he had charted, and to concentrate power even more firmly in his own hands and in those of trusted Nazis. At the same time, the power and influence of traditional conservative élites, on whom the Nazi dictator had been dependent at the outset of his rule, waned perceptibly. By early 1938, the old guard effectively had been sidelined. In November 1937 Schacht had resigned as Economics Minister and General Plenipotentiary for the War Economy (a post to which he had been appointed in May 1935) and Göring had replaced him as the dominant figure in economic policy. In February 1938 a far-reaching shake-up of the armed-forces leadership left the supreme command of the army in Hitler's own hands, after War Minister Werner von Blomberg resigned (following revelations that he had recently married a former prostitute) and the Supreme Commander of the Army General Werner von Fritsch was dismissed (on trumped-up charges of homosexuality). And in the wake of the Blomberg–Fritsch crisis, Joachim von Ribbentrop (Hitler's foreign-policy adviser and from 1936 to 1938 German Ambassador in London) replaced Konstantin von Neurath as Foreign Minister in February 1938.[102]

In each of these cases, important influences restraining Hitler and the headlong drive to war were removed. With the arrival of Ribbentrop at the Foreign Ministry, German foreign policy took an increasingly radical and undiplomatic turn, with Hitler completely in control (and egged on by his bellicose new Foreign Minister). With his resignation as Economics Minister, Schacht's efforts to reign in government spending on armaments and to keep Germany integrated in a multilateral trading system came to an end. In Göring Hitler had someone dominating economic policy who favoured autarky and believed, as he (Göring) stated in July 1936, that 'carrying out [...] the armaments programme according to schedule and planned scale is *the* task of German politics' and who was not about to let rational economic considerations stand in his way.[103] As a result of the Blomberg–Fritsch crisis – by placing the command of the Army in his own hands, abolishing the War Ministry and creating instead the 'Supreme Command of the Wehrmacht' (*Oberkommando der Wehrmacht*, OKW) and putting the pliant General Wilhelm Keitel at its head – Hitler had established his outright dominance over the armed-forces leadership. In foreign policy, economic policy and military policy, Hitler's position was now unchallenged.

Hitler's headlong rush to war nevertheless continued to raise concern among the military, most importantly with the Chief of the Army General Staff, General Ludwig Beck. When Hitler made clear his determination to go to war to destroy Czechoslovakia in 1938, Beck (who had been one of the chief architects of the massive rearmament drive during the first four years of Nazi rule) began to get cold feet. In May 1938, when the prospect of conflict with Czechoslovakia seemed imminent, Beck surveyed Germany's military position and concluded gloomily that, given the armament of Germany's potential opponents, her lack of powerful allies and, especially, her poor economic position ('worse than in 1917/18'), 'Germany cannot run the risk of a long war'.[104] In Beck's view, an attack on Czechoslovakia would lead to war with France and Britain, a war which Germany would lose, and after plans for the invasion of Czechoslovakia were made ready at the end of May he pressed the point in two further memoranda. Although Beck's misgivings about going to war against Czechoslovakia were widely shared, his military colleagues proved unwilling to face down their commander-in-chief. Beck was isolated, and his caution served only to confirm Hitler's contempt for a traditional military élite which seemed reluctant to use the military machine the Nazi dictatorship had provided.

If the main thrust of Nazi policy during the 1930s was the drive to war, the domestic policies of the regime need to be viewed as subordinate to this end. For Hitler, the function of domestic politics, of propaganda and of the Nazi Party was to ensure that the German people would take up the historic task he was placing before them. Popular measures – putting Germans back to work, creating imposing propaganda spectacles, or promoting an extreme nationalist cultural agenda – were exploited to mobilize support for the regime and its warlike aims. For those whose resisted the message there was ruthless suppression of dissent. It was, as the title of one collection of studies on domestic policies in Nazi Germany had it, a policy of 'fear, reward, discipline and order'.[105] However, as recent research has demonstrated, the Nazi police apparatus, while it may have been terribly effective, was not all that large.[106] Far from being a huge 'all-knowing, all-powerful and omnipresent' organization, the Gestapo was relatively small and dependent upon the cooperation of the civilian population to carry out its tasks. Without the willing collaboration of Germans prepared to help the police, to inform on and denounce their neighbours and even their spouses and parents, the police of the Third Reich would not have been able to function so effectively. The sad fact is that they enjoyed considerable support from the German people as they went about their duties in the service of the Nazi regime.[107]

When Hitler arrived at the Reich Chancellery in 1933, he had only two fellow members of the Nazi Party in his cabinet, and both were responsible for the police: Wilhelm Frick at the Reich Interior Ministry, and – more importantly, in terms of direct control over police forces – Hermann Göring at the Prussian Interior Ministry. However, the figure who emerged at the head of the Nazi police state and concentration-camp empire was neither Frick nor Göring but the leader of the SS, Heinrich Himmler. Himmler's position in January 1933 had not been terribly auspicious, as head (since 1929) of the 56,000-strong SS, which formally was subordinate to Ernst Röhm's SA. Yet the *Reichsführer-SS* managed very quickly to establish himself first as Acting Chief Commissioner of Police in his native Munich and then as Political Police Commandant for the whole of Bavaria; on 20 March, he announced the opening of a concentration camp under SS control at Dachau, near the Bavarian capital – a camp which was to become the model for what was to follow. Over the following year Himmler assumed command of the political police forces in almost all the German states, and on 20 April 1934 Göring appointed the SS leader Inspector of the Secret State Police (Gestapo) in Prussia – shortly before the SS murdered the SA leadership and thus earned its independence from its erstwhile parent organization.

Two years later, Himmler was undisputed master of German policing. With the reorganization of the police in June 1936, the *Reichsführer-SS* was charged with the 'unified integration of police functions in the Reich' and became 'Chief of the German Police'. The police were organized into two 'main offices': the 'order police' (*Ordnungspolizei*) under *Polizeigeneral* Kurt Daluege, comprising the police on the beat

(*Schutzpolizei, Gemeindepolizei* and *Gendarmerie*); and the 'security police' (*Sicherheitspolizei*) under *SS-Gruppenführer* (and head of the SS 'Security Service', the SD) Reinhard Heydrich, comprising the 'political police' (essentially the Gestapo) and the criminal-investigative police (*Kriminalpolizei,* or *Kripo*). With their own intelligence organization (the SD), their own paramilitary organization (the SS), control of Germany's concentration camps and command of the entire German police, Himmler and Heydrich headed a police apparatus outside the control of the Interior Ministry, able to operate independently of legal norms, and beyond the reach of the Reich Justice Ministry and the courts (which the Gestapo felt unnecessarily impeded the fight against crime).[108] The Gestapo and *Kripo* may have been relatively small, and they could not do everything; however, they could do anything, and the German people knew it.

Himmler and Heydrich did not recruit ruffians or simple-minded thugs to run the Nazi police. They recruited and promoted well-educated, well-trained experts, 'high flyers' whose ideological commitment and ruthlessness was combined with technical competence.[109] For example, Heinrich Müller – 'Gestapo-Müller', the wartime head of the Gestapo and a key figure in the campaign to murder Europe's Jewish population – was a career police officer who had entered police service at the age of nineteen and was not even a member of the Nazi Party when, in July 1936, Heydrich appointed him to head the most important section – Section II, Domestic–Political Affairs – of the Gestapo.[110] What Heydrich most sought in his subordinates was not the 'ability to express opinions' but first and foremost 'the absolute functioning of his area of responsibility' (*das absolute Funktionieren seines Ladens*).[111] Such men could carry out their duties without having to worry about legal constraints; their task was to defend the Nazi 'racial community' against its supposed enemies, and this justified whatever actions were required. According to Heydrich, writing in the legal periodical *Deutsches Recht* in 1936, National Socialism (unlike liberal concepts of the state) 'stems not from the state but from the people. [...] Accordingly, we National Socialists recognize only the enemy of the people. He is always the same, he forever remains identical. He is the opponent of the racial, ethnic and spiritual substance of our people.'[112]

*

Just who comprised this arch 'enemy of the racial, ethnic and spiritual substance of our people' was obvious. From the very start, the Nazi regime had set about making its racist ideology real, aimed first and foremost against Germany's Jews. No sooner had Hitler consolidated his position in government, then discriminatory measures were targeted at the Jews. After the boycott of Jewish businesses at the beginning of April 1933, antisemitic legislation was brought in to restrict Jews' employment. On 7 April 1933 the government enacted the Law for the Reconstitution of the Professional Civil Service, which stipulated that 'civil servants who are not of Aryan descent are to be sent into retirement' (with an exception made – at the insistence of Reich President von Hindenburg – for those who had served in the military during the First World War).[113] In the autumn of 1933, Jews were prohibited from working in the performing arts or the media. From the summer of 1934 they were no longer allowed to gain legal qualifications. With the introduction of conscription in May 1935, they were banned from serving with the German military. Then, on 15 September 1935, during the Party Rally, the Reichstag was called to Nuremberg to pass the so-called Nuremberg Race Laws. This legislation – the Law for the Protection of German Blood and German Honour, which prohibited marriage and sexual intercourse outside marriage between Jews and non-Jews, and the Reich Citizenship Law, which deprived Jews of German citizenship – effectively destroyed the remnants of the liberal, Enlightenment foundations of the German state.[114] The fundamental principle whereby all those within its territory were regarded as equal before the law had been abrogated. The Nazi state had become explicitly a racial state, in which legislation and citizenship were based upon pseudo-biological principles about 'the purity of German blood' and upon the presupposition of an eternal racial struggle between peoples.

Banning marriage and sexual relations between Jews and members of the Aryan racial community and introducing a new racial definition of a 'Reich citizen' with the Reich Citizenship Law – decreeing that a 'Reich citizen is only a state subject with German or related blood who through his behaviour demonstrates that he is willing and suitable loyally to serve the German people and Reich' – left the German government with a difficult question: how was one to define who was a person 'with German or related blood' and who was a Jew? The answer –

which defined a Jew as someone 'who is a descendent of at least three racially completely Jewish grandparents' and went on to define various categories of racial hybrids (*Mischlinge*)[115] – did not go so far as the definition which had served to exclude Jews from the armed forces in May 1935,[116] but it was hardly scientific or watertight. For there was no clear definition as to how one could determine whether a grandparent was Jewish, other than that their own grandparents had been regarded as Jewish – something which, could it have been discussed openly, would have exposed the spurious nature of supposedly scientific racism. But that was not really the point. The Nuremberg Laws served an important purpose: as Cornelie Essner has pointed out, they 'gave the National Socialist state a codified definition of the Jew which allowed it to turn a Utopian vision into reality: the Utopian vision of a "clean differentiation" between one substance defined as foreign ("Jewish blood") and another substance ("German blood") which so to speak was identical'.[117] As such, the Nuremberg Laws provided a legal framework for discrimination, persecution, expropriation and, eventually, murder.

It was not just the German state which turned on the Jews. Although reactions among Germans to the Nuremberg Laws were ambivalent,[118] there can be little doubt that state-sponsored antisemitism had its effects on popular opinion. While the excesses of Julius Streicher's shameless antisemitic newspaper *Der Stürmer* met with scant approval, in the report of the exiled SPD on conditions and opinions inside the Third Reich in January 1936 it was admitted that: 'Generally one can observe that the National Socialists actually have managed to deepen the gulf between the people and the Jews. The perception that the Jews are another race is universal today.'[119] Antisemitic prejudice fuelled antisemitic practice, as Germans took advantage of helpless Jewish neighbours, vented their hatred against Jews and used the officially sanctioned climate of antisemitism to line their own pockets. Towns and villages competed in attempts to intimidate Jews, posting signs that announced to Jews that they were unwelcome.[120] Businessmen took advantage of the misfortune of Jewish competitors, buying businesses at knock-down prices from Jews desperate to sell.[121] Jewish firms were boycotted. 'Protest rallies' were organized by Nazi Party groups in answer to the alleged 'insolent and pushy behaviour' of Jewish entrepreneurs. Customers of Jewish shops might find themselves photographed by Nazi Party members, and those who traded with Jews (for example, with Jewish cattle dealers) might find their names recorded in the antisemitic newspaper *Der Stürmer*.[122] Jewish children were bullied at school. Jews became easy targets for extortion; and in a country where Jews could no longer expect the protection of the law there was little sense in reporting such incidents to police.[123]

Despite the obstacles they faced in doing so, many Jews managed to emigrate from Nazi Germany during the 1930s, leaving sadly depleted Jewish communities behind. In Osnabrück, for example, the Jewish community which had numbered 380 when Hitler came to power was only 265-strong in the spring of 1935.[124] By the beginning of 1938 (before their numbers were increased through the *Anschluss* of Austria), of the roughly 525,000 Germans registered as Jews in 1933 only about 350,000 remained.[125] Altogether, before Jewish emigration was stopped completely during the war, between 270,000 and 300,000 had been able to flee Germany.[126] Some (particularly in the early years) fled across the border to France or Switzerland; some went to the United Kingdom (where about 40,000 found refuge); many looked to a future in Palestine (where 55,000 settled); most hoped for new life in the United States (which took 132,000); others found their way to Argentina, South Africa, Australia and Shanghai (for which one did not need a visa).[127] Of those who remained in Nazi Germany, an increasingly large proportion were the elderly.

Although there was something of a pause in the Nazi campaign against the Jews after the Nuremberg Laws were passed – during the 1936 Olympics (the winter games held in Garmisch-Partenkirchen and the summer games in Berlin) an attempt was made to rein in the ugly public face of Nazi antisemitism – that changed dramatically in 1938. At that point the Nazi onslaught against the Jews was accelerated and radicalized through Nazi expansion in Europe; the path to war and the path to genocide were closely linked. On 12 March 1938, after mounting German pressure on the Austrian government to agree to the appointment of a Nazi (Arthur Seyss-Inquart) as Federal Chancellor, German troops marched across the Austrian border and put an end to the rump Austrian Republic which had resulted from the break-up of the Habsburg Empire in 1918. Fascist Italy, which had stepped in to prevent a German take-over when Austrian Chancellor Engelbert Dollfuss was assassinated by Nazis in July 1934, this time bowed before her Axis partner.[128] When Hitler returned to his native land as its undisputed master, he was met with tremendous enthusiasm; a quarter of a million people turned out to hear him speak at the Heldenplatz in Vienna, the city where before the First World War he had led a depressing existence as a homeless vagrant.[129] That he received so ecstatic a welcome, that his radical course had been so stunningly successful against the odds, that the western powers had done nothing to stop him – not to mention that he had gained a huge strategic advantage over Czechoslovakia – made Hitler more convinced than ever that his hand was guided by Providence. 'The result was', as Franz von Papen (at that time German Ambassador in Vienna) subsequently put it, 'that Hitler became impervious to the advice of all those who wished him to exercise moderation in his foreign policy'.[130]

The *Anschluss* of Austria into the Reich led not just to public expressions of joy, but also to the immediate introduction into Austria of the antisemitic legislation already on the books in Germany. After the Germans arrived in Austria, Himmler and Heydrich prominent among them, there followed a terrible wave of political repression and anti-semitic violence. Thousands of Socialists and Communists were taken into 'protective custody', and persecution and violence enveloped Austria's Jewish population, which numbered some 200,000 and was concentrated overwhelmingly in Vienna (whose 170,000 Jews comprised one tenth of the city's population and were now the largest Jewish community in the Greater German Reich). Jews were assaulted on the streets, humiliated and forced to do menial tasks before jeering Aryans. Jewish property was plundered; the homes of Jews were searched and often ransacked, and Jews were taken into custody in a frenzy of violence which drove many to suicide and many more desperately to seek ways to leave the country. This marked a qualitative change in the antisemitism unleashed by the Nazis, as did the setting up in August 1938 in Vienna of an Office of Jewish Emigration (headed by Adolf Eichmann) to increase the numbers of Jews leaving the country and to rob them of their possessions as they left. Both in the severity of the violence against the Jews and in the creation of administrative machinery for the expropriation of Jewish property, Vienna provided a model for things to come.[131]

The next giant step down the 'twisted road to Auschwitz'[132] was taken in the wake of the next major foreign-policy *coup* by Hitler. This was the pogrom, the so-called Night of Broken Glass (*Kristallnacht*) orchestrated by Joseph Goebbels and carried out by the SA within weeks of Hitler's take-over of the Sudetenland following the Munich Agreement. The sort of violence which had overwhelmed Vienna's Jews in March 1938 was now organized, coordinated and extended throughout the Greater German Reich. The spark for the nationwide pogrom had its origins in the expulsion by the German government, at the end of October 1938, of roughly 17,000 Polish Jews (some of whom had Polish citizenship, some of whom were stateless) then living in Germany. The Polish government refused to admit them all, leaving some 8,000 stranded at the frontier town of Zbaszyn.[133] Among those expelled were the parents of seventeen-year-old Herschel Grynszpan (who had been born in Hanover, had Polish citizenship and was living with his uncle in Paris at the time). When Grynszpan learned of his parents' fate, he bought a revolver and, on 7 November, headed for the German Embassy in Paris, where he shot the first German diplomat he saw, the Third Legation Secretary Ernst vom Rath. Vom Rath died of his wounds on the afternoon of 9 November (the fifteenth anniversary of the Nazis' 1923 putsch attempt). That evening, Goebbels delivered a ferociously antisemitic speech, in which he noted that 'spontaneous' actions were already taking place against synagogues. Viktor Lutze, the SA Chief of Staff, informed his subordinates that synagogues and Jewish businesses would be the targets of 'spontaneous' actions; and the police were instructed not to intervene.[134] An orgy of violence followed: in the next twenty-four hours over a thousand synagogues and Jewish prayer houses were set alight and damaged, and roughly 200 synagogues destroyed; Jewish cemeteries were vandalized throughout Germany; over a hundred Jewish homes were set alight; thousands of Jewish shops were looted and their windows smashed; hundreds of Jews were injured and nearly 100 were killed.[135] 30,000 Jewish men were taken away to concentration camps (Dachau, Buchenwald and Sachsenhausen), from which they emerged at the beginning of 1939 terrified and often with their health broken, and Germany's Jews collectively were required to pay 'a contribution of

1,000,000,000 Reichsmarks to the German Reich' in order to make good the damage which had been done to their property (so that German insurance companies would not suffer due to claims made against them).[136] The Nazi regime had deliberately unleashed a violent pogrom, in which innocent, defenceless Jews were arrested, attacked and murdered, their property destroyed, their places of worship set on fire. German popular reactions to the pogrom, and especially to the unsightly mess it left on the streets, were not exactly favourable; according to SPD informants, after the pogrom 'the great majority of the German people' condemned the rioting, and registered disgust at 'this vandalism'.[137] However, few could imagine where the terrible logic of Nazi anti-semitism was headed.

After the November 1938 pogrom, the restrictions placed on Jews were tightened further. In August 1938 they had been forced to add 'Israel' (for men) and 'Sarah' (for women) to their names; and from October their passports were stamped with a large red 'J'.[138] On 12 November the government decreed that Jews had to transfer their retail businesses to Aryans, and three days later all Jewish children were expelled from German schools. By the end of 1938 Jews could not run businesses, attend public concerts or plays, send their children to German schools, or drive motor vehicles. The occupations whereby they still might earn a living were increasingly limited.

The aftermath of the pogrom also brought Hermann Göring to the centre of the frame. In addition to his responsibilities for the Luftwaffe and preparing the German economy for war, in November 1938 Göring was put in overall charge of dealing with the 'Jewish Question' – a task delegated to Reinhard Heydrich (who was responsible for accelerating Jewish emigration).[139]

While the explosion of antisemitic violence moved the Nazi regime's anti-Jewish policies to the forefront of public consciousness in late 1938, preparation for war remained the major preoccupation for Hitler and his lieutenants. The bloodless victories of 1938, which brought Austria and the Sudetenland 'home into the Reich', also brought much-needed labour and foreign exchange to the Nazi war economy – in particular some 600,000 unemployed Austrians and Austria's gold and foreign-currency reserves.[140] The take-over of the Sudetenland in October 1938 also brought welcome reserves of labour into the Reich. At the same time, these triumphs further increased Hitler's prestige, and after the Munich Agreement which had delivered the Sudetenland into German hands it became even more difficult for the generals to oppose his plans for future aggression. Nevertheless, Hitler himself did not regard the Munich settlement with great satisfaction. Although Germany had gained the Sudetenland (and with it Czechoslovakia's border fortifications) without a shot being fired, the Nazi dictator had been denied the military triumph he desired and thus the destruction of Czechoslovakia.[141] Within a few weeks of German troops having entered what had been Czechoslovak territory, Hitler ordered that preparations be made for the 'liquidation of the remainder of Czechia'.[142] He did not want partial successes won at the conference table; he wanted the destruction of Germany's opponents through war. To achieve this, it was necessary that the German people too should not be satisfied with partial successes achieved by peaceful means. In the Nazi racial struggle, there was no room for peaceful compromise, and the German people had to realize this.

On 10 November, shortly after the Wehrmacht marched into the Sudetenland and immediately after the *Kristallnacht* pogrom, Hitler spoke before 400 German journalists and publishers in Munich.[143] It was not the pogrom and reactions to it which were the subject of Hitler's speech, but the attitude of the German people to the prospect of war and the role of propaganda in shaping public opinion. Echoing convictions that he had expressed years before in *Mein Kampf*,[144] Hitler asserted that National Socialism had undertaken an 'enormous educative job', the 'slow preparation of the German people' for the great task ahead. However, the widespread fear of war and the tremendous popular relief when the Sudetenland crisis came to a peaceful conclusion – the fact that the Munich Agreement had appeared to the German people, according to one SPD informant, 'a beautiful fairy tale'[145] – gave him cause for concern. Hitler informed the assembled journalists:

> For years circumstances have compelled me to talk about almost nothing but peace. Only by continually stressing Germany's desire for peace and her peaceful intentions could I achieve freedom for the

German people bit by bit and provide the armaments which were always necessary before the next step could be taken. It is obvious that such peace propaganda also has its doubtful aspects, for it can only too easily give people the idea that the present regime really identifies itself with the determination to preserve peace at all costs. That would not only lead to a wrong assessment of the aims of this system, but above all it might lead to the German nation, instead of being prepared for every eventuality, being filled with a spirit of defeatism which in the long run would inevitably undermine the success of the present regime. It was only out of necessity that for years I talked of peace. But it was now necessary gradually to re-educate the German people psychologically and to make it clear that there are things which must be achieved by force if peaceful means fail. To do this, it was necessary not to advocate force as such, but to depict to the German people certain diplomatic events in such a light that the inner voice of the nation itself might gradually begin to call for the use of force. That meant, to portray certain events in such a way that the conviction automatically grew in the minds of the broad mass of the people: If things cannot be settled amicably, force will have to be used, but in any case things cannot go on like this.[146]

The task was clear. The German people had to be infused with the will to war. 'Somehow I think', he continued, 'that this disc, this pacifist disc, has now played itself out as far as we are concerned'; the only remaining way forward was 'to tell the truth quite brutally and ruthlessly, no more and no less'.[147]

Even more revealing, and of tremendous significance for the war to come, was the speech which Hitler delivered to army commanders assembled in the Kroll Opera House (where the Nazi parliament met after the Reichstag building had been burned out in 1933) on 10 February 1939, concerning the 'Tasks and Duties of the Officer in the National Socialist State'. The military leadership, now forbidden any 'interference' in political decision-making and effectively reduced to the status of a functional élite whose job was to carry out the military tasks assigned by Hitler,[148] was told quite explicitly what the game was about:

In the next great war this time peoples really will be involved. One

says that world views, ideologies, are involved. It is peoples, gen-
tlemen! [...] Today it is recognition of race, it is peoples, which now
clash. It therefore is obvious that [...] the symbolism of this struggle
also will be quite different. The next struggle will be a pure war of
ideology [*Weltanschauungskrieg*], i.e. consciously a war of peoples
and races [*Volks- und Rassenkrieg*].[149]

As to his own position in all this, Hitler spelled it out to the army
leadership in unmistakable language:

> I have taken it upon myself to solve the German question, i.e. to solve
> the German problem of space. Be aware that, so long as I live, this
> thought will dominate my entire existence. Be convinced further that,
> if I believe at some moment to [be able to] take a step forward in this
> regard, I would act in an instant, that I thereby would never shrink
> from the most extreme measures, because I am convinced that this
> question must be settled one way or the other.[150]

The message was clear: Hitler, embodying the will of the German people,
was in charge and would lead Germany into war come what may. The
task of the armed forces was not to debate the wisdom of marching
down the path to a 'war of peoples and races' but to confine themselves
to operational planning and tactics and to do what they were told.
Concerns remained about the risks involved, and cautious voices – e.g.
of Admiral Wilhelm Canaris, the head of the military intelligence service
(*Abwehr*), and General Georg Thomas, head of the Military-Economic
and Armament Office – tried to present information demonstrating
that, should war come soon, Germany's resources were far inferior to
those potentially at the disposal of the western powers. Even General
Wilhelm Keitel, the compliant Chief of the Wehrmacht High Command,
voiced misgivings about a possible two-front war.[151] However, by 1939,
with the most vocal critics either dismissed or neutralized and Hitler's
star so obviously in the ascendent, the armed-forces leadership ultimately was prepared to do the Nazi leader's bidding despite the huge risks
involved. Germany had been turned into an armed camp, with an
armaments programme and a military establishment which could not
be maintained for long in peacetime. The armed-forces leadership did

not want to disarm, and ultimately this left them with little choice but to follow where Hitler led and to use the arms he had provided.[152] That this may have constituted an overestimation of what a medium-sized European power might be able to achieve, that this threatened to squander the security which Germany had come to possess through economic and military recovery, or that this was a racist and criminal undertaking, did not really enter the picture.

During 1939 the pace of Nazi aggression quickened further. In mid-March Hitler made good his intention to liquidate 'rump Czechia' (*Rest-Tschechei*). Using conflict between the Prague government and Slovakia as a pretext, Germany dictated a Slovak declaration of independence and during the night of 14–15 March the Wehrmacht entered Czechoslovakia – effectively tearing up the Munich Agreement signed less than six months previously. German forces met with no military resistance, and on 16 March a triumphant Hitler announced from Prague Castle the incorporation of Bohemia and Moravia into the Reich as a Protectorate. (with former Foreign Minister Konstantin von Neurath as Protector). As a result, the German war machine gained not only large quantities of high-quality arms and ammunition but also the substantial Czech armaments industry.[153] A week later, the Lithuanian government bowed to German demands for the Memelland, which had been taken from Germany under the terms of the Versailles Treaty and which had a largely German population. Although it was not realized at the time, this minor triumph at Lithuania's expense marked something of a turning-point, for when Hitler arrived at the port of Memel with a German naval squadron at dawn on 23 March, he was celebrating his last bloodless conquest.

By the spring of 1939 the focus of German military planning had shifted to Poland, and this time neither the target for Nazi expansion nor the British and French governments were prepared to allow Germany further conquest without a fight. Planning for the invasion of Poland had begun soon after Germany was handed the Sudetenland – despite the Non-Aggression Pact which the German government had signed with her neighbour to the east in 1934, despite earlier hopes that Poland might join with Germany as a satellite in an anti-Bolshevik crusade, and despite the participation of Poland in the carve-up of Czechoslovakian territory which had followed the Munich Agreement. Within a few weeks of the destruction of Czechoslovakia, on 3 April, the decisive point was reached: Keitel ordered that plans for 'Case White' – *Fall Weiss*, the invasion of Poland – be ready to be put into operation by 1 September 1939.[154]

Of all the consequences of the Versailles Treaty settlement, Germans had found the so-called 'bleeding frontier' with Poland – the loss of Posen, most of West Prussia and much of Upper Silesia, the creation of the 'Free City' of Danzig and the separation of East Prussia from the remainder of the Reich by the Polish corridor – most difficult to accept. However, Hitler did not want simply a revision of the Versailles Treaty. The coming war would be fought not merely to recapture what had been lost in 1918, but would be a 'war of ideology, i.e. consciously a war of peoples and races'. The goal of the coming attack on Poland was not to return Danzig to Germany, abolish the Polish corridor and retake eastern Upper Silesia; it was to liquidate the Polish state. According to Hitler, in a statement made to the Commander of the Army Walther von Brauchitsch on 25 March, 'Poland then will be so smashed that it no longer will need to be considered as a political factor for decades'.[155] On 23 May Hitler made it clear to his generals that, in his view, the choice of 'the Pole' as his target was not taken lightly:

> Poland always will be on the side of our opponents. Despite the Friendship Treaty, Poland always had the intention of exploiting any opportunity against us. Danzig is not what this is about. For us it is a matter of the expansion of living space in the East and the securing of our food supply.[156]

Hitler was keenly aware that his policies were regarded as highly risky. However, as he reminded his military leaders on 17 August, only two weeks before the onslaught on Poland was to begin the Second World War, 'there is no success without risk, neither politically nor militarily'.[157] By this point, Hitler had become thoroughly convinced of his own genius, and his generals were in no position to contradict him. Furthermore, he was convinced that the war against Poland would remain just that, and that the western powers would not intervene. ('The men that I met in Munich will not make a new world war.')[158] The Non-Aggression Pact with the Soviet Union – revealed to a stunned world on 23 August after months of negotiations behind the scenes – may have been a hard pill to swallow for those convinced of the anti-Bolshevik mission of Nazism, but it also made the prospect of a war limited to Poland appear more likely. Hitler, it seemed, had Poland where he wanted her; his generals had put the Wehrmacht at the disposal of his expansionist policies; his war could now begin.

As we know, things did not work out quite as Hitler had gambled that they would. On 3 September 1939 the United Kingdom and then France declared war on Germany. Instead of a limited war against Poland (leaving the bigger wars for later), Nazi Germany had precipitated a major European conflict. In this the Nazi dictator had miscalculated. However, in another sense he was proved absolutely correct: for the war which Nazi Germany unleashed at 4.45 in the morning of 1 September 1939 very quickly revealed itself to be, as Hitler had envisaged, a 'war of ideology [...] a war of peoples and races'.

....

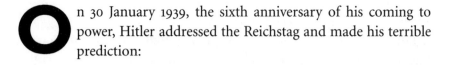

CHAPTER THREE

NAZISM AND THE
SECOND WORLD WAR

On 30 January 1939, the sixth anniversary of his coming to power, Hitler addressed the Reichstag and made his terrible prediction:

> If the international Jewish financiers inside and outside Europe should succeed in plunging the nations once more into a world war, then the result will not be the Bolshevising of the earth, and thus the victory of Jewry, but the annihilation of the Jewish race in Europe.[1]

This chilling and oft-quoted statement may not be hard evidence of a specific plan to murder the entire Jewish population of Europe, but it was, in a real sense, the Nazi declaration of war. The terrible themes which lie at the centre of the history of Nazism – war, the anti-Bolshevik crusade, and racist mass murder – were inextricably linked. From the perspective offered by Nazism, war and racial struggle were, in the final analysis, the same.

The Second World War offered the Nazi regime the opportunity to restructure the racial composition of the European continent, a project which meant the abandonment of rational political (and military) calculation in the criminal hope of creating a racist Utopia. In war the Nazi regime would attempt the 'realization of the unthinkable' – the extermination of an entire people.[2] War liberated Nazism from the constraints which hitherto had inhibited the fulfilment of the terrible logic of its racist ideology. It allowed Nazi ideology to be made real.

It was with the assault on the Soviet Union that the full horrors of

Nazism were realized. The goal of eradicating the 'Jewish-Bolshevik' regime of the USSR together with its supposed biological underpinning (the Jewish 'race'), combined with the aim of conquering a huge colonial area suitable for German settlement, the decimation of the Slavs and their subjugation by the Germans, and the creation of a gigantic economic region capable of withstanding blockade and achieving autarky.[3] Nazi war was not simply the stage for genocide, the context in which campaigns of mass murder could be carried out. War was itself an expression of the applied racism of the regime. Nazi war was racial struggle; Nazi racial struggle was war.

Of course, Germany's Second World War was neither the first nor the only conflict in recent history to involve racist genocide and extreme brutality. The armed forces of Fascist Italy had liberally used poison gas in Ethiopia in 1936.[4] Japanese wartime conduct towards the Chinese during the 1930s and 1940s and the horrors that Japanese forces visited upon the populations of Nanking and Manila[5] were monstrous crimes against humanity. Nor was the Allied war effort completely free of racial prejudice. The practice of racial segregation in the US armed forces and the wartime detention of Japanese-Americans in the western United States are chapters of American history which do not exactly justify pride. However, Nazi war had a different quality. Here, racism was not just part of the ideological framework which shaped the behaviour of politicians, generals and soldiers. Nazi war was racial war, fought for conquest and plunder conceived in limitless terms. It was not fought in order rationally to defend national interests or to ensure national security; it was fought in order to redraw the racial map of Europe through violence and mass murder.

Nevertheless, the war which Germany unleashed in September 1939 may have appeared, initially at least, as a conventional war. This was a European war, involving more or less the same powers that had fought the last time round, with Germany once again facing the 'arch-enemy', France. Memories of the First World War, not visions of a gigantic racial struggle to come, dominated public consciousness. When Hitler announced to the Reichstag on 1 September 1939 that Germany was at war with Poland, he appeared in military uniform and declared that 'I now want nothing else than to be the first soldier of the German Reich', and went on to proclaim: 'I therefore have put on once again that coat which was once the most sacred and dear to me. I will take it off again only after victory, or I will not survive the outcome.'[6] The Nazi dictator, the front-soldier of the trenches of 1914–18, swore that 'there never will be another November 1918 in German history'. This language resonated powerfully in a country still deeply affected by the experiences of the 1914–18 conflict and the November Revolution, and it reflected the fundamental importance to Hitler of his own experience of the First World War as he steered Germany into the Second.

On 1 September 1939, after months of mounting diplomatic pressure in support of German territorial demands, Nazi Germany launched a stunningly successful military campaign which subjugated Poland in a matter of weeks. Attacking from three sides, the Wehrmacht quickly overwhelmed Polish forces. In little over a week after German troops crossed the Polish border, the city of Lodz had fallen and the Wehrmacht stood at the gates of Warsaw; soon thereafter (once it was absolutely clear that the Germans would be victorious), on 17 September, the Soviet Army joined in, taking control of the eastern half of what had been independent Poland; by 27 September Warsaw had surrendered to the Germans, and on 5 October, a mere five weeks after the war began, Hitler entered the Polish capital in triumph. The military campaign was short and bloody; only in comparison with what came later would the roughly 15,000 German military dead in September 1939[7] (to say nothing of the Polish military casualties, which numbered over 100,000 dead and a million taken prisoner)[8] seem insignificant.

However, if the Polish campaign appeared a conventional war to the near-sighted, the nature of the German occupation quickly revealed itself as part of something far more sinister. The outbreak of war, the establishment of an occupation regime to rule what many Germans regarded as an inferior people, and the bringing of nearly two million eastern-European Jews under German control,[9] allowed Nazism rapidly to develop its murderous potential. The conditions of war served to break down normative constraints on the behaviour of the German conquerors, as they came face to face with people who appeared to confirm racist prejudices. Goebbels, visiting Lodz at the beginning of November 1939, recorded his impressions of the 'Polish Manchester', with its large Jewish population, in his diary:

Lodz itself is a dreadful city. [...] Drive through the ghetto. We got out and looked everything over closely. It is indescribable. These are not human beings, these are animals. Therefore it is not a humanitarian operation but a surgical one. One has to make incisions here, and quite radical ones. Otherwise some day Europe will perish from the Jewish disease. Drive over Polish roads. This is Asia already. We will have a lot to do in order to germanize this region.[10]

He was not alone in having such thoughts. Thousands of German soldiers, policemen, officials, and administrators in conquered Poland had their first encounter with an economically underdeveloped eastern Europe impoverished by war, and what they saw all too often appeared to confirm a racist Nazi world-view.

Not only did the encounter with 'Asia' seem to offer confirmation of racist ideology and prejudice; it also gave rise to hitherto unimaginable inhuman fantasies. For example, in a conversation with Chief of the Army General Staff Franz Halder on 2 February 1940, Himmler spoke of putting two and a half million Jews to work building a huge anti-tank ditch along the entire length of the German–Soviet demarcation line.[11] The sudden conquest of millions of allegedly inferior human beings fuelled a mentality whereby rational political or economic (to say nothing of moral or ethical) constraints seemed to evaporate. With the outbreak of war and the stunning successes of German arms in the '18-day campaign' in Poland, publicly trumpeted as battles which had been 'unique in the history of the world' and won by the 'soldiers of the best army in the world',[12] anything appeared possible.

It did not take long before the self-styled architects of a racist 'new order' in Europe looked to put their ideology into practice. Plans were hatched for the removal of hundreds of thousands of Poles and Jews from regions (e.g. West Prussia and the Warthegau) annexed to the Reich, in order to make room for ethnic Germans (coming from territories overrun by the USSR in the autumn of 1939) and to make these annexed regions purely 'German'. Shortly after the successful conclusion of the Polish campaign, on 7 October 1939, Hitler named Himmler Reich Commissar for the Consolidation of Germandom. The head of the SS and of

Germany's police and security apparatus thus was installed formally as the architect of the new racial order in Europe and endorsed proposals to deport a million Jews and Poles from the areas newly annexed to the Reich by February 1940.[13] Although logistical problems made it impossible to realize such grandiose plans so quickly, the consequences this had for the occupied population over the next few months were dreadful enough: by the spring of 1940, nearly 130,000 Poles and Jews had been deported in the most brutal manner. Altogether, hundreds of thousands of Poles were expelled from their homes in areas annexed by Germany;[14] and hundreds of thousands of Germans were resettled from their homes in the Baltic, Yugoslavia, Bulgaria, Bessarabia and eastern Poland, often to be given furniture, household goods and dwellings which had been robbed from those just expelled.[15]

While Poles were deported in their hundreds of thousands, the Jews in the newly annexed *Reichsgaue* were to be deported in their entirety. However, deporting all the Jews was easier said than done. While just about everyone in the Nazi leadership, from the *Gauleiter* in the newly annexed districts to those charged with administering the General Government of Poland (chief among them the Governor, Hans Frank), wanted to get rid of the Jews, no one was keen to take them.[16] Plans to expel Jews were frustrated repeatedly as they collided with unwelcome realities, including problems of transport, not to mention how to house and feed hundreds of thousands or even millions of destitute deportees. The period from late 1939 until mid-1941 witnessed a succession of plans and discussions about 'solving' the 'Jewish question' – the dimensions of which were made vastly greater through the conquest of the main areas of Jewish settlement in Europe – through mass deportation, whether this be into the 'Generalgouvernement' or into some sort of 'Jew reservation' (*Judenreservat*) along the German–Soviet demarcation line near Lublin,[17] to Madagascar (an idea developed at the initiative of the German Foreign Office and taken up with some enthusiasm by Hitler in the summer of 1940),[18] or to some unspecified location in the east. While such plans for a 'territorial solution' to the 'Jewish question' might perhaps seem less horrific than the systematic campaigns of mass murder which in fact were carried out from the second half of 1941 onwards, they too were conceived as a genocidal 'final solution' to the Jewish question. Had they been realized, the result almost certainly would have been the deaths of millions of people, dumped in inhospitable territories without means of sustenance. The failure to realize these plans, combined with the rapid decomposition of normative behavioural constraints in the context of war and a growing belief among the Nazi élite that anything was possible, would eventually open the gates to Auschwitz.

That, however, lay in the future. Within weeks of the German invasion of Poland, the institutional framework for genocide had taken shape. On 27 September 1939, the same day as Warsaw fell to the Nazis, Himmler put Heydrich in charge of the new Reich Security Main Office (RSHA), which combined the Security Service (SD) of the SS, the Gestapo, the Criminal Police and the intelligence services under a single organizational umbrella. By the time the RSHA was formed, however, the radicalization of police repression and the escalation of racial persecution was already well advanced. During the months before the outbreak of war, as relations between Germany and Poland deteriorated, the SD had already begun to prepare for what was to come – planning the creation of *Einsatzgruppen* to follow directly behind the invading army to deal with real and imagined enemies of Nazi rule, and preparing intelligence reports about possible opponents of German forces (including reports about 'Jewry in Poland').[19] Shortly before the German invasion, at the end of August 1939, guidelines were issued for the 'foreign operations of the Security Police and the SD' for 'combating all elements opposed to the Reich and to Germans'.[20] When the invasion began, and with the approval of the Wehrmacht, *Einsatzgruppen* of the Security Police followed immediately behind the invading armies, making preparations (ranging from the compilation of lists to arrests and actual deportations) for the deportation of Jews from areas to be annexed by the Reich.[21] During the first days and weeks of the military campaign, German security forces began deporting Jews from their homes and shooting hostages in order to discourage Polish resistance to German rule.[22] Anger at Polish killings of ethnic Germans at the outset of the military campaign and fears of guerrilla activity combined with racial prejudice to justify a sudden escalation of violence by German police forces almost immediately after war broke out. War provided the trigger for a quantitative and qualitative escalation of Nazi racist violence.

With the military campaign against Poland, Reinhard Heydrich's hour had come. On 7 September he stipulated that 'the leading section of the population of Poland should as far as possible be eliminated' and sent off to concentration camps, while the rest were to be denied anything but the most basic education.[23] On 9–13 September, before the military campaign was two weeks old, he travelled to Poland to inspect what his police commandos were doing. On 20 September, Hitler informed the army leadership of the planned deportation of Poles from what had been western Poland and the intention to force Jews into ghettos,[24] and the following day Heydrich told the heads of the *Einsatzgruppen* of the provisional measures which would need to be taken to deal with the 'Jewish question': concentrating the Jews in the larger towns, and making the territories annexed outright to the Reich (Danzig–West Prussia and the Warthegau) 'free of Jews'.[25] Heydrich spoke of setting up a 'Jew reservation' to the east of Crakow. Police and Party leaders in Prague, Vienna and Kattowitz (in Upper Silesia) began planning the deportation of Jews from their areas. Between 18 and 26 October Adolf Eichmann organized the deportation of some 4,700 Jews from Moravia, Kattowitz and Vienna to a railway station at Nisko, in the district of Lublin.[26] The intention had been to establish a transit camp from which to shift Jews into an unspecified 'Jew reservation' further east. In the event, the Nisko project proved a fiasco, as scant provision had been made for the arrivals, and within days it was stopped on orders from above. Nevertheless, the idea of deporting Jews into the Lublin district was not abandoned, and the Nisko action provided a foretaste of the deportations to come.

The failure of the Nisko action did not signal a halt to the racist violence in Germany's first military conquest. During the autumn of 1939, Jews who attempted to cross the demarcation line with Soviet-occupied Poland were shot, and Heydrich's demands for the 'liquidation of the Polish élite' were put into practice as German 'self-defence' (*Selbstschutz*) organizations, under the command of police *Einsatzgruppen*, murdered between 20,000 and 30,000 Poles.[27] While Hitler spoke of his intention to maintain a low standard of living for Poles (who would be 'cheap slaves'), of the need to expel 'all rabble' from the German-occupied territory[28] and of how the Poles were 'more animals than humans',[29] German police and the SS were putting Nazi ideology into practice. (It was also in occupied Poland that Jews were first compelled to wear Stars of David on their outer clothing when, on 23 November 1939, the 'Governor' Hans Frank took up Heydrich's proposal and decreed that all Polish Jews over the age of ten would be required to wear such identification.)[30] During October and afterwards, once military action had ended, mass shootings of civilians became common and tens of thousands of Poles and Jews were killed.[31] The Army commander in Posen, who viewed with alarm the conduct of the SS and its tendency to become a 'state within a state', noted in November that 'there have been public shootings [by SS formations] in almost all larger towns'. He went on:

> In some districts all the Polish owners of landed estates have been arrested and interned with their families. Arrests are almost always accompanied by looting.
>
> In the cities deportations have been carried out whereby blocks of flats are cleared out at random and the inhabitants loaded on to lorries at night and taken to concentration camps. Here too looting constantly occurs. [...]
>
> In many cities actions against Jews were carried out which degenerated into the worst excesses. In Turek on 30 October 1939 SS lorries drove through the streets under the command of a high-ranking SS leader, whereby people on the street were beaten indiscriminately with horsewhips. Ethnic Germans too were among those attacked. Eventually a number of Jews were herded into a synagogue and forced to crawl among the pews, singing, while being beaten constantly by the SS with whips. They then were forced to drop their trousers in order to be beaten on their naked backsides. One Jew who soiled himself out of fear was forced to smear the excrement in the faces of other Jews.[32]

This wave of violence did not amount to a systematic campaign of mass murder such as later would overwhelm the Jewish population. However, its ideological inspiration was clear, and an important line had been crossed. As Michael Wildt has noted, what occurred once war broke out in Poland was of a different quality than what had occurred when the Germans marched into Austria, Bohemia and Moravia. Arbitrary arrest, physical assault and even murder of political and 'racial' 'enemies' by Nazi police were not new; what was new was the deportation and murder by the police and the SD of whole groups of people deemed to be racially inferior. According to Wildt: 'In Poland SS leaders, who in the Reich Security Main Office later were responsible for the "Final Solution", learned to think in "large dimensions" and to act radically up to and including [committing] mass murder'.[33]

It is not only with its treatment of the Jews that Nazism developed its murderous potential during war. The outbreak of war also saw the launching of the Nazis' so-called euthanasia campaign – the destruction of 'lives unworthy of life'. In the weeks after German forces invaded Poland, and at the initiative of the *Gauleiter* installed in the newly annexed territories, there began a systematic killing of residents found in psychiatric institutions in the new *Reichsgaue* of Wartheland and Danzig–West Prussia. Between September 1939 and the spring of 1940, more than 10,000 mentally handicapped people – including many who had been shipped in from institutions in Pomerania – were shot or gassed.[34] Within the Altreich as well, the constraints to murder were lifted; as Detlev Peukert noted, with the invasion of Poland Hitler not only began the struggle for the domination of Europe but simultaneously also opened a 'domestic front' in the racial struggle.[35] A few weeks after the outbreak of war, Hitler's enabling letter – which he backdated to 1 September, the day on which war had been declared – launched the 'T4-Action' (after the street address of the office involved, at Tiergartenstrasse 4 in Berlin). As a result, over the following two years roughly 70,000 patients in psychiatric institutions were gassed; even after Hitler called an official end to the campaign on 24 August 1941 (following protests in particular from the Catholic Church), the murder continued. Altogether, the campaign claimed the lives of well over 100,000 psychiatric patients, mentally and physically handicapped people, as the future of the 'Aryan race' was to be secured through the murder of the congenitally handicapped. Here, too, the crimes launched in autumn 1939 were to lead to even worse – as the skills developed in the T4 Action and the 'technical' personnel who had gained experience in gassing people would find ample scope for their further deployment when the Nazi regime set in motion its 'Final Solution' of the 'Jewish question' in 1941 and 1942.[36]

*

The war provided the context for the Nazi assault on another 'domestic front' as well: the struggle against crime. German courts played their part, and made increasing use of the death penalty (rising from 139 death sentences passed in 1939 to 1,292 in 1941 and 4,457 in 1942).[37] However, the main initiative was taken not by the courts but by the police. Guided by an ideology which attributed social behaviour to innate racial characteristics, Germany's criminal investigative police geared up for a campaign to create a 'people's community without criminals' – by eliminating those regarded as 'habitual criminals' and 'asocials'.[38] This was a campaign which had begun well before the outbreak of war; however, wartime conditions (and the increase in recorded crime) accelerated it considerably after 1939. Altogether, between 1933 and 1945 the German criminal police sent more than 70,000 people classified as 'habitual criminals' and 'asocials' to concentration camps; fewer than half survived.[39] This was to have been only the beginning: estimates by Nazi 'experts' in 1940 of the numbers of German citizens who supposedly were innately criminal and deviant ranged between one and 1.6 million.[40] What was in store for repeat offenders, prostitutes and those leading allegedly dissolute and immoral lives, had Germany not lost the war, can well be imagined.

Nazi determination to shape the racial community was expressed not only in campaigns to remove the allegedly inferior but also in concern to encourage the propagation of Aryans. As we have seen, propaganda exhortations and material incentives had been used to encourage 'child-rich' families during the 1930s, and the regime displayed understandable anxiety about the drop in the birth-rate which was an inevitable consequence of the war, with millions of young men away in uniform, many never to return. With the outbreak of war, measures were introduced to facilitate marriage for the racially fit: provisions were made for 'war marriages', which involved dropping requirements about age and length of military service which hitherto had applied to soldiers who wanted to marry; and 'long-distance marriages' allowed a prospective husband and wife to make their declarations of marriage at separate times and places. As a result, hundreds of thousands of couples who had spent little time together married and then were separated for much of the war. These marriages often came under considerable strain when the husbands finally returned (sometimes after years in prisoner-of-war camps).

In this, however, the fate of women in wartime Nazi Germany was not fundamentally different from that of women in other combatant countries or in Germany during the First World War. What was unique to Nazi Germany at war was the institution of post-mortem marriages, authorized in a decree by Hitler in November 1941. These were marriages of pregnant single women approved after the father had fallen in battle and declared to have been concluded on the day before the man's death. Although this option never was publicized, altogether some 18,000 women became post-mortem brides (allowing them to claim widow's pensions and their children to be legitimate and thus able to claim an inheritance). While these women comprised only a tiny fraction of the more than one million German widows who the war left in its wake, 'corpse marriages' were perhaps a quintessential expression of Nazism – linking the regime's racially inspired pro-natalism with the awful consequences of Nazi war.[41]

The main concern of the Nazi leadership, however, was the military situation and the conduct of the war. Once Hitler had donned 'once again that [military] coat which was once the most sacred and most dear' to him in September 1939, he spent his time increasingly at his military headquarters, away from the centre of government in Berlin. In addition to his special train, the Nazi leader had more than a dozen headquarters constructed during the war (although he did not actually use them all). The best-known was the vast 'Wolf's Lair' (*Wolfsschanze*) complex at Rastenburg deep in the forests of East Prussia, which functioned as his headquarters from June 1941 until November 1944.[42] The concentration on the conduct of the war effectively removed the dictator, and with him the nerve centre of the Nazi regime, from civil administration. It also meant that Hitler had scant contact with the German civilian population or first-hand knowledge of their tribulations in wartime (and, unlike Churchill, he never visited sites of bomb damage).

After the rapid subjugation of Poland, the main challenge – that posed by the French and the British – remained to be faced in the west. On 9 October 1939, just three days after he proclaimed the successful conclusion of the Polish campaign to the Reichstag, Hitler ordered that plans be prepared for the invasion of France, Belgium and the

Netherlands. However, first it was the turn of Denmark and Norway, which were attacked by Germany on 9 April 1940. The Danes surrendered the following day; the Norwegians, however, put up more spirited resistance, with some Allied help, and did not surrender unconditionally to the Germans until 10 June. In the meantime, the main drama was unfolding in France and Belgium, where German armies had been stalled for four years in the trenches in 1914–18. This time, it was very different. After repeated postponements and changes in military planning, the invasion in the west began on 10 May 1940. As in the Polish campaign during the previous autumn, the Wehrmacht proved stunningly successful. The Netherlands were overrun in a matter of days, surrendering to Germany on 15 May. Belgium held out only a little longer, with the Belgian government abandoning Brussels on the 16th, Antwerp falling to the Germans on the 18th, and Belgium formally surrendering on the 28th. French forces collapsed in the face of the German onslaught in June, with German troops arriving in Paris on the 14th and the French compelled to sign an armistice at Compiègne on the 22nd.

Within six weeks, Nazi Germany had conquered the Low Countries, driven British forces off the Continent, and conclusively defeated what many had believed was the world's most powerful army (taking 1.9 million French prisoners in the process). France was divided into four zones: the largest, comprising the northern half of the country and the entire Atlantic coast, fell under direct German occupation; in central and southern France a French government was set up under the aged First World War hero Marshal Philippe Pétain and Prime Minister Pierre Laval; Alsace and Lorraine were annexed by Germany; and in the extreme south-east a small occupation zone was created for Italy.

Of all the military campaigns launched by the Nazi regime, the stunningly successful assault in the west most resembled a conventional (as opposed to a racial) war. However, the 1940 campaign affected the development of Nazi war in a number of crucial respects. First, by defeating the 'arch enemy' which had held German troops at bay for four years between 1914 and 1918, the haunting memories of the First World War, of the suffering and bloodshed which had resulted from the military stalemate on the western front and of the subsequent defeat, were expunged. In effect, Hitler, the former front-soldier, had finally won the First World War. Second, the German military, looking back upon their stunning success in northern France, success which had been achieved at remarkably little cost in men and materiel when compared with what had happened a quarter of a century before,[43] discovered Blitzkrieg. This, it seemed, was the tactic which had enabled the Wehrmacht to overcome all odds – and, the generals convinced themselves, would do so again.[44] Third, through this victory the Nazi regime, and its leader, reaped a phenomenal harvest of popular support. Even those who had been less than enthusiastic about Nazism now rejoiced in the triumph of German arms. Friedrich Meinicke, doyen of the German historical profession and later the founding rector of the Free University in Berlin, wrote to a colleague on 4 July of his 'joy, admiration and pride at this army': 'And the reconquest of Strasbourg! ... That was stupendous, and it may well be the greatest positive achievement of the Third Reich in four years to have built up such an army of millions and to make such achievements possible.'[45] War and military conquest brought the Nazi regime and German people together as never before.

On 6 July 1940, after spending the previous eight weeks overseeing the German offensive in the west, Hitler returned to Berlin in triumph amidst scenes of frenzied rejoicing. The contrast with the sullen, apprehensive atmosphere in which the declaration of war had been greeted the previous September, when Germans could not help but think back on the enormous suffering and losses which had resulted from the 1914–18 conflict, could not have been greater. Never in the history of the Third Reich had its leader enjoyed such popular acclaim. The great fear of a repetition of the blood-letting of the trenches was lifted.

Forcing the French to sign the armistice at Compiègne in the same railway carriage as that in which German forces had surrendered in 1918, Hitler buried the negative memory of the lost First World War. Nazi Germany seemed to have achieved the impossible. What once was regarded as Germany's most powerful military opponent had been crushed in a matter of weeks and at comparatively little cost; the war appeared won; the Soviet Union had been neutralized through the Non-Aggression Pact. German troops stood unopposed from Brest on the Atlantic coast to Brest-Litovsk on the River Bug; only Britain remained to be defeated. Peace, victorious peace, Germans hoped and believed, seemed in the offing. As the SD noted in a report on 6 June 1940, when the outcome of the campaign in the west already was clear: 'With the victorious conclusion of the heavy fighting in Flanders, many among the population now believe that the worst is over. The hope for a speedy end to the war is most widespread.'[46] But Germans who believed that the worst was over and peace was around the corner were profoundly mistaken.

The way in which they were mistaken reveals a great deal about the nature of Nazism and its relationship to war. At this point it would have made sense for the German government to have used its virtually impregnable position to consolidate its conquests and seek peace. Instead, Hitler chose the opposite path. In the euphoria of the victory over France, with the whole of Europe from Warsaw to the Pyrenees at his feet, the Nazi leader again turned his gaze eastwards. On 21 July, barely a month after the French had signed the armistice at Compiègne, Hitler issued orders to the Supreme Army Command to begin planning an invasion of the Soviet Union, and at the Obersalzberg on the 31st he announced formally to his military commanders his decision to invade and 'dispose of' the USSR in May 1941. The little local difficulty posed by the United Kingdom would have to wait (not least since Germany lacked the military equipment necessary for a successful amphibious landing or for overcoming British air defences). The 'collapse of Russia' would cause the British to come to their senses and give up the fight. The Wehrmacht leadership, which independently of Hitler had begun investigating possibilities for a limited war against the Soviet Union, was ready to oblige.[47]

In the meantime, however, the Nazi war machine was compelled to take a detour through the Balkans. This was precipitated by Hitler's Fascist ally, Mussolini. After having entered the war in the west only once it had become clear that France was defeated, in late 1940 Fascist Italy launched its own aggressive military adventure in south-eastern Europe. After protesting against the allegedly 'non-neutral' behaviour of the Greeks towards Italy and immediately after the rejection by Greece of an Italian ultimatum, on 28 October Italy attacked its neighbour on the other side of the Adriatic. Very soon, however, the Italian forces found themselves driven back, with their positions in Albania threatened and the Greeks capturing town after town; by the end of December, Mussolini was compelled to turn to Hitler for help. Intense diplomatic pressure on Bulgaria and Yugoslavia to join with Germany in a Tripartite Pact, and to allow the Germans access in order to aid their Italian ally, was followed by a series of events which drew the Nazi regime deep into the Balkans. On 27 March 1941, two days after the Yugoslav government bowed to German pressure and signed the Tripartite Pact, anti-German demonstrators took to the streets of Belgrade and other Serb cities and the government was overthrown in an anti-German *coup*. Then, on 6 April, the German forces, together with Italian and Hungarian troops, invaded both Yugoslavia and Greece. This time, the Axis succeeded. On 17 April, less than two weeks after the campaign had begun, Yugoslavia surrendered. The subjugation of Greece took a little longer, but by the end of April the whole of Greece was in Axis hands.

In a sense, the campaigns in the Balkans, triggered by Italian failures and the unexpected *coup* in Belgrade, were a diversion from the main objective – the subjugation of the Soviet Union. The assault on Greece and Yugoslavia had been launched in order to clean up a mess left by Italian military failure and to secure Germany's southern flank before the main show began. The invasion of the USSR was postponed until the second half of June 1941, although it appears that concerns about the weather and logistics, rather than Germany's Balkan adventure (as Hitler was to claim in 1945), caused the start of the Barbarossa campaign to be put back.[48] Nevertheless, the conquest of the Balkans should not be dismissed as peripheral to the Nazi project. As in Poland in 1939, here Nazi war, brutal occupation policies and racist mass murder came together, and Serbia became the second country (after Estonia) occupied by the Germans to be declared 'free of Jews' (*judenfrei*).[49] From the beginning of the German occupation of Yugoslavia, immediately after the capitulation of the Yugoslav army on 17 April 1941, the practice of hostage-taking and reprisals (which, as we have seen, began with the Polish campaign of 1939) became common – now perpetrated not just by German security police but by the Wehrmacht as well. German troops could have been in no doubt as to what was expected of them should the Serbs refuse to submit. According to the orders given to one unit:

Any resistance will be broken with ruthless severity. Anyone found with a weapon in his hand while resisting or fleeing is to be shot on the spot. [...] Furthermore, in disorderly regions hostages are to be taken who may be shot if there is continued enemy resistance. Any considerate behaviour will appear to German troops as weakness and is wrong.[50]

Theory was put into practice, when the shooting of a German officer in the village of Donji Dobric on 21 April led to the destruction of the entire village by the Germans.[51] The principle, given expression by General Maximilian von Weichs in the wake of the incident at Donji Dobric, was that Serb men were assumed guilty unless proven otherwise: 'Should an armed gang appear in a region, then all the men capable of bearing arms who are apprehended in the vicinity of the gang are to be shot unless it immediately can be demonstrated beyond doubt that they have no connection with the gang.' To encourage the others: 'All those shot are to be hanged, their corpses are to be left hanging.'[52]

More generally, the conquest of Yugoslavia and Greece brought into the Nazi empire both a complicated mix of ethnic tensions and a further substantial number of Jews. The latter included some of the oldest Jewish communities in Europe, most prominently the 50,000-strong Jewish population of Saloniki, the vast majority of whom would be deported and then murdered at Auschwitz between March and August 1943. There, as previously in occupied Poland and elsewhere, the arrival of German forces on 9 April 1941 was followed by anti-Jewish measures: the closing down of Jewish newspapers, the arrest of the Jewish leadership, the confiscation of Jewish homes and property, the public humiliation of rabbis and the seizure of the Jewish hospital by the Wehrmacht.[53] By that time, the pattern had been well established: wherever the Germans set foot in their war of conquest, they put Nazi racist ideology into practice. German occupation authorities knew what was expected of them, and they did it.

Of course, the main stage for the Nazi project lay not in the Balkans but in the east, with the assault on the USSR. This was to be a lightning campaign, in which the aim was 'to crush the Soviet Union in a swift campaign even before the end of the war against England'.[54] Traditional assessment of the 'Russian character' (that Russians supposedly were dull-witted and shied away from taking decisions or responsibility), memories of Germany's occupation of wide stretches of Ukraine, Belarus, Russia and the Baltic countries during the First World War,[55] and a belief in the poor military leadership of the Red Army (a belief reinforced by its unimpressive performance in the Russo-Finnish War) and in German technical superiority, underpinned the conviction shared throughout the German military leadership that the Wehrmacht would achieve rapid victory over the Russian 'clay colossus'.[56] The scale of the undertaking was enormous: on 22 June 1941 German forces would attack the USSR on a 2,130 kilometre front with 3,050,000 men and 3,350 armoured vehicles.[57] Unlike the campaigns against Poland, Denmark and Norway, France and the Low Countries, and even those in the Balkans, the invasion of the Soviet Union was conceived of as a war of extermination from the outset. As with Hitler's underestimation of Soviet strength, the Wehrmacht leadership did not dissent from this. This war was to be conducted without reference to internationally accepted legal norms. The fact that the USSR had neither acknowledged the 1907 Hague Convention on Land Warfare nor ratified the Geneva Convention of 1929 on the handling of prisoners of war offered the Nazi regime a spurious and welcome legitimation for its brutal treatment of the Soviet enemy – treatment which resulted in millions of deaths. On 17 March Hitler first hinted at what later would become the notorious Commissar Order of 6 June 1941, when he let it be known at his military briefing that Stalin's intelligentsia 'must be exterminated'.[58] In a speech to his assembled generals less than two weeks later, on 30 March, Hitler expanded on his vision of the ideological war of extermination to be waged against the USSR. Bolshevism was, in Hitler's view, 'the same as asocial criminality'; Communism was an 'enormous danger for the future'. Therefore, according to the Nazi leader:

> We have to dissociate ourselves from the standpoint of soldierly com-
> radeship. The Communist is from beginning to end no comrade. It
> is a war of extermination. If we do not conceive it as such, then we
> may defeat the enemy but in 30 years' time we again will be facing the
> Communist enemy. We are not fighting a war in order to conserve
> the enemy.

The war against the Soviet Union would include 'extermination of the Bolshevik commissars and the Communist intelligentsia', and there was no question of being inhibited by legal norms:

> The struggle must be conducted against the poison of subversion. This is not a question of military courts. The leaders of the troops must know what this is about. [...] The troops must defend themselves with all the means with which they are attacked. Commissars and GPU [secret police] people are criminals and must be treated as such.[59]

From the outset of the Second World War, German occupation forces in Poland had perpetrated massacres and engaged in campaigns to wipe out the Polish intelligentsia and élites. However, with the Commissar Order a new stage in Nazi war was reached: planned, systematic mass murder, explicitly ordered by the head of state and of the armed forces, and directly involving the army. As Wilhelm Deist has pointed out, 'the war got a new quality, the Wehrmacht became an instrument in a war of race and extermination'.[60]

Hitler made it clear that (as Franz Halder noted in the margins of his war diary), with the attack on the USSR, 'the struggle will be very different from the struggle in the west'.[61] Legal norms would be dispensed with, and the conquered population would be treated without mercy. A few weeks later the requirement that crimes committed by members of the Wehrmacht against civilians should be prosecuted was lifted explicitly, and battalion commanders were urged to take 'collective violent measures' where necessary against entire villages.[62] None of this aroused objections among troop commanders. On the contrary, deep-seated prejudices and resentments derived from memories of the military collapse and revolution of 1918 made them quite receptive to demands for a merciless struggle to be conducted against the 'Jewish-Bolshevik' enemy in the east.[63] This found its echo in orders issued for the Barbarossa campaign by Wehrmacht commanders. At the beginning of May 1941, General Erich Hoepner offered the Tank Group he commanded the following instructions for how to conduct the upcoming campaign:

The war against Russia is an essential stage in the struggle for the existence of the German people. It is the old struggle against the Slavs, the defence of European culture against a Muscovite-Asiatic flood, the warding off of Jewish Bolshevism. This struggle must have as its goal the smashing of present-day Russia and therefore must be conducted with unprecedented harshness. Every military engagement must in its planning and execution be guided by the iron will to achieve the merciless, complete extermination of the enemy. In particular there is to be no mercy for the representatives of the present-day Russian-Bolshevik system.[64]

During the summer of 1941, as German military columns were streaming eastwards, Hitler spoke freely of his intention 'to raze Moscow and Leningrad to the ground, in order to prevent that people remain there who we would have to feed in winter'.[65] Inhumanity and hubris crystallized in the brutal fantasies of a racist dictator, and were reflected in the attitudes of his generals. Most famously, on 10 October 1941 Walter von Reichenau, the Commander of the Sixth Army, issued an order which revealed the extent to which Barbarossa was regarded as an ideological racial crusade:

The fundamental aim of the campaign against the Jewish-Bolshevik system is the complete smashing of the power of and the eradication of Asiatic influence in the European cultural realm. Duties hereby also arise for the troops which go beyond the customary, one-sided military tradition. The soldier in the East is not only a fighter according to the rules of the art of war, but is also the bearer of a merciless racial [*völkisch*] idea and avenger for all the bestialities which are committed against Germans and related peoples. Therefore the soldier must possess *complete* appreciation for the necessity of the harsh but justified sanctions against the primitive Jewish race [*jüdisches Untermenschentum*]. It has the additional purpose of nipping revolts against the Wehrmacht in the bud, which experience tells us always are instigated by Jews.[66]

This order, which Hitler regarded as 'splendid', was remarkable not least for its thoroughly Nazi terminology, from one of the Wehrmacht commanders most sympathetic to the Nazi message. No less revealing is the order issued a little over a month later, on 20 November, by General Erich von Manstein, then commanding the 11th Army in the Crimea (where partisans were becoming a growing problem). He, too, made it clear that 'the Jewish-Bolshevik system must be exterminated once and for all' and that 'never again must it step into our European living space'. Significantly, he went on to underline the importance of traditional conservative military values, of selflessness and the need to 'intervene with utmost rigour against arbitrary behaviour and self-enrichment, against running wild and indiscipline, against any breach of soldierly honour'.[67] The context in which those under Manstein's command were expected to guard against 'any breach of soldierly honour' was remarkable: an anti-partisan struggle which included mass executions of Jews living in the Crimea. The most barbarous behaviour was viewed as part of a crusade for European civilization against alleged 'Asiatic' barbarism, conducted with 'soldierly honour'.

Indeed, soldierly honour played remarkably little part in how the Wehrmacht treated the huge numbers of Soviet soldiers it captured, particularly the hundreds of thousands of troops taken prisoner in the great encirclement campaigns in the summer of 1941. In one of the greatest crimes ever committed by a professional army, the Wehrmacht treated those it took prisoner in this campaign not to internationally agreed standards of care, but to systematic neglect which can only be described as mass murder: of the roughly 5.7 million Soviet soldiers who fell into German hands, at least 3.3 million met their deaths as a result of decisions taken neither to feed them adequately nor to house them decently, nor to care for the wounded or ill effectively.[68]

Hitler was right that 'the struggle will be very different from the struggle in the West' in another sense as well, but not one he had foreseen. Although Barbarossa had been planned as a 'lightning war', although the three million soldiers who streamed over the Soviet border on 22 June 1941 made swift initial progress (moving 200 miles eastwards and capturing the White Russian capital of Minsk within a week), and although Hitler spoke of taking Moscow in August,[69] German forces did not achieve the hoped-for swift victory. Instead, they experienced serious resistance from the outset. For the first time, the Wehrmacht did not appear invincible. Although Soviet forces had been taken by surprise, were tactically overwhelmed, saw their forward positions overrun and had millions of their soldiers captured, and although the USSR lost huge amounts of territory containing a large portion of its industrial capacity and some of its best agricultural land, the Soviet armed forces did not collapse as the Polish, Dutch, Belgian and French armies had done before them. They formed, as Army Commander Walther von Brauchitsch admitted in late July 1941, the 'first serious opponent' that the Wehrmacht had had to face.[70] Despite suffering huge numbers of casualties – far greater than those suffered by the German invaders – Soviet troops were able to resist and to inflict serious losses on the Wehrmacht. Indeed, more German soldiers were killed in action during June, July and August 1941 than had lost their lives in the conflict during the entire period from September 1939 to May 1941.[71] By the end of 1941, over a quarter of the entire German army in the East had been either killed (173,722) or wounded (621,308) or were missing in action (35,873).[72]

By mid-August it had become clear that the Germans had underrated their military opponent. As Chief of the General Staff Franz Halder admitted, 'we underestimated the Russian colossus, which had consciously prepared for war with the complete ruthlessness which is peculiar to totalitarian states':

> This assessment applies no less to organization than to economic resources and to transport facilities, but above all to purely military capability. At the start of the war we reckoned with roughly 200 enemy divisions. Now already we count 360. These divisions are certainly not armed and equipped as we would do [our own], and often they are poorly led tactically. But they are there.[73]

As autumn progressed, German forces continued to seize great swathes of territory and take vast numbers of prisoners – in particular in the Ukraine, where on 19 September Kiev was captured along with 650,000 Soviet prisoners (the largest number of prisoners ever captured in a single battle). However, the Germans' problems of supply, which had presented difficulties from the outset of the Barbarossa campaign, were becoming ever greater. The unexpectedly rapid victory over France had led the German military leadership to overestimate the importance of operational skill as opposed to logistical planning and support, and the consequences were now becoming apparent.[74] By November the weather was making movement and supply increasingly difficult, while Soviet forces continued to offer stiff resistance. Then, at the beginning of December, with German troops at the gates of Moscow and temperatures reaching –37° Celsius, the Red Army counter-attacked. For the first time, German forces were driven back, and there was according to Franz Halder a 'serious "crisis of confidence" among the troops'.[75] The first campaign which had been planned at the outset as a Blitzkrieg had turned into a long, unimaginably bloody and ultimately doomed undertaking. Nazi fantasies of being able to do anything had collided with reality.

It was with the war of extermination against the USSR that Nazism and war reached their symbiotic extreme. This was apparent from the beginning of the Barbarossa campaign, when the *Einsatzgruppen* – the mobile killing squads of the Security Police and the SD – were permitted by the Wehrmacht to operate in its rear operational areas.[76] The RSHA, under Himmler and Heydrich, thus gained effective control, with the agreement of the army, over the 'securing by the police of the newly occupied eastern regions'.[77] As we have seen, similarly designated squads had already been in action from the beginning of the German occupation in Poland. Whereas in Poland the numbers of victims had been in the thousands, in the occupied Soviet territories they soon were in the hundreds of thousands. *Einsatzgruppen*, police battalions and Waffen-SS brigades now engaged in the wholesale slaughter of the Jewish population within their reach. In June and July, Jewish men of military age were murdered; from August and September women and children were killed as well; and in September and October there began the systematic extermination of entire Jewish communities.[78] Of the roughly 5.1 million Jews registered in the USSR before the war, about three million lived in territories which were occupied by German forces; of these, roughly two million were murdered.

One *Einsatzgruppe* was formed for each of the three main Wehrmacht Army groups (North, Centre and South) invading the Soviet Union, and a fourth was with the German 11th Army which was operating with Romanian forces. Each was motorized, with between roughly 600 and 1,000 men in its ranks (including the drivers and police and Waffen-SS personnel assigned to it).[79] Their task was to liquidate any and all people who might pose a threat to German rule and its world view. As set out by Heydrich on 2 July 1941, they were 'to execute':

> all functionaries of the Comintern (and all professional Communist politicians in general),
>   the senior, middle-ranking and radical junior functionaries of the Party, the Central Committee, the regional and district committees, People's Commissars,
>   Jews in Party and State positions, miscellaneous radical elements (saboteurs, propagandists, snipers, assassins, agitators, etc.)[80]

While this obviously offered broad targets for the 'executions', it left considerable room for independent initiative, and in practice the *Einsatzgruppen* cast their net even wider. A report of the *Einsatzgruppe* C (which operated in northern and central Ukraine) from the beginning of October 1941 listed the following categories and grounds for the executions carried out by its commandos:

> Political functionaries, looters and saboteurs, active Communists and exponents of political ideas, Jews who have gained release from prison camps under false pretences, agents and informers of the NKVD, people who played an important role in the deportation of ethnic Germans by giving false evidence or in corrupting witnesses, Jewish sadism and vindictiveness, undesirable elements, asocials, partisans, *Politruks* [political instructors in the Soviet Army], danger of plague and epidemics, members of Russian gangs, guerrillas, providing Russian gangs with food, insurrectionists and agitators, youths running wild, Jews in general.[81]

Alongside the *Einsatzgruppen*, there were various SS formations (answerable directly to Himmler) allotted 'security' tasks in the occupied USSR from July 1941, as well as a growing number of police battalions (composed largely of local collaborators).[82] Not only was their net cast so wide that almost anyone could be shot as an alleged threat to Nazi rule, but Jews' very existence was regarded as a threat and thus as justification for murder. As was stated explicitly in a report about a police campaign near Leningrad in February 1942, 'membership of the Jewish race' itself justified execution.[83]

With the launch of the Barbarossa campaign, German policy against the Jews had taken a fateful turn. After it had become clear that the mass deportation of Europe's Jewish population somewhere to the east could not be realized, the Nazi regime embarked on a widespread campaign of 'ethnic cleansing', followed by a gigantic programme to transport millions of Jews to extermination camps whose purpose was the rapid, efficient, industrialized mass destruction of human life.

The combination of ideological exhortation, criminal orders for the liquidation of various groups of people, independent initiative on the part of the various killing squads on the ground and a complete lack of sanctions for criminal behaviour characterized the way the Nazis' wartime campaigns of mass murder were committed. Specific instructions by the Nazi dictator, whose main preoccupation remained the military conflict, were not required.

During the second half of 1941, mobile killing squads in the occupied USSR progressed to annihilating entire communities. Between June and November 1941, the majority of the Jewish men in Serbia were killed by the German occupation forces (the SD, the military administration and the Wehrmacht, acting on their own initiative and in brutal response to partisan activity).[84] In October, mass executions of Jews began in Galicia.[85] From October, Jews were deported from Germany, Austria, Bohemia and Moravia to the east – some to ghettos (e.g. in Lodz/Litzmannstadt), some directly to their deaths by shooting (e.g. in Riga); and at Chelmno, near Lodz, and at Belzec in the district of Lublin, the first extermination camps were being built, while at Auschwitz gas chambers were used to kill Soviet prisoners of war branded 'fanatical Communists'.[86] Yet, as the fateful year of 1942 began, the main element of the as yet unsolved 'Jewish question' lay in the General Government, where some two million mostly undernourished Jews, many now huddled in desperately crowded, disease-ridden ghettos, were still alive.

It was against this background that Reinhard Heydrich called the now infamous Wannsee Conference, originally scheduled for 9 December

1941 but postponed until 20 January 1942. At this meeting, Heydrich as the head of the RSHA presented to representatives of various ministries the outlines of a comprehensive Europe-wide 'solution' to the 'Jewish question' and sought to iron out questions of organization and operational responsibility.[87] The systematic extermination of millions of Jews in the gas chambers of Chelmno, Belzec, Sobibor, Treblinka and Auschwitz could now unfold. As the spring of 1942 dawned, the racial war of extermination combined with the comprehensive campaign to destroy the entire Jewish population of Europe. Having been robbed of their property, restricted in all aspects of their daily lives, herded into ghettos, subjected to random massacres and then to the mass-murder campaigns of the *Einsatzgruppen*, now the remaining Jewish population in German-occupied Europe was to be transported to extermination camps in occupied Poland in order to be killed.

Although the German population back home was not informed of the full horrors of what was being done to the Nazis' supposed 'racial enemies', some news inevitably filtered through. The millions of soldiers fighting on the eastern front could hardly have been completely unaware of what was happening to Jewish settlements and in Jewish ghettos, or the campaigns of the *Einsatzgruppen* in the Wehrmacht's rear operational areas, and some were willing to speak about these horrors when home on leave. Rumours of mass shootings made their way back home, and did not always provoke sympathy for the victims. To take one piece of evidence among many, a young woman architectural student in Austria wrote in her diary on 13 November 1941 (as the bloody campaigns of the *Einsatzgruppen* were at their height):

> Norbert Berger told me yesterday that Russians taken prisoner are divided into three camps: the deserters and those who surrender without resistance, the many Communists, and the Jews. The last two, as well as the Jews we send to Poland, are shot on the spot. Norbert sees nothing wrong with that!!! [88]

The climate of state-sponsored antisemitism emboldened those who hated Jews and intimidated those not inclined to support such inhumanity. Within Germany, restrictions on Jews had become ever tighter in the wake of the invasion of the USSR: from the beginning of September

1941, Jews in the Reich were forced to wear yellow Jewish stars on their clothing – a move which appears to have provoked positive responses among the German population[89] – and they faced new restrictions in their daily lives (depriving them of telephones, newspapers and ration cards for many important foodstuffs). Outside Germany, Jews were being slaughtered in hitherto unimaginable numbers, often in plain sight of Wehrmacht soldiers. One way or another, the society of the Third Reich was becoming conscious of (and complicit in) the Nazi regime's most monstrous crimes.

Monstrous as it was, the campaign to murder Europe's Jews formed just one part of the Nazi racist programme. Of all the civilian victims of the Nazi barbarism during the Second World War, Russians probably constituted the largest single group of dead. The Nazi campaign for a 'solution to the Gypsy question' – by persecution and involuntary sterilization before the outbreak of war, to wartime deportations, mass murder by *Einsatzgruppen* and Wehrmacht units in the occupied USSR, gassings and mass shootings and the creation of a 'Gypsy camp' at Auschwitz-Birkenau – did not differ substantially in its aim or methods from the campaign to exterminate the Jews, although the numbers involved were smaller.[90]

Furthermore, the crimes which the Nazi regime succeeded in carrying out were dwarfed in their scope by plans which Nazi 'experts' – in the Reich Security Main Office and the Race and Settlement Main Office of the SS, as well as the Economic Staff East (*Wirtschaftsstab Ost*) created by the Wehrmacht to plan the exploitation of the conquered USSR[91] – were developing for the future Nazi empire. The fate envisaged for the subjugated east included de-industrialization, the elimination of the 'superfluous' urban population and the conversion of the area into a huge source of raw materials and agricultural produce for Germany. For the moment, the immediate needs of the German war economy had priority, as Göring (who had overall responsibility for economic policy in the east) spelled out in November 1941, but in the long run 'the newly occupied eastern regions will be exploited economically from colonial points of view and with colonial methods'.[92] Vast programmes of settlement were foreseen, with Germans going out to 'civilize' the conquered wild east. To bring this about, up to 50 million people, mostly Slavs, would be expelled from lands between Germany and the Urals to make room for racially 'valuable' settlers. The long-standing structural problems which had plagued German farming for decades would thus be solved, and the concern that Germany's own agricultural land was insufficient to feed her people would be met by settling Aryan farmers on the 'living space' in the east. What is more, the idea of creating thousands of German agricultural estates in Ukraine formed an important part of Heinrich Himmler's 'socialism of good blood', of the Utopian dream whereby all racially pure Germans could share in the Nazi *Volksgemeinschaft*. No doubt there were many German soldiers fighting in the east who shared the thoughts of the young Heinrich Böll, hardly a fanatical warrior for the Nazi racial state, who wrote to his mother from a military hospital at the end of 1943: 'I long greatly for the Rhine, for Germany, and yet I often think of the possibility of a colonial existence here in the east after a victorious war.'[93]

The vision of a 'socialism of good blood' involved not just the forced transfer of millions of people but also their murder. In the run-up to the invasion of the USSR, plans were hatched which, based on the assumption that the war would lead to a downturn in German agricultural production and that the Wehrmacht would need to draw on the food resources of the territory it occupied, callously foresaw the starvation of millions of people: 'In this connection x-million people undoubtedly will starve if we extract what we need from this country.'[94] According to general plans for the exploitation of Soviet territory presented by experts working under Herbert Backe, State Secretary in the Reich Ministry for Food and Agriculture (and the person in charge of Germany's wartime food supply), on 23 May 1941 (as the Barbarossa campaign was being planned): 'Many tens of millions of people will be superfluous in this area and will die or have to emigrate to Siberia.'[95] If tens of millions of Russians would have to starve to death in order to ensure that food supplies were available for the Wehrmacht, so be it.[96] In characteristically brutal fashion, Göring put it in a nutshell in August 1942: 'If people are going to starve, then it will not be Germans who starve but others.'[97] That these murderous plans, subsumed under the general rubric of the General Plan East, were not translated into reality was due not to any pangs of conscience on the part of the technocrats who were so fascinated with them, but to the military success of the Allies in defeating the Third Reich.

The brutality of Nazi occupation policies and of the Wehrmacht's war of extermination was amplified by the partisan war which confronted German forces in Soviet territory. During the opening phases of the Barbarossa campaign, the civilian populations in the western portions of the USSR (Belarus and Ukraine) reacted to the invaders in an ambivalent manner, with many (particularly the non-Russians) regarding the Germans as liberators from an atheist Stalinist Communism which had brought collectivization, terror and misery to millions. The Soviet Communist Party and state reacted as well: a week after Wehrmacht units crashed into Soviet territory, on 29 June 1941, the Central Committee issued a directive which included a paragraph (not then made public) calling for 'partisan detachments and sabotage groups' to be organized for 'action with units of the enemy army, for kindling partisan war everywhere and anywhere, for blowing up bridges, roads, telephone and telegraph lines, destroying dumps and the like'. When he finally spoke to the Soviet population by radio on 3 July, Stalin ordered a policy of scorched earth and the spread of partisan warfare, and two weeks later (on 18 July), the Central Committee provided more detailed guidelines for 'the organisation of the struggle in the rear of the German troops', to be led by Party and state functionaries.[98] For the USSR, too, the war on the eastern front was to be a conflict unlike what had gone before, and its call for partisan warfare behind the lines allowed the Germans to link the campaigns against the Jewish civilian population with those conducted against the partisans. Hitler welcomed the opportunity this presented, as he explained (to Rosenberg, Lammers, Keitel, Göring and Bormann) on 16 July: 'The Russians now have issued an order for partisan war behind our lines. The partisan war also has its advantage: it gives us the opportunity to exterminate whatever is opposed to us.'[99]

Initially the Soviet call for resistance met with little popular response. However, once the brutal exploitative intentions of the Nazi conquerors became apparent, and even more so once the war began to turn against the Germans in late 1941 and 1942, this changed. In the summer of 1941 small groups of partisans began to organize and the Wehrmacht met with resistance behind the front lines. Such activity came to pose a real threat to German military forces and the German administration (and exploitation) of conquered Soviet territories. It gave substance to fears of guerrilla activity (as Prussian forces had experienced after their victory in the Franco-Prussian War from the *franc-tireurs*); it gave rise among German soldiers to 'a furious rage against these fellows';[100] it appeared to confirm racist stereotypes of eastern Europeans as dangerous, threatening and deserving extermination; and it led to the most brutal reprisals and vicious campaigns to 'cleanse' so-called 'bandit areas' – campaigns inextricably entwined with Nazi genocide. For an army whose soldiers had been schooled in racist ideology, confronting conquered peoples living in supposedly primitive conditions, having been told to conduct their war with merciless harshness, the fear that the conquered civilian population posed a constant danger provided justification for the most brutal measures. As the German Supreme Army Command noted in a directive in late July 1941, 'The troops available for securing the conquered eastern areas will, considering the vast expanse of these stretches, suffice only if the occupying power meets all resistance, not only by legally punishing the guilty, but rather by spreading that type of terror which is the only means of removing from the population any appetite for opposition.'[101]

Of course, the interactions between German forces and subjugated peoples in fact were rather more complicated than this implies. During the first year or so of the occupation it was not Soviet partisan brigades but roaming bands of thieves which posed the main security problem facing the police formations serving the Germans, formations generally recruited from among the local population.[102] What is more, German security forces were aware that unnecessarily harsh behaviour could drive more people into the arms of the partisans, and there were rear-area Army commanders in Russia who viewed the indiscriminate attacks on civilians as 'excessive'.[103] As was spelled out in April 1942 to one of the Wehrmacht Security Divisions responsible for the anti-partisan campaign in Central Russia, 'it must be made clear to every soldier that any civilian he mistreats might join the partisans and face him with a gun the next day'.[104] Yet that same Security Division was also told by its commander General Pflugbeil the same month that the 'aim of any combat engagement is not to drive the enemy back, but to exterminate him'.[105] The more the Germans exploited the conquered population – in particular, the more they sought forcibly to recruit Soviet citizens to work in Germany, which drove many to flee their homes rather than allow themselves to be shipped off to the Reich, and as food shortages became acute and taxation and requisitioning increased – the more people joined the partisans. And as more people joined the partisans and the partisan war became more intensive, the more harsh were the measures that German security forces believed necessary to control a vast population in a vast territory with the relatively few, poorly trained men at their disposal.[106] Subjugated peoples were driven by the cruel German occupation regime to behave in ways which confirmed negative racist stereotypes, and thus provided apparent justification for still harsher measures. The result was a spiral of violence which was the inevitable consequence of a racist ideological crusade to exploit and enslave allegedly inferior peoples.

The partisan war took on increasingly serious dimensions after German forces experienced their first setbacks at the gates of Moscow and the prospect of a German victory no longer appeared inevitable. The few tens of thousands of active partisans at the beginning of 1942 grew to roughly 120,000 during the second half of that year, and the numbers of people involved and the amounts of territory they controlled mounted substantially thereafter.[107] As the plunder by the German authorities increased (with rising agricultural delivery quotas, the seizure of crops and livestock, and the deportation of people for forced labour) and the partisan campaign and the areas effectively controlled by partisans grew, so, too, the violence which was supposed to suppress partisan activity increased. In the first eleven months of the war against the Soviet Union, German forces managed to liquidate some 80,000 alleged partisans (with 1,094 dead registered on the German side).[108] Increasing partisan activity led to increasingly radical responses, culminating in an order, issued by the Armed Forces High Command in December 1942, that the 'struggle against bandits both in the East and in the Balkans' be waged with 'the most brutal means' and that those engaged in this were 'therefore entitled and required to employ any means in this struggle, including against women and children, if it leads to success'. It went on to prohibit the prosecution of any German engaged in the anti-partisan campaign.[109]

By the second half of 1942, the partisan war was posing a significant challenge to the Germans' ability to control and administer the vast territories they had conquered. According to a report of the *Reichs-kommissariat Ostland* about the development of the partisan movement between July 1942 and April 1943:

> As matters stand today a large portion of last year's harvest is anni-hilated, farms burnt, dairies and industrial and commercial enter-prises destroyed, and almost the entire administrative apparatus which we set up in the district cities, towns and villages simply no longer exists. The population is completely intimidated and as a result of the long reign of the partisans in many cases has lost confidence in the power of the Germans.

The prescribed remedy, as always, was the application of yet more force: 'a substantial reinforcement of military and police forces is urgently necessary and the arming of these forces with heavy weapons is required' and 'hostages from individual villages must be selected who will be shot if there is an attack on these villages or if looting and destruction takes place on state farms. If that still does not work, then one must resolve to liquidate entire villages.'[110]

This, in turn, offered the opportunity to kill yet more Jews, some of whom indeed chose partisan activity rather than submit meekly to deportation and thus appeared to confirm the Nazi clichés about 'Jewish Bolshevism'. For example, following Operation Swamp Fever (carried out against partisans between 21 August and 21 September 1942), the head of the SS and police in the *Reichskommissariat Ostland*, Friedrich Jeckeln, boasted that not only were '49 bandit camps, bunkers and strongholds, as well as many villages located in the swamp regions, which served as hiding places, smoked out and destroyed', but also '389 armed bandits were shot in the fighting', 1,274 people suspected of being partisans were sentenced and shot, and '8,350 Jews were executed'.[111] Partisan activity offered pretext and justification for the murder of the Nazis' supposed racial enemies.

Reprisals and massacres committed by German forces were not con-fined to eastern and south-eastern Europe. Of course, the overwhelming majority of the victims of Nazi atrocities were in the east, but as the war dragged on German forces committed atrocities in the west as well, in

France and Italy as well as in Ukraine and Russia. Indeed, the behaviour of German forces in the east and west converged as the war progressed, and the practice of reprisal was remarkably similar whether it took place in France, Italy, Serbia or Russia. Fear of partisan activity combined with a desire for revenge for past attacks and contempt for conquered peoples, as well as the 'technocratic production of order'.[112] Villages suspected of harbouring resisters were surrounded. The men were shot, and in extreme cases so were the women and children (as in the famous case of Oradour-sur-Glane in June 1944, where Waffen-SS troops locked the village's women in the church, then shot and burned them).[113] Women suspected of fighting with the partisans were regarded as degenerate and thus meriting execution. Not just Waffen-SS units but also regular Wehrmacht units (as in Kommeno in Greece and Padule di Fucecchio in Northern Italy) were responsible for the massacre of women and children as well as of men.[114] The practice of Nazi war led inexorably to atrocities against civilians, and not just by the Waffen-SS and not just in the east.

Nevertheless, it was in the great war of extermination in the east that 'the barbarisation of warfare'[115] was most extreme. A number of factors came together to make this so. First, the Wehrmacht was sent into battle with criminal orders which sanctioned murder on a massive scale. This combined with a broadly held belief that eastern European people were primitive and dangerous, ideological indoctrination by the Nazi regime, and experiences – not least, seeing eastern European Jews in the poverty-stricken *shtetl* – which appeared to confirm negative racist stereotypes. Added to this, conditions on the eastern front were extremely harsh. There was sustained heavy fighting, fierce resistance by the Red Army and increasingly by partisan units. The exhausted troops, many of whom had had to march for hundreds of miles (for the Wehrmacht was not a truly motorized army – men marched and goods generally were moved by horses), were often ill, hungry and extremely cold during the winter months. Unlike the short victorious campaigns of 1939 and 1940, the fighting on the eastern front went on and on. Wehrmacht units often had little respite, and suffered tremendous numbers of dead and wounded. On the Russian steppes there stretched out before the German soldiers the prospect of seemingly endless war – a gruesome marriage of Nazi fantasy and nightmarish reality.

All this had an effect on the attitudes of German soldiers, and made it all the easier for them to accept and repeat anti-Semitic racist opinions: to assert that (as one corporal wrote in July 1941) the 'enemy is not made of real soldiers, they are guerrillas and killers'; to regard Russians as 'no longer human beings, but wild hordes and beasts, who have been bred by Bolshevism during the last 20 years'; to see before them 'what the Jewish regime has done in Russia'; and to believe, as one German NCO wrote in August 1942, that 'we must and we will liberate the world from this plague, this is why the German soldier protects the Eastern Front'.[116] German soldiers were able to convince themselves that they were 'fighting for a just cause',[117] that (in the words of one private) 'Such a huge battle has never before taken place on earth. It is the greatest battle of the spirits ever experienced by humanity, it is waged for the existence or downfall of Western man and the highest values which a people consciously carries on its shield.'[118] Certainly not all German soldiers shared such convictions, or felt them all the time. Many soldiers had deep misgivings about the atrocities they saw committed by their comrades and in Germany's name.[119] However, such statements – together with the record of the conduct of German military forces in the territories they conquered – show the extent to which Nazism had got under people's skin.

Towards the end of 1941, as the campaign against the Jews was entering its most comprehensively murderous phase, the Nazi regime had had to deal with military failure for the first time. Despite suffering enormous losses during the first weeks and months of the war, the Red Army had not buckled and the Soviet Union had not collapsed. At the gates of Moscow, the Wehrmacht found itself on the defensive as Soviet forces counter-attacked and drove the Germans back. In the crisis of December 1941, Hitler took two decisions which would have enormous consequences for the Nazi regime and the war it was fighting. On 11 December, following the Japanese attack on Pearl Harbor, Germany declared war on the United States. Vastly overestimating German military capabilities and spectacularly underestimating the military potential of the United States, Hitler ensured that roughly three-quarters of the world's human and material resources now were united against the Axis. Then, on 19 December, faced with the failure of the Wehrmacht to achieve victory over the USSR, the physical and psychological collapse of Army Commander von Brauchitsch (who on 15 December had confessed to

Franz Halder that he no longer saw a 'way out in order to rescue the army from the difficult situation')[120] and the possibility that the German lines might crumble, Hitler accepted von Brauchitsch's resignation and assumed direct personal command of the Army (as 'Supreme Commander of the Army' in von Brauchitsch's place).[121] Hitler's decision to take personal command revealed both his contempt for military professionals ('Anyone can do a bit of operational command')[122] and the importance of his experience of the First World War. Announcing this decision to his soldiers, the Nazi dictator told them:

> I already know war from the four years of the mighty struggle on the western front in 1914–1918. As a simple soldier I experienced the horrors of almost all the great battles. I was wounded twice and in the end was threatened with blindness. Therefore nothing that torments you, that burdens you, that worries you, is unknown to me.[123]

The front-soldier of the First World War was convinced that he knew best how to fight the Second.

With the German invasion crumbling before Moscow, Hitler insisted that the Wehrmacht hold its positions at all costs and 'without regard to the consequences'.[124] 'Every man must defend himself where he is.'[125] In taking this decision, Hitler may have saved the German forces from collapse before Moscow. However, the significance of this tactic extended far beyond what occurred in December 1941. The idea that German troops should hold their ground 'without regard to the consequences', should fight to the last man and the last bullet in seemingly hopeless situations, became fixed in the minds of the Nazi leadership and of Hitler in particular. He certainly convinced himself that, as he put it in May 1942, the fact 'that we got through this winter and today are again in a position to move into battle victoriously [...] is thanks only to the courage of the soldier at the front and my firm will to hold fast, cost what it will'.[126] Over the coming months and years, commanders who held out against impossible odds – such as Major General Theodor Scherer, the commander whose outnumbered and surrounded troops held out against Soviet forces at Cholm for 107 days between January and May 1942 – were accorded the highest praise.[127] (Scherer was decorated personally by Hitler.) Commanders who chose to retreat or surrender rather than have their troops die fighting against impossible odds – such as General Erich Hoepner, who withdrew his troops from the gates of Moscow in January 1942 rather than see them needlessly slaughtered, or Field Marshal Friedrich Paulus who surrendered at Stalingrad in 1943 – were cashiered and/or condemned as traitors to the German *Volk*. The fact that Hitler's tactics were vindicated at Moscow in 1941 set a terrible pattern for the years to come, when again and again German units would be expected to hold their positions and fight to the last man. This had reinforced Hitler's confidence in himself as military commander and his conviction that a racially superior German *Volk* could defeat a materially superior enemy provided that they had the proper strength of 'will' and fanatical, resolute leadership.

Back in the real world, the failure to achieve a Blitzkrieg victory over the USSR in 1941 fundamentally undermined the Nazi war. Soviet forces might have suffered enormous casualties, but they could call on reinforcements more easily than could the Wehrmacht, which was sustaining losses which were increasingly difficult, if not impossible, to replace. During the five months from November 1941 to the beginning of April 1942, the Wehrmacht lost roughly twice as many men (killed, wounded, missing and ill) as it gained through replacement; the situation with regard to transport, whether motor vehicles or horses, was even more imbalanced; and the fighting power of army units was falling due to a lack of experienced officers and specialists as well as the exhaustion of men, horses and materiel.[128] Nazi Germany was overstretched. Having been turned back at the gates of Moscow and having declared war on the most productive country on earth, Germany now desperately needed more labour, and looked increasingly to foreign workers to supply it (a theme to which we shall return below).

After the Germans' near disaster before the Soviet capital and Soviet successes in Ukraine, however, the Wehrmacht recovered sufficiently to launch huge new offensives. These succeeded in capturing new swathes of Soviet territory, and once again it seemed possible that the Nazi war might reach a triumphant conclusion. After bitter fighting in the Crimea during the spring of 1942, the main German military thrust this time round, Operation Blue – concentrating on the southern portion of the eastern front and aiming at Stalingrad and the Caucasus – was launched on 28 June 1942. As in the previous year, the Wehrmacht scored impressive successes, rapidly capturing large amounts of territory, taking the city of Rostov on the Don on 24 July and reaching the Volga near Stalingrad less than a month later. On 23 August the swastika flag was planted atop Europe's highest peak, Mt Elbrus in the Caucasus. However, German forces overextended themselves, as they had done during the previous year, and this time the Soviet military leadership had learned from past mistakes. The tide was set to turn.

Although it may not have been appreciated at the time, October 1942 marked a fundamental turning-point in Nazi Germany's war. Not only had the strategic initiative passed from the Wehrmacht to the Red Army, but Hitler was also confronted by the fact that his forces could not bring the war to a successful conclusion on their own. The Nazi regime might hope for a stalemate or that the Allied coalition might fall apart, but the Wehrmacht no longer could deliver victory; at best, it could deliver only war without end. This stark fact frames the second – and in terms of casualties, by far the more destructive – half of Nazi Germany's war. On the defensive, without a realistic prospect of victory, the Wehrmacht kept fighting for another two-and-a-half years. Nazi war became more radical than ever, and at this point fundamental and revolutionary changes were instituted in the recruitment of army officers, opening up the officer's career to all levels of society. Hitler had his revenge on 'the calcified Wehrmacht old gang', supplanting, as MacGregor Knox has pointed out, 'the Prusso-German *Offizier* by the National Socialist "Führer-personality"', which resulted in a 'people's officer corps' 'committed unto death to careers open to talent in war and mass murder'.[129]

Back at the front, the setting for the great military turning-point was the city of Stalingrad, stretched out for some 12 miles along the Volga. The battle for Stalingrad raged for over five months, from the German assaults of late August and September to the encirclement of German forces in the city on 23 November and the eventual surrender of Field Marshal Friedrich Paulus on 31 January 1943 (the other pocket of German forces, in the north of the city, held out until 2 February). It was a battle which proved incredibly brutal and bloody, ending with street-by-street, house-by-house fighting in bitter cold. Hitler had attached tremendous importance to the capture of the city, named after the Soviet dictator in 1925, and refused to allow his troops either to withdraw, even after they had been encircled and a break-out to the west offered their only chance to avoid annihilation or capture, or to surrender, when doing so might have saved at least some of the tens of thousands of wounded, freezing and starving remnants of the German Sixth Army. This time, Hitler's determination that his troops hold their ground and fight to the last, a tactic which earlier had been vindicated (at Cholm, Demyansk and, of course, at Moscow), had catastrophic consequences. By refusing the forces surrounded in Stalingrad permission to attempt to break out of the city when it might still have been possible to do so, the 'greatest military strategist of all time' and veteran of the trenches of the First World War sealed the fate of over 100,000 German soldiers in the greatest defeat yet suffered by the Wehrmacht. Of the once 300,000-strong German Sixth Army trapped in Stalingrad, between 30,000 and 45,000 had been flown out wounded, half were killed or died of cold, and over 100,000 surrendered to the Russians – of whom only about 6,000 survived captivity to return to Germany.[130]

The surrender at Stalingrad was regarded by broad sections of the German population as a turning-point in the war.[131] However, the shock of the defeat did not cause the Nazi regime to reassess its catastrophic course. How could it? On the one hand, the Allied policy of 'unconditional surrender', agreed by Churchill and Roosevelt at Casablanca on 24 January 1943, left no room for compromise; on the other, such a reassessment would have been the negation of what the Nazi regime and its ideology were about. Nevertheless, the defeat at Stalingrad signalled a shift in the regime's propaganda and its tactics for securing popular support for continued fighting. Against a background of the grim news from Stalingrad, chronic labour shortages and huge military losses which could not be made good, a new and essentially defensive message was conjured up to guide Nazi propaganda: that unless all resources were mobilized, Germany could lose the war, and that this in turn would lead to the horrors of Russian occupation and Bolshevism being visited upon the German people. The campaign was, in an ironic allusion to the German Labour Front's leisure organization 'Strength through Joy', dubbed one of 'Strength through Fear'.[132]

The most powerful expression of this new message – that the German people should be spurred on to greater efforts by stressing the seriousness of Germany's predicament and the fearful consequences of defeat – was Goebbels' great performance of 18 February 1943. Emphasizing the 'gravity of the situation' and a supposed determination to 'look the facts in the face, however hard and dreadful they may be', and with Albert Speer (who was demanding drastic measures to increase armaments production) at his side, Goebbels followed the 'tragic battle of Stalingrad' with his famous call for 'total war' at a rally of the Berlin Nazi Party at the city's 'Sports Palace' auditorium. In a speech broadcast to the nation, Goebbels invited his audience to scream its approval for a 'total war', 'a war more total and radical than anything that we can even imagine today'.[133] The popular response, at least in the short term, was overwhelmingly positive. According to the report of the SD on 22 February, a public 'whose morale again had reached a low point as a result of the development on the eastern front, above all the alarming news of the evacuation of Charkov [which had been retaken by Soviet forces on 16 February], was virtually longing for a clear description of the situation'.[134] It was this aspect of the speech, and in particular 'the announcement of the most radical application' of total-war measures which 'everywhere had met with the greatest approval'.

Goebbels ended his 'total war' speech with the cry, echoing Theodor Körner's call in 1813 during the Wars of Liberation against Napoleon: 'Now, people rise up and let the storm burst forth!' His audience in the Sports Palace stamped their approval. Yet this was no programme for extracting Germany from the terrible hole which Nazism had dug for it, and upon reflection the German people knew it. Even in the immediate aftermath of the speech, popular anxieties remained focused on the eastern front and on the tremendous losses which the Wehrmacht had suffered and was likely to suffer in the near future.[135] Within a few weeks the resonance of Goebbels' speech had faded, and scepticism grew. The SD reported in mid-March 1943: 'People say that on the surface little has changed and the energy which initially gripped the population [after Goebbels' speech] has fallen back into indifference and scepticism. Of the storm which – according to Reich Minister Dr. Goebbels' peroration at the Sports Palace rally – was supposed to burst forth among the people, there is no trace.'[136] The concerns of everyday life in wartime, the mounting military casualties, the bombing, the fear of what was happening on the eastern front (and what might happen if and when the Russians arrived in Germany) dominated popular consciousness. The broad basis of consent which the regime previously had enjoyed – as it succeeded in reviving the economy, reversing the Versailles settlement and winning a series of stunning military victories with surprisingly low (German) casualties – was being undermined. The Nazi leadership may have fantasized about having the people 'rise up', but by this point in the war the main concern for most of their subjects was just to survive.

The defeat at Stalingrad, together with the setbacks in North Africa (where Rommel's forces had been turned back at El Alamein in late October and the Allies successfully landed in Morocco and Algeria in early November), left Nazi Germany, although still in control of most of the European continent, effectively without a military strategy. As the military historian Bernd Wegner has observed: 'Hitler and the military leadership entered the year 1943 *without* any overall strategic concept – a fact which fundamentally differentiates this year of the war from all those which preceded it.'[137] The vast Barbarossa campaign of 1941 had aimed to annihilate the Soviet military and bring about the collapse of the USSR, and the huge offensives of 1942 (in which, among other things, the USSR's oil fields were to be conquered) had aimed to remove vital resources from Soviet control. Their failure, the setbacks in North Africa, the expectation of an Allied landing in western Europe which tied down many German soldiers in anticipation of the assault,[138] and the fact that German forces now were largely on the defensive, left the Nazi regime without a military or political strategy. The armed-forces leadership were aware of the huge and growing imbalance of forces to their disadvantage, and yet never seriously discussed that this meant, over the medium term, that Germany's military position was hopeless. To quote Bernd Wegner once again: 'Characteristically, there was in the "Führer state" at this time no longer even a forum in which questions of major strategy could have been discussed.'[139] Unlike the United Kingdom or the United States, in Germany a systematic, comprehensive evaluation of overall strategy was almost completely absent.[140]

This was not simply a consequence of faulty organizational structures. For an ideologically driven regime whose goal was unlimited expansion and the racial restructuring of the European continent through war, there were no rational strategic options to pursue. Instead, when the

4 November 1923. Five days before the putsch, paramilitary groups march through Munich after the foundation stone for the Bavarian war memorial had been laid, with Hitler (bare-headed, holding a walking stick) among those reviewing the formations.

The 'Day of Potsdam', 21 March 1933. The 'new Germany' claims legitimacy from the old, as a deferential Chancellor Hitler bows before Reich President von Hindenburg, dressed in his Field Marshal's uniform.

The Wehrmacht displays its heavy artillery at the Nuremberg Party Rally in September 1937.

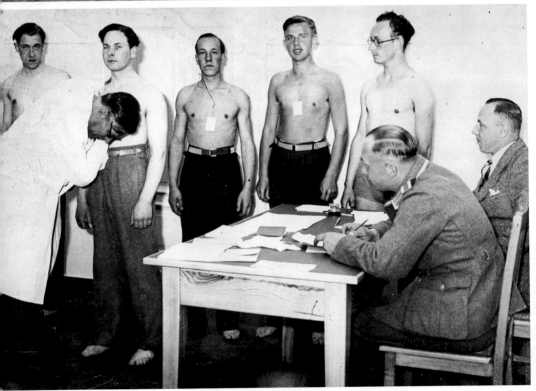

Berlin, June 1935. Members of the birth cohort of 1914–15 are examined by a military doctor for conscription.

Jews in Vienna are forced to scrub the streets after the *Anschluss* in 1938.

Berlin, November 1938. Passers-by inspect the damage done to a Jewish-owned shop during the so-called 'Night of Broken Glass'.

LEFT: The Front soldier of the First World War returns as conqueror in 1940. After the fall of France, Hitler visits a site near Vimy, in Flanders, where he had fought in 1917.

BELOW: Hitler observes a moment of silence at the cemetery where the youthful German volunteers who fell at Langemarck in November 1914 were buried.

RIGHT: 6 July 1940. At the height of his popularity after the defeat of France, Hitler greets ecstatic crowds together with Göring from the balcony of the Reich Chancellery.

TOP: Some of the 400,000 Soviet soldiers taken prisoner during the first three weeks of the 'Barbarossa' campaign. Very few would survive German captivity.

ABOVE: December 1943. Victims of the Allied bombing are laid out for identification in a hall decorated with Christmas trees in Berlin.

TOP: 1 May 1945. Germans flee from the advancing Soviet forces across a damaged railway bridge over the Elbe at Tangermunde.

ABOVE: 2 May 1945. Soviet tanks roll past the Reichstag building, a red flag flying from its roof.

3 May 1945. German soldiers are led away into captivity by Soviet troops in the Berlin district of Kreuzberg.

The consequence of Nazism and war. A British soldier uses a bulldozer to push bodies into a mass grave after the liberation of the concentration camp at Bergen-Belsen.

Chief of the Wehrmacht Staff Alfred Jodl spoke on 7 November to assembled government and Nazi Party leaders about 'the strategic position at the beginning of the fifth year of war', he had little to offer beyond the assertion that in November 1918 Germany had been 'broken not at the front, but at home' and a reference to the 'ethical and moral foundations of our struggle'. Jodl summed up, in astounding testimony to an inability or unwillingness to think in rational strategic terms and to the extent to which Nazism had permeated the professional military mentality:

> At this hour I want not to speak from the mouth but to acknowledge from the deepest recesses of the heart,
>> that our trust and our faith in the Führer is limitless,
>> that for us there is no higher law and no more sacred duty than to fight to the last breath for the freedom of our people,
>> that we want to rid ourselves of everything soft and disloyal,
>> that all the threats of our enemies only will make us even tougher and more determined,
>> that we will not surrender to the cowardly hope that others could save us from Bolshevism, which will sweep everything away if Germany falls,
>> that we would defend even the ruins of our *Heimat* to the last bullet, because it is a thousand times better to live in ruins than to live in slavery,
>> that we will win because we must win, for otherwise history would have lost its meaning.[141]

However, it was not world history but the German military élite which had lost its bearings, an élite which had so distanced itself from military professionalism and become so corrupted by the Nazi racial state that, instead of developing a rational strategic perspective, it could assert only that 'we will win because we must win'. During the First World War, it should be remembered, when Germany's military position had become hopeless in the summer of 1918, the military leadership – and, in the end, even that subsequent propagandist for 'total war' Erich Ludendorff – faced the fact that the war could not be won and demanded that Germany seek an armistice.[142] During the Second World War, when

Germany's military position became hopeless, such rational assessment of the military situation was not an option.

The fact that there was no forum left in which overall strategy could be discussed is a reflection of the character of the Nazi state, in which the coordination of policy had been undermined by institutional Darwinism and extreme personal dictatorship. More specifically, the inability to formulate strategy and the willingness of the generals to commit their troops to suicidal battles during the last years of the war was a consequence of what Bernd Wegner has described as the step-by-step 'military seizure of power' by Hitler.[143] This gradual take-over – by becoming first Supreme Commander of the Wehrmacht, then Supreme Commander of the Army as well, then assuming practical command of the operations of individual army groups and effectively reducing the Wehrmacht leadership staff to a personal office – in the end left the military leadership without responsibility for military strategy. More generally, this process signified the domination not of politics by the military (as many generals had hoped for in 1933) but of the military by (Nazi) politics. That the Wehrmacht had surrendered itself to Hitler and Nazi ideology, had willingly engaged in a war of racial extermination and had abandoned moral responsibility and military rationality would leave it with no choice in the end but to fight for a criminal and vastly destructive lost cause.

Following the surrender at Stalingrad, the Wehrmacht was thrown on to the defensive. On 8 February Soviet forces took Kursk; on 12 February they recaptured Rostov; on 16 February Charkov, Ukraine's second largest city; on 3 March they took Rzhev, 100 miles to the west of Moscow. Yet German forces were far from beaten. Experienced and desperate, they managed to mount a major counter-offensive, beginning on 19 February (the day after Goebbels had delivered his 'total war' speech) and lasting until 17 March. In so doing they managed to stabilize the front in Ukraine and to recoup some of their losses – most importantly, re-taking Charkov on 14 March, a success which a hopeful German public seized upon as a 'turning-point of the Second World War'.[144] Although, with hindsight, it is apparent that by this time Nazi Germany no longer had a realistic hope of winning the war, nevertheless to a people convinced of their superiority over a 'primitive' enemy there still seemed grounds for believing in the possibility of victory. The

Wehrmacht remained a formidable force; severe military setbacks had not led to a precipitate German military collapse, and German forces – even with their backs to the wall – remained capable of effective fighting.

The late-winter counter-offensive by the Wehrmacht was to be followed by a third major offensive once the weather had improved. Initially planned for the spring, it was not until the summer that the Wehrmacht was able to mount Operation Citadel, designed to encircle and destroy the Soviet forces in the Orel-Belgorod salient near Kursk. Unlike the massive attacks against the USSR in 1941 and 1942, however, this time (in the words of Gerhard Weinberg), 'the aim was to seize the initiative and win a great tactical victory, not a knock-out blow'.[145] This time the Soviet military leadership anticipated the German attack and were able to bring it to a halt within a matter of days. Launched on 5 July, five days before the Allied landing in Sicily, Citadel was the greatest tank battle in world history and the last major German offensive on the eastern front. Altogether, the Germans deployed 900,000 men and 2,700 tanks against Soviet forces totalling more than 1,300,000 men and over 3,400 tanks. Soviet forces were well prepared for the Germans, who managed to advance only a few miles and at tremendous cost.[146] Although German forces inflicted enormous losses on the Red Army – indeed, far greater than those they suffered themselves – by 13 July the offensive had stalled, to be followed by successful Soviet campaigns driving the Germans westwards. At Kursk, the German forces were outgunned and outmanoeuvred; the Red Army had won 'the most important single victory of the war'.[147] No longer did the Wehrmacht enjoy the advantages of surprise, tactical superiority and better training which had brought it such impressive successes in 1941 and in the summer of 1942. Launching the gigantic battle of Kursk effectively speeded up the German defeat, for although the Red Army suffered far greater losses than did the Wehrmacht, the Wehrmacht had much greater difficulty in replacing men and materiel. On 23 August Charkov was again in Soviet hands. On 6 November the Red Army had retaken Kiev. The writing was on the wall.

But who was reading the writing on the wall? Certainly not Hitler, committed as he was to a racial war in which there could only be either victory or destruction. Hitler had been fond of using an apocalyptic rhetoric of 'either/or', of domination or annihilation, and by 1943 he had steered Nazi Germany into a position where sooner or later it would face annihilation. However, unlike their leader, the German population were reading the writing on the wall. They were becoming increasingly fearful and pessimistic about the course of the war and, within the limits imposed by a terroristic police state, critical of the government. The relationship of the German people to Nazism had always contained a certain degree of ambivalence. There had been approval of much that the Nazi regime succeeded in doing, agreement with at least parts of the Nazi 'world view', and an opportunist acceptance of the benefits of a redistributive, egalitarian *Volksgemeinschaft* to be achieved through what Götz Aly describes as the 'popular unity of economic, social and racial policy'.[148] Yet this approval coexisted with everyday concerns which had little to do with the horrible visions which transfixed Hitler and Himmler and spurred the drive to redraw the racial map of Europe through mass murder.[149]

German business interests also tended towards realism rather than apocalyptic Nazi fanaticism. Businesses had to deal with practical problems, and felt the need to look ahead rationally to a world after German defeat. In September 1943 the supervisory board of the Deutsche Bank, for example, was discussing contingency plans for the decentralization of their bank, in order to be prepared for the possibility of defeat and subsequent Allied occupation.[150] During the later stages of the war, the management of Daimler-Benz looked to the future, becoming 'increasingly preoccupied with the development of an overall strategy for the immediate post-war period', a strategy which would ensure that the company maintained productive capacity after the inevitable German military collapse.[151] The Nazi leadership might have committed itself, and the empire it ruled, to an increasingly radical and irrational racist crusade and a suicidal final struggle, but many within that empire realized that, apocalyptic Nazi visions notwithstanding, life would have to go on.

The summer of 1943 marked the last time – with the exception of the Ardennes Offensive (the 'Battle of the Bulge') at the end of 1944 – that the Wehrmacht had been able to take the initiative. Instead, the German armed forces now were compelled to fight a defensive war. On the eastern front, the Wehrmacht faced offensive after offensive by a Red Army which succeeded in recapturing large tracts of the territory it had lost in the first two years of the 'Great Patriotic War'. Despite periodic and often impressive tactical successes, in which the Wehrmacht was able to hold positions and even drive Soviet forces back temporarily, the initiative now definitively lay in the hands of Nazi Germany's Communist enemy. In the west, there was no longer any hope of invading Britain, which had become a huge base for the North American troops being amassed for an eventual landing across the Channel. The German tactic was essentially to hold on to what had been conquered in 1940 and await the inevitable opening of a second front. In the south, with Allied forces on their way to taking Sicily, Mussolini was deposed at the end of July 1943 as Italian Fascist resolve dissipated in the face of Allied military successes. The new government in Rome, with Marshal Pietro Badoglio as its Prime Minister, signed a secret armistice with the Allies at the beginning of September and surrendered openly a few days later, while Mussolini (who had been arrested by his erstwhile underlings) was rescued on 12 September by German forces and set up in his rump Fascist Republic of Salò in the Italian north. On the seas, the high hopes that the German Navy's U-boat campaign would cut Allied supply lines had not been realized. In the air, the Allies had established their superiority not only over German-occupied territories but also over Germany itself. German cities were being pounded by ever greater numbers of Allied bombers and, while the German air defences were able to inflict serious casualties on Allied bombing crews, the days when the Luftwaffe could carry the war to the cities of the enemy were largely over. In the occupied territories, whether in Russia or France, Greece or Yugoslavia, German authorities and their local collaborators faced an increasing problem of resistance and sabotage, as the brutality of the occupation regime and the growing realization that Germany would lose the war drew ever greater numbers into the resistance struggle. And the losses of territory which Germany suffered in 1944 meant the loss of raw materials vital to the war effort: the oil fields at Ploesti in Romania, the iron-ore reserves of Lorraine, the Belgian iron and steel industry. Europe, from the German perspective, was now a besieged and battered 'fortress' – *Festung Europa*.

The last two years of war saw the step-by-step destruction of Fortress

Europe while the Wehrmacht – faced on the one hand with Allied demands for 'unconditional surrender' and on the other with a political leadership unwilling to consider compromise or surrender – could do little but try to keep Allied forces at bay and hope for a miracle. The way in which the German military responded to the impossible position in which it found itself had profound consequences, for the greatest number of German casualties came in the final two years of the war. That is to say, according to figures compiled by Rüdiger Overmans,[152] over three million German soldiers died for absolutely nothing, when there was no real chance of Germany avoiding defeat.

The story of Nazi Germany's war during 1944 is one of attempts, sometimes successful and more often not, by the Wehrmacht to resist the tide, and of successful Allied offensives which pushed the Germans back hundreds of miles. 1944 opened with the Red Army crossing the 1939 Polish border, on 4 January, after having advanced 170 miles in two weeks. At the end of January, the 900-day siege of Leningrad was lifted. On 15 March Soviet forces reached the River Bug, which had been the starting-point for the Barbarossa campaign in June 1941, and in April the Russians reached the borders of Romania and Slovakia. On 6 June, the long-promised second front finally was opened when the British, Canadians and Americans landed on the beaches of Normandy – an invasion which was followed a little over two weeks later, on 22 June (the third anniversary of the launching of Barbarossa), by a huge Soviet offensive against the German Army Group Centre along a 450-mile front. On 3 July Soviet forces took the Belorussian capital of Minsk, or what was left of it. By the beginning of August they had reached the Baltic coast to the west of Riga and the Lithuanian city of Kaunas, cutting off the Wehrmacht's Army Group North and all road links between Germany and the Baltic countries. With the loss of Riga on 13 October, the Army Group North was confined to the Curland and could only be supplied by sea. Towards the end of August, as Soviet troops arrived at its borders, Romania's government was overthrown, the country switched sides and declared war on Germany. In the west, by the beginning of July the Allies had been able to land over 900,000 men in France. In late July they had made their breakthrough at Avranches; by 17 August they had taken Chartres and Orleans; and by 23 August Paris had been liberated. In southern France the Allies landed on 15

August between Cannes and Toulon. And on 21 October, after weeks of heavy fighting, American troops captured Aachen, the first German city to fall to Allied forces.

Rather than face the reality of a lost war, the Nazi regime did just the opposite. The option of facing reality was extinguished with the failure of the attempt by Claus von Stauffenberg to assassinate Hitler at the dictator's East Prussian headquarters at Rastenburg on 20 July 1944. Deeply disturbed by the prospect of looming catastrophic defeat, conservative officers and associated figures – including former Chief of Staff Ludwig Beck – had hoped to depose the fanatical, uncompromising Nazi leader and his entourage and then negotiate a peace, to rescue what might still be rescued from the disastrous situation. That is to say, the aim of the bomb plot of July 1944 was to substitute a regime which had no strategy but to fight, kill and die, and no goal but to go down in flames in a gigantic, apocalyptic final battle, with a regime which would seek a strategy for dealing with a rapidly deteriorating military situation. That might have been a naïve hope, but it does not mean that the failure of the plotters in July 1944 was without important consequences. The plotters were rounded up, tried and killed; and the last shred of respect which Hitler had possessed for the officer corps disappeared as his worst suspicions and prejudices were confirmed. The failure of the attempt on Hitler's life removed any possibility of curbing the destructive radicalism of the Nazi regime, and was followed by unparalleled bloodshed. Hitler's survival in July 1944 effectively led to the deaths of millions more people during the last and most murderous year of the war.

The failure of the bomb plot was followed by yet further radicalization of the regime, and of its relationship with the Wehrmacht and its officer corps – symbolized by the substitution on 23 July 1944 of the 'German greeting' (with the arm outstretched) for the traditional military salute. More importantly, following the unsuccessful assassination attempt, Hitler approved the move to total war which his Minister for Armaments and War Production, Albert Speer, had been urging before the bomb went off at Rastenburg.[153] On 25 July 'total war' was declared for a second time, as Hitler issued his decree 'on the application of total war' and named Goebbels Reich Plenipotentiary for Total War.[154] Goebbels set to work with a radical agenda, which included extending the normal working week from forty-eight to sixty hours, closing down universities insofar as they were not engaged in matters necessary for the war effort, banning exhibitions, shutting the casinos at Baden-Baden, Zoppot (near Danzig) and Baden near Vienna, and forbidding journeys of over 100 kilometres without a special permit.[155] However, while Goebbels' efforts may have aroused 'great expectation' among the German people for a short period, the resulting measures certainly could not alter the course of the war.[156] Germany was doomed to defeat whether or not the casino at Baden-Baden had to close its doors.

More important for the lives (and deaths) of people still within the Nazis' grasp than the increase in the responsibilities of Goebbels were the powers which now accrued to Heinrich Himmler. Himmler was not only appointed Commander of the Replacement Army in July 1944, but in September he also was given oversight of prisoners of war – thus granting him command over important areas once reserved for the Wehrmacht[157] – and by the end of 1944 he had roughly 590,000 fighting men under his command in the Waffen-SS (compared with about 150,000 at the end of June 1941).[158] At the end of November 1944, Hitler also appointed Himmler commander of German forces on the Upper Rhine, which had become the front line as American forces approached the Reich.[159] As Germany headed for defeat, responsibility for the conduct of the war was moved increasingly from the Wehrmacht and into the hands of the most radical exponents of Nazism.

That the Nazi regime remained on a course characterized by radicalism, racism and death was demonstrated by two important developments. First, the slaughter of the Jews did not cease just because the Nazis were losing the war and Soviet forces were closing in on the killing fields in the east. (The Red Army liberated the Maidanek extermination camp near Lublin on 23 July 1944.) Instead, there seemed almost to be an urgency to finish the job before it was too late. Beginning in May 1944, Eichmann and his staff began deporting the Jews of Hungary – the last major Jewish population left in Europe, numbering some 750,000 people – to their deaths at Auschwitz. By the end of June, half of them had been killed, and, after a temporary pause, the deportations continued into the autumn.[160] At the same time, on 6 August 1944, the last of the ghettos, at Lodz, was liquidated and its remaining 60,000 inhabitants were sent to the gas chambers of Auschwitz. (Most of the ghettos had already been liquidated on Himmler's orders in the summer of 1943.) Despite the fact that defeat was staring the Nazi regime in the face, it persisted in its attempt to restructure Europe's racial composition through mass murder.

Second, during the summer of 1944, after the Allied landings in Normandy, German casualties reached levels never before seen, not even with the defeat at Stalingrad. July and August 1944 proved the bloodiest months yet for the Wehrmacht; over 215,000 German soldiers were killed in July and nearly 350,000 were killed in August.[161] With defeat unavoidable, the Nazi regime persisted in sending its soldiers to their deaths in hundreds of thousands. In September 1944 Himmler, speaking before the assembled commanders of the various military districts about calling up not only those born in 1928 (as was on the cards for the coming January) but also the cohort born in 1929, declared: 'It is better if one young cohort dies and the people are saved than if I spare the young cohort and an entire people of 80–90 million dies out.'[162] Shortly thereafter, the regime resorted to a sort of Nazi *levée en masse*, with Hitler's call – made public on 18 October 1944, the anniversary of the 'Battle of the Nations' against Napoleon in 1813 – creating the *Volkssturm*.[163] Supposedly embodying the spirit of the *Landsturm* of 1813, the *Volkssturm* was to bring all men between the ages of sixteen and sixty capable of bearing arms into an 'army of millions of idealists' who would prefer death to giving up the 'freedom' of the German people.[164] Although the military value of the poorly armed *Volkssturm* was virtually nil, this did not stop Hitler from calling on teenagers and old men to fight and to die in a lost cause. Instead of rational strategy and rational politics, all that Nazism had to offer, in the end, was an apocalyptic vision of bloodshed, destruction and death.

Where rational planning could not be disregarded, even once the war had turned against the Nazi regime, was the economy. Whatever the fantasies of the Nazi leadership and whatever the propaganda about the need for fanaticism to overcome adversity, the supply of weapons, vehicles, fuel, food, uniforms and bullets depended on the efficient organization of production and distribution. During the rise as well as the fall of Germany's military effort, her armed forces were dependent upon the capacity of the German economy, and the economy of German-occupied Europe, to produce what was needed to keep fighting. This is not to suggest that the Nazi economy was a rational, capitalist economy driven essentially by the profit motive. Of course, there had been a great deal of money to be made through the war economy, from the plunder of conquered territories from the Atlantic to the steppes of Ukraine, and from the exploitation of slave labour – not to mention the huge opportunities for corruption which the Nazi dictatorship offered its faithful servants.[165] However, it would be mistaken to conclude, as it was once fashionable to do, that the underlying logic of Nazism was unbridled capitalist exploitation, that the aim of the Nazi leadership was to provide capitalist interests with opportunities to make vast profits through war and plunder. While there was little compunction in German boardrooms about taking advantage of the commercial opportunities presented by war, the Nazi regime was no puppet of big business. It was not private companies but the Four-Year Plan and the Reichswerke Hermann Göring – which had secured state control over resources needed for war, which profited massively through the expropriation of Jewish property, which became a huge employer of foreign and POW labour, and which became the largest firm in German-dominated Europe – which spearheaded Nazi Germany's industrial expansion across a subjugated continent.[166] The Nazi project was about restructuring Europe through war and mass murder, not about securing German capitalism. As Michael Thad Allen has observed in his recent study of the SS business empire and its exploitation of slave labour, the goal was not necessarily to make profit. Rejecting what it saw as mindless liberal-capitalism, the SS 'based its modernity on productivism and racial supremacy'.[167] The currency of Nazism was not money, but racist violence.

The organization and direction of the Nazi war economy may be divided into two fairly distinct phases, which roughly paralleled the course of Germany's war. The change occurred in 1942, shortly after the Wehrmacht had been turned back at the gates of Moscow and after Hitler had expanded his European war into a world-wide conflict by declaring war on the United States. In February 1942 Hitler appointed his favourite architect, Albert Speer, to be Minister for Armaments and

Munitions, replacing Fritz Todt, who had died in a plane crash near Hitler's headquarters in Rastenburg. Although Speer did not rush to impose radical organizational changes on armaments production, his privileged access to Hitler and lack of responsibility for what had gone before put him in a strong position, from which his ministry was able quickly to displace both Göring's Four-Year-Plan machinery and the Wehrmacht's War Economy and Armaments Office, headed by General Georg Thomas, as the bureaucracy responsible for war production.[168] Speer worked closely with industry, minimizing the interference of the military in the organization of war production, and (successfully) seeking to increase production through centralization and greater efficiency (rather than through further conversion from civilian to military production).

Although it may be tempting to regard the years 1939–41 as the phase of a limited war economy based on a strategy of Blitzkrieg – of short wars which would not require massive armament in depth – and followed by the phase of a total-war economy from 1942 to 1945, there are reasons to doubt this division. Although German armaments production trebled between 1941 and 1944 despite the increasingly heavy Allied bombing, and although the Nazi regime had been reluctant to impose extreme economic burdens on the German civilian population and thus risk a repetition of the revolution of 1918, the less impressive production figures for the first years of the war were not less impressive for want of trying. During the first three years of war, the concentration of the German economy on military needs could be seen on a number of fronts. There had been a sharp decline in consumer expenditure per capita between 1939 and 1942 – considerably more so than was the case in the United Kingdom at the same time.[169] In wartime Germany, rates of savings, which had been encouraged by government, increased hugely; between 1939 and 1941 deposits in savings-bank accounts grew more than fivefold, a development which signalled the restriction of civilian consumption and effectively provided additional funds to be channelled into the war effort.[170] Levels of taxation, already high, rose significantly between 1939 and 1941. Although the greater part of Nazi Germany's war was financed by borrowing and although Hitler repeatedly displayed reluctance to allow his Finance Minister to raise taxes,[171] central government tax receipts were more than 70 per cent higher in 1941 than they had been in 1938 (and receipts from income and business taxes more than doubled).[172] In 1939–40 military spending by the German government was more than double the (already high) levels of the previous year, and by 1941–2 they had nearly doubled again.[173] By 1941 the claims of the armed forces on Germany's non-food production were approaching 50 per cent.[174] This amounted altogether to a phenomenal militarization of the German economy in order to wage global war.

The problem was that the militarization of the German economy had not been well managed. This is where Albert Speer came in. In the words of Richard Overy, 'The great success that Speer had in multiplying war output by 1944 was not a result of converting more civilian resources to the war effort, but of using the resources already converted more rationally.'[175] Speer oversaw a concerted drive to rationalize production, to reduce costs and labour inputs, to increase production efficiency, to improve administration and tighten control over the use of raw materials, factory equipment and labour, to reduce the number of different types of weapons in production, to adopt new production methods and to impose standardization across German industry.[176] While the move towards the rationalization of production was already under way when Speer became Armaments Minister in early 1942, he enjoyed a great advantage in getting his objectives met: Hitler's support. The result was a 'production miracle' in the German armaments industry, brought about by making better, more efficient use of resources and keeping the Wehrmacht out of economic decision-making. Despite the difficulties caused by Allied bombing, Germany managed to produce nearly twice as many rifles in 1944 as in 1941, over three times as many hand grenades, over seven times as many howitzers, and over three times as many aircraft.[177] The fact that Germany had the weapons to continue fighting to the bitter end, causing the deaths of millions of people in the last two years of the war, was to no small degree the achievement of Albert Speer.

The Nazi war economy was not merely an economy at war; it was an economy of racial war and plunder. The economic assets of subjugated peoples, beginning with the assets of Jews within Germany and then throughout Europe, were looted. Jewish-owned banks ended up in the clutches of German banks;[178] Jewish-owned factories and shops were taken over by Germans who enriched themselves at others' expense, and tens of thousands of Germans took advantage of wartime auctions of the personal property left behind as Jews were deported to their deaths. In a study of 'aryanization' in Hamburg, Frank Bajohr has noted that from February 1941 until April 1945 scarcely a day went by without stolen Jewish property being auctioned off to the public.[179] The Nazi regime systematically plundered the economic resources of the countries it conquered, with little or no concern for what this might mean for their populations. Productive capacity throughout occupied Europe was harnessed to the Nazi war machine; agricultural produce was taken to ensure that the German consumer would not suffer food shortages, even if this meant that millions of people in Eastern Europe might starve to death. At a conference held on 7 and 8 November 1941 to discuss how to increase the performance of the German war economy, Göring had observed that bringing large numbers of able-bodied Soviet labourers to work in Germany and taking foodstuffs from the occupied USSR to the Reich would lead to a catastrophic deterioration in the food supply for the people there under German occupation, which in turn could lead to 'the greatest mortality since the Thirty-Years War'.[180] But no matter. Already on 4 November daily food rations in cities in the conquered Soviet territories had been fixed at roughly 1,200 calories for those engaged in 'useful' work and roughly 850 calories for those not working in ways deemed beneficial to the Germans; children under fourteen and Jews were allocated a mere 420 calories per day.[181] This was, quite simply, a recipe for starvation – so that Germans might eat.

The demands of the war economy, the militarization of society and the structures of the racial state intersected most clearly in the exploitation of foreign labour. The serious labour shortages which the Germans had faced before the outbreak of war were exacerbated by the huge wartime increases in armaments production and the conscription of millions of men into the armed forces. By the end of 1944, of the 12,889,000 German men between the ages of eighteen and thirty-eight (i.e. those born between 1906 and 1926), 10,627,000 – or over 80 per cent – were under arms.[182] Yet, in contrast to what occurred in the United Kingdom and the United States, where the participation of women in the work-force grew by roughly 50 per cent during the war, in Nazi Germany between 1939 and 1944 it barely increased.[183] The way the Nazi regime sought to square the circle was to employ millions of foreign labourers – workers recruited or conscripted in countries occupied by German forces, prisoners-of-war, and slaves in the SS concentration-camp empire.

The recruitment of workers in occupied territories had begun within days of the invasion of Poland and accelerated after the failure to achieve a rapid victory over the Soviet Union, as German manpower increasingly was drawn into the armed forces. Already by September 1941 roughly 3.5 million foreign labourers (including POWs) were working in the Reich, and the crisis of manpower after the military setback at Moscow in December was overcome largely through the exploitation of Soviet labour. Force was used from the outset to acquire labour from occupied Soviet territory: within months of invading the USSR, the Wehrmacht conscripted Soviet citizens to work for the occupation forces, and on 19 December 1941 the Eastern Ministry issued an ordinance stating that 'all inhabitants of the occupied Eastern territories are under a public obligation to work according to their capacity' – thus providing a legal basis for coercion.[184]

Propaganda, financial inducements and quotas of labourers which local authorities had to deliver through 'conscription operations' brought over a million Soviet labourers to Germany by the end of 1942. By November 1942 there were 4.66 million foreign workers in Germany, with most of the increase coming from the USSR, and Germany continued to recruit large numbers of foreign workers during 1943 and 1944. At its peak, in 1944, roughly a quarter of the labour force of the Greater German Reich was foreign: in August 1944, 7,651,970 million foreigners – 5,721,883 civilian labourers and 1,930,087 prisoners of war – were registered as working in the German economy, comprising 26.5 per cent of the 28,853,794 people employed in Greater Germany.[185] Nearly half those employed in German agriculture (2,747,238 out of 5,919,761, or 46.4 per cent) were foreign, as were over one third of those employed in mining (433,790 out of 1,289,834) and nearly one third of those in the construction industry (478,057 out of 1,440,769). The largest contingents were Soviet (2,126,753, including 631,559 POWs), Polish (1,688,080, including 28,316 POWs), and French (1,254,749, including 599,967 POWs). Of the total of 5,721,883 civilian labourers registered in August

1944, one third (1,924,912) were women; generally, the lower an ethnic group's position in the Nazi racial hierarchy, the greater the proportion of women among the foreign labourers in Germany (with over half the civilian workers from the USSR being female).

The presence of millions of foreign workers intensified German fears of the supposedly primitive people working in the Reich. In September 1942, for example, the Chief State Prosecutor in Nordhausen (in Thuringia) became particularly agitated about 'Russians running around loose' and committing 'the gravest acts of violence'. He concluded:

> The Russians, who think completely differently than we do and who are on a much lower cultural level, cannot be judged according to our standards, i.e. they cannot be dealt with and sentenced according to our laws. To punish Russians for, for example, theft from fields, theft of food, vagrancy and breach of contract with penalties which are normal for Germans would be an absurdity and would not be suitable for eliminating this extremely dangerous vagabondage, which has become a real public nuisance. It therefore is understandable that the State Police attempt to get on top of these cases and to 'liquidate' the Russians.[186]

Germans feared what the foreign labourers might get up to, and worries about the 'plague' of foreigners, alongside the assumption that they 'think completely differently than we do', provided apparent justification for harsh police controls. Racist policies fuelled racist assumptions, and vice versa.

The same was true in the realm of sex. The German authorities, from Himmler on down, were anxious that the presence of so many foreigners should not lead to sexual relations across supposed racial boundaries. Concern to maintain the dignity of German women and the supposed purity of the German race combined with anxiety about the allegedly 'animal' lust of the foreign men who had been brought into the Reich in their millions during the war. Harsh penalties were imposed on those who transgressed: a male Polish or Russian labourer who had sexual intercourse with a German woman during the war could face execution (sometimes by public hanging, with fellow foreign labourers forced to watch), and in 1944 between two and three Soviet workers per day faced execution orders for illegal contact with German women. The numbers of German women sent to concentration camp for forbidden contact during the war approached ten thousand annually.[187] And to meet the sexual needs of foreign male workers, foreign prostitutes were provided, something which Hitler had urged wherever large numbers of foreign labourers were concentrated and which Himmler had begun to organize within weeks of the outbreak of war.[188]

The presence of foreign labourers throughout Germany placed racism at the centre of everyday life. It was not the murder of the Jews, which was committed largely out of sight to the east, or the deaths of millions among the conquered peoples of Eastern Europe, but the presence of foreign labourers almost everywhere in Germany which reinforced racist ideology through everyday practice. Foreign workers were employed in subordinate positions, generally to do the heavy and dirty work which Germans preferred not to do themselves; they often were poorly housed and poorly clothed; personal contacts and friendships between Germans and foreign labourers (although not infrequent) were officially discouraged, not least through harsh police measures; and the millions of exploited foreign labourers comprised an ever-present potential threat to Germans should the Nazi system break down. Germans grew to accept, and where possible to profit from, the racial hierarchies enforced by the Nazi state; they became linked to the Nazi regime through a combination of prejudice, opportunism, greed and fear.

The most vicious exploitation of foreign labour occurred in the SS concentration-camp and slave-labour empire, where people quite literally were worked to death. Of all the Nazi concentration camps, perhaps the worst was Mittelbau-Dora. Opened in 1943 near the Thuringian city of Nordhausen (otherwise noted for its production of spirits) and occupying a vast system of gigantic tunnels which had been built in the mid-1930s to house Germany's strategic oil reserve and which extended for 11 miles under the Thuringian hills, Mittelbau-Dora was used for armaments production – most famously (but not exclusively) for the assembly of the V2 rockets which fell on London during the last year of the war.[189] Conditions were terrible: the prisoners, forced to work and sleep in cold, damp tunnels, quickly fell victim to lung infections;

those who entered the camp in a healthy condition were lucky if they survived more than a few weeks.

As in all concentration camps, at Mittelbau-Dora there existed a racial hierarchy, with Jews at the bottom and subject to especially harsh treatment. Yet, surprisingly perhaps, a national group which fared particularly badly was the Italians, hundreds of whom landed in the camp after Mussolini's overthrow in July 1943.[190] The harsh treatment meted out to the Italians casts an interesting light on Nazi war. After the collapse of Mussolini's government, some 600,000 Italian troops who had refused to continue fighting for the Axis were deported to Germany and put to work in conditions similar to those which Soviet labourers had to endure.[191] These Italian prisoners of war too were regarded as lesser human beings, as the prejudices which many Germans had long held about their erstwhile Fascist comrades in arms now could be expressed openly. What is more, during the last two years of the war Wehrmacht units engaged in a series of massacres in the northern part of Italy which they continued to occupy, massacres which claimed the lives of over 9,000 Italian civilians (including at least 580 children under the age of fourteen) and 11,000 military personnel.[192] Prejudice combined with desire for revenge against an unfaithful ally[193] as Italians, too, were allocated their place in the deadly racial hierarchy.

During the early years of the war, the horrors unleashed by the Nazi regime had not really impinged on the daily lives of most German civilians. Provided that they were not 'tainted' with 'Jewish blood', were not regarded as 'life unworthy of life' due to disability, had not been involved in political opposition, had not been classified as habitual criminals and did not get caught up in the prison and concentration-camp system, German civilians initially were hardly affected. Taxes were raised, men mobilized, foreign countries occupied (offering new possibilities for tourism in uniform, which confirmed racist ideology to soldiers who came as conquerors), natives massacred. Yet until the second half of 1941, most Germans remained largely unscathed by the wars that their regime had launched. Military casualties still were relatively low, living standards had not yet declined drastically, and German cities and towns had not yet been bombed as were Warsaw, Rotterdam and Coventry. However, this changed dramatically in the second half of the war, as the violence of war came to Germany with a vengeance, in particular with the bombing. Few aspects of the Second World War made so deep and lasting an impression on Germans as did the bombing of their cities. Hundreds of thousands of Germans were killed, millions were made homeless, millions were evacuated or fled from endangered urban centres into the safer countryside.[194] The shattering of their physical environment, of the buildings and urban landscapes with which they had grown up, had long-lasting consequences. Fixed points in the lives of millions of Germans were obliterated and, as we shall see, Germans emerged from the rubble in 1945 with a profound sense of their own victimhood.[195]

After some relatively minor raids during the first two years of war, the Allied bombing of German cities began in earnest in the spring of 1942, with the British 'area bombing' of Lübeck by 234 RAF planes on the night of 28–9 March. In the words of the official British history of the 'strategic air offensive', the 'outstanding success' of the Lübeck raid 'was a convincing demonstration of what could be achieved by the tactics of concentrated incendiarism'.[196] The 500 tonnes of bombs which fell on Lübeck that night formed only the beginning. A month later, from 23 to 27 April, it was the turn of Rostock. On 31 May 1942 RAF Bomber Command flew the first thousand-bomber raid, against Cologne, where 1,130 aircraft dropped 1,500 tonnes of bombs on the city in ninety minutes. In 1943 the US Air Force joined in, with its attack on Wilhelmshaven on 27 January. During the spring and summer of 1943, the cities of the Ruhr industrial region were hit again and again, and then in late July and early August the most terrible example of what 'area bombing' could achieve occurred with Operation Gomorrha – the attack on Hamburg. Between 24 July and 3 August, four great waves of bombers dropped their loads of explosives and firebombs on Germany's premier port city and 'gateway to the world'. On 28 July the bombing of Hamburg caused the first man-made firestorm, which created such powerful air currents that it fed itself by sucking in human and material debris and which reached temperatures of 1,000 degrees centigrade at its core. At least 30,000 people were killed; nearly one million fled the city; roughly half of Hamburg's dwellings were destroyed and another 30 per cent badly damaged.[197] In the following months, city after city in

western and central Germany was bombed; in November 1943 the air
Battle of Berlin began; during 1944, as the front neared Germany and
more cities came within easy reach of Allied bombers and Germany
could not produce sufficient aviation fuel for all its new fighter aircraft,[198]
the bombing campaign intensified; and in the first months of 1945 the
bombing reached its peak, in terms of tonnage dropped,[199] with the
destruction of Magdeburg (in January), Dresden (in February) and
Swinemünde and Würzburg (in March).

At end of this campaign, the German urban landscape consisted
largely of piles of rubble. In Cologne, which was the target of 262
bombing raids during the war, 200,380 of the city's 252,000 dwellings
were destroyed. Whereas at the beginning of the war Cologne had
contained 768,000 inhabitants, at its end only about 100,000 were living
in the rubble.[200] In Hamburg, of the 552,484 dwellings which had stood
in 1939, less than half – 266,592 – were left in 1945. In Berlin, 556,000 of
the city's pre-war housing stock of 1,502,383 dwellings were destroyed.
Some smaller cities suffered even greater proportional destruction:
Hanau (near Frankfurt am Main) lost 88.6 per cent of its dwellings; in
Paderborn, 95.6 per cent of all dwellings were destroyed; in Düren (near
Aachen), the figure at the end of the war was an almost unimaginable
99.2 per cent.[201] The bombs fell on supporters and opponents of the
regime alike, on the old and the young, on Germans and on foreigners
trapped in German cities. On 3 and 4 April 1945, when the Thuringian
city of Nordhausen was bombed, some 8,000 of the 65,000 people then
in the overcrowded city were killed, including 1,300 concentration-camp
prisoners housed in barracks.[202] Altogether, over 500,000 people were
killed by the bombing in Germany – some estimates reach nearly
600,000 – and more than 800,000 were injured. In the last four months
of the war alone, when the bombing campaign was at its most ferocious,
at least 130,000 people died.[203]

If Nazism had brought revolutionary changes to people's lives
through constant mobilization, police terror, physical and social mobil-
ity, militarization, conquest, plunder and racial hierarchy, it was the
bombing which more than anything else destroyed the order and security which Germans cherished. Bombing not only damaged morale; it
also contributed mightily to what Neil Gregor, discussing the effects
of the bombing in Nuremberg, has described as a 'process of social

dissolution, in which the dominant process was a successive reduction of horizons to the level of local community, family and the individual'.[204] Social organization, social networks and social solidarities were shattered, in what Bernd Rusinek has described in his history of Cologne during the last year of the war as 'the increasing chaos of the social terrain'.[205] Together with the physical environment, society and community were being smashed, leaving individuals to look out for themselves in cities and towns plagued by petty and not-so-petty criminality and among growing indifference to human suffering. As one observer in March 1944 put it, noting the callousness with which bombed-out Berliners came to be treated as their numbers mounted, 'now a more raw wind is blowing'.[206] Perhaps most disturbing was that the sight of the corpses became part of everyday life as the Third Reich went down in flames. The disposal of so many thousands of dead posed enormous difficulties for the authorities, in cities where infrastructure had largely been destroyed. When the city of Heilbronn, for example, suffered a massive air raid on 4 December 1944 in which more than 70,000 fire-bombs were dropped, more than one third of the buildings in the city were destroyed, a further quarter were severely damaged and about 6,500 of the city's roughly 60,000 inhabitants were killed. For days after the raid, groups of police, soldiers and workers roamed the city, removing corpses from cellars of buildings to be buried.[207] These experiences would haunt survivors for the rest of their lives, in particular those who had been children during the war and came of age in post-war East and West Germany. As one survivor of the bombing raid which destroyed much of Magdeburg on 16 January 1945, who as a seven-year-old saw his grandmother burned alive, put it nearly fifty years later: 'This terrible experience burned itself into us for ever. I have never got over it.'[208]

The bombing campaign was one sign among many that ending the war was the only way to stop the German people's suffering. Yet the Nazi regime remained unwilling to seek peace. Indeed, even when Germany was riding high after the defeat of France, at no point had there been serious discussion about how the war might be brought to an end. Nazi Germany had no 'exit strategy' from war. German foreign policy, such as it was, essentially consisted of keeping Germany's allies tied to the Reich as it went down to defeat. German military strategy, such as it was, consisted of trying to ward off the inevitable collapse while shedding as much blood as possible. And through it all, the terrible machinery of genocide continued to operate, with the deportation and murder of the Jews of Hungary in 1944 and the death marches of Jews and other camp prisoners during the last months and weeks of the war.

In the end, Nazi Germany achieved something quite remarkable: total defeat. For the first time in modern history, a developed industrial state fought to the very last, surrendering only once enemy troops had captured the seat of government in street-by-street fighting which cost both the invaders and the defenders hundreds of thousands of casualties. Not even imperial Japan held out to the bitter end, choosing instead to bow to the inevitable after atomic bombs had been dropped on Hiroshima and Nagasaki. But German troops continued fighting even as Soviet forces approached the garden of the Reich Chancellery.

That they did fight to the bitter end surprised even many functionaries of the regime, obsessed as they were with the spectre of November 1918. Typical of official anxieties about popular morale were those expressed by Eduard Frauenfeld, the head of the Nazi Party's propaganda office in Vienna, in September 1944. According to Frauenfeld, 'the hope that we still ever could bring the war to a victorious conclusion has sunk to zero'; 'as a result', he warned, 'the danger of the repetition of the events which unfolded in November 1918 is imminent', 'despondency' and 'complete indifference' to calls to fight on were growing, and 'negative hopes' ('ah, if we lose the war, it won't be so bad!') had become widespread.[209]

Yet the spectre never materialized. At the end of the Third Reich, there was no repetition of what had occurred in Germany and Austria in November 1918, the fears of a Nazi leadership haunted by the military collapse and political revolution which had ended the First World War notwithstanding.[210] Certainly many Germans came to feel, as one muttered in an air-raid shelter in Berlin at the end of March 1945, that 'if our soldiers were as clever as in 1918, the war already would be over'.[211] However, in 1945 Germany experienced not a re-run of the 'covert military strike' or the domestic unrest which had culminated in political revolution in 1918, but an economic and military collapse during a terrible 'final struggle' in which collective action proved impossible and most people looked no further than to their own survival.

In early 1945, the odds against survival reached their peak. Not only was the bombing campaign against German cities and towns at its most intense, but Allied offensives from east and west brought the land war on to German territory with unparalleled ferocity. In the west, on 3 January the Allies counter-attacked after the failure of the Wehrmacht's Ardennes offensive. Then in the east, on 12 January, the Soviet Army began its great offensive, charging forward from the Vistula to the Oder in less than three weeks, and precipitating the flight of millions of Germans westwards. The result was casualties on a colossal scale – so much so that Germany in January 1945 became the site of what perhaps was the greatest killing frenzy the world has ever seen. Certainly the last months of the war were, for Nazi Germany, by far the most bloody. In January 1945 alone, more than 450,000 German soldiers lost their lives (a considerably greater number of soldiers than either the United Kingdom or the United States lost during the entire war). In February, March and April, the number of German military dead approached 300,000 per month.[212] That is to say, over one quarter of Germany's entire military losses during the Second World War occurred in the last four months, when it was obvious that there was no possibility of a German victory and no military rationale for continuing to fight.

In the wake of the failed bomb plot, successful Allied offensives in east and west, and the capture of Aachen by American forces, Hitler became more determined than ever that radical National Socialism would displace traditional militarism. On 25 November 1944 he issued an order which effectively undermined the established military hierarchy, demanding that any officer who lacked the 'indispensable qualities for the struggle' – 'energy, willingness to take decisions, firmness of character and strength of belief, and hard unconditional readiness for action' – 'must step down'. 'If a troop leader [...] must give up the fight, then he must first ask his officers, then the non-commissioned officers, and then the men, if one of them wants to carry out the task and continue the fight. If this is the case, he is to transfer command – without regard to rank – and fall in.'[213] Under the pressure of a lost war, military rationality crumbled before a faith in the value of 'will'. Where traditional military values had failed, Nazi fanaticism was expected to succeed.

At the end of March 1945, General Alfred Jodl, the man who on 7 May 1945 was to sign the capitulation of the German Armed Forces at Reims, wrote in his diary, 'if one no longer has any reserves, then fighting to the last man makes no sense'.[214] Although Jodl discovered 'sense' a bit late in the day (and too late to save him from the hangman's rope at Nuremberg in 1946), he was right. However, by the spring of 1945 the Nazi war effort had little to do with sense. Commanders abandoned their responsibility for the survival of the soldiers under their command and deliberately put their troops into hopeless positions where they were surrounded, expected to fight to the last bullet, and could look forward only to death.

Hysterical demands were issued to continue the struggle, to display 'fanatical will' in the face of hopeless odds. Among the most shrill voices was that of Admiral Karl Dönitz, who had been appointed Commander-in-Chief of the Navy in January 1943 and whom Hitler was to name as his successor (and who after the war tried to present himself as a responsible military leader concerned about the survival of his troops and the German population). Only weeks before unconditional surrender, on 7 April 1945, Dönitz called upon all naval officers to fight to the bitter end:

> In this situation one thing matters: to continue fighting and despite all the blows of fate still to bring about a turning-point. [...] Fanatical will must enflame our hearts. [...] Our military duty, which we fulfil unwaveringly whatever may occur to the left and right and all around us, makes us stand courageously, firmly and loyally like a rock of resistance. Anyone who does not behave thus is a scoundrel. He must be strung up with a placard tied around him: 'Here hangs a traitor.'[215]

This appeal so impressed Martin Bormann, Hitler's *éminence grise* at the Party Chancellery, that he circulated it to the entire Nazi Party leadership.

Given what we know of Germany's war against the Soviet Union, it perhaps is not surprising that German soldiers continued to fight to the bitter end against the Red Army. The conduct of Nazi Germany's war in the east left German soldiers in little doubt about what might be in store once the Red Army arrived in Germany and had an opportunity for revenge. German propaganda reinforced the menacing spectre of savage, bloodthirsty subhumans arriving from the east – most strikingly after the Soviet capture of the East Prussian town of Nemmersdorf in October 1944, when 'the gruesome Bolshevik crimes in East Prussia', including pictures of mutilated corpses of German victims, were 'featured prominently and effectively and commented upon with extreme severity' in German news propaganda so as to arouse the greatest possible fear.[216] The spectre of barbarous 'Asiatic' hordes in Red Army uniform was presented repeatedly to the German people, up to the last days of the Reich. In his eleventh-hour 'Call to the Soldiers of the Eastern Front' on 15 April 1945, for example, Hitler warned that should the Soviet Union prevail, 'old men and children will be murdered and women and girls will be reduced to being barracks whores' while 'the remainder marches off to Siberia'.[217]

Yet while Germans were prepared to expect the worst from the enemy to the east, the Nazi propaganda did not necessarily stir up the associations which the regime desired. A report of 'confidential information' drafted shortly after the discovery of the Nemmersdorf atrocity, noted that:

> Citizens are saying it is shameful to feature these [photographs of German victims at Nemmersdorf] so prominently in German newspapers. [...] They [the Nazi leadership] must surely realize that every intelligent person, upon seeing these victims, will immediately think of the atrocities we have committed on enemy soil, yes even in Germany. Did we not slaughter the Jews by the thousands? Don't soldiers repeatedly tell of Jews who had to dig their own graves in Poland? [...] We have only shown the enemy what they can do with us should they win.[218]

It was not just fear of the Slavic 'sub-humans' who were closing in on Germany but also guilt and well-founded fears of revenge which drove Germans to continue their hopeless struggle against the foe from the east.

The same cannot quite be said of the struggle in the west, however, and yet here, too, German forces fought fiercely to the bitter end.[219]

Indeed, the motive behind the Ardennes Offensive of December 1944 had been, as Hitler put it, 'to make it clear to the enemy that [...] he can never count on our capitulation, never, never'.[220] While German forces had failed to achieve the desired breakthrough in Belgium and to recapture the port of Antwerp, during late 1944 and early 1945 the Wehrmacht inflicted on US forces the highest casualties they experienced during the entire war; and the surrender of 9,000 surrounded GIs on 19 December in the Schnee Eifel was the most serious defeat which US forces suffered in Europe. Even in April 1945 – when there was no conceivable remaining rationale for offering resistance to the Americans – German forces killed almost as many GIs as they had monthly on average since the landings at Normandy![221] The first German city to fall to American troops, Aachen, was captured on 21 October 1944, but it was only after another six months of bloody fighting that American soldiers could shake hands with their Soviet allies at Torgau on the Elbe (on 25 April 1945, the same day as the Red Army surrounded German forces in Berlin). The war in the west had not been a war of extermination; it was not an ideologically inspired racial struggle as the war in the east had been, and western prisoners of war generally fared far better in German captivity than did Soviet prisoners of war. Nevertheless, in the end the Nazi leadership called for a final struggle scarcely less radical in the west than in the east, and German forces fought to the finish not only against the Russians but also against the British and Americans.

As the war entered its final stages, Hitler became increasingly determined to leave only 'scorched earth' behind. Already in the previous summer, as Allied forces were nearing the borders of the Reich, the Nazi dictator had spoken of his intention to turn this destructive dream into reality, but there was little enthusiasm for a scorched-earth policy in German industry.[222] However, in March 1945 the matter came to a head. Faced with an utterly hopeless military situation and the collapse of German industry, and with Albert Speer now pleading for an end to hostilities,[223] Hitler rejected any thought of an armistice and issued his famous Nero Order of 19 March 1945. He instructed that 'all military, communications, industrial and logistics installations as well as material assets within Reich territory which the enemy can use for continuing his struggle either immediately or in the foreseeable future are to be destroyed'.[224] Significantly, he assigned responsibility for carrying out this final campaign of destruction not to the military (who were supposed to help as required) but to the Nazi Party *Gauleiter* and Reich Defence Commissars. With final defeat only weeks away, Hitler abandoned any thought for how 'his people' might survive the conflict he had launched.

At this point, Speer, whose organizational talents as Armaments Minister had contributed so mightily to prolonging the war (and whose ministry was not mentioned in Hitler's Nero-Order), saw fit to confront his leader.[225] After the collapse of Germany's offensive in the Ardennes and with the rapid advance of the Red Army, it had become clear to Speer that there was no alternative not only to defeat but also to unconditional surrender. The Armaments Minister, whose power had been on the wane since late 1944 and whose ministry no longer directed a coherent armaments economy,[226] now tried to save what he could. On 29 March Speer wrote to Hitler, stressing that 'until this point I believed whole-heartedly in a good end to this war' but going on to say that 'I no longer can believe in the success of our good cause if in this decisive month we simultaneously and systematically destroy the basis of the life of our people. [...] We must not destroy that which generations have built.' He concluded by urging his leader 'therefore not to inflict this step to destruction on the people'.[227] Although Speer's resolve crumbled in Hitler's presence,[228] in the following weeks he did what he could to subvert the Nero Order. In this he was not alone; others in his ministry, as well as many local politicians, were loath to see the complete destruction of what was left of their country. By this point, the dictator's orders were no longer necessarily being obeyed – and in the chaos and economic paralysis enveloping Germany in March 1945 there was probably not enough explosive still available to carry out the order anyway.[229] Hitler's radical policy could not be put into practice. The grip of the Nazi regime was finally beginning to loosen.

As the war came to Germany with full force in 1944 and 1945, it became less a matter exclusively for the military. The last months of the war saw a resurgence of the Nazi Party, which had been largely eclipsed after Hitler established his dictatorship and again after Germany went to war. However, as the war-related destruction came to dominate the lives of Germans and the efforts of local government, as the Allies closed in on the Reich, and as the prestige of the Wehrmacht plummeted along with Germany's military fortunes, the NSDAP came back into its own. Increasingly, the party assumed responsibility for organizing the home front, as the home front came ever closer to being the military front. Control of civil defence within the Reich was placed not with the military but with regional Reich Defence Commissars, who generally were the Nazi Party *Gauleiter* of their regions, while the military was limited essentially to its operational tasks at the front.[230] Although the Wehrmacht had supported the idea of creating militia units for some time, when the *Volkssturm* was called into being in the autumn of 1944 it was not the Wehrmacht but Martin Bormann (as head of the Party Chancellery) and Heinrich Himmler (as Commander of the Replacement Army) who issued the instructions.[231] In the final phase of the racial 'struggle for existence', Hitler chose to keep control of the new militia units out of the hands of the military establishment. If the Wehrmacht could not deliver the final battle of racial war, then the party would!

This opened the door to the senseless and suicidal tactic of trying to turn every German city and town into a fortress, in which the invading Allied armies would suffer the maximum casualties and be bled white. Looking ahead to the arrival of Allied forces in Germany, Hitler had demanded in September 1944 that 'every block of houses in a German city, every German town must become a fortress on which the enemy is either bled to death or in which its defenders are buried beneath [the rubble] in man to man combat'.[232] What had happened to German forces in Stalingrad was now supposed to happen to British, American and Soviet forces in German cities from Aachen to Breslau. If the Soviet Union's war had its turning-point in the terrible street-by-street fighting in Stalingrad, then Germany would achieve a similar revival of fortunes through maximum bloodshed on the streets of German towns and cities. The war would become a gigantic battle of attrition, in which a racially superior and fanatically committed German people would grind down Allied armies and break the will of Allied soldiers to keep fighting.[233]

The message was repeated again and again, in an increasingly hopeless situation. On 12 April 1945 – less than a month before the unconditional military surrender – Himmler ordered: 'No German city will be declared an open city. Every village and every city will be defended and held with all means.'[234]

What this meant in practice was illustrated by the case of Breslau. The Silesian metropolis had largely escaped Allied bombing but held out as 'Festung Breslau', surrounded by Soviet forces from mid-February, until 6 May 1945 – four days after Berlin had fallen to the Red Army. By the time Breslau capitulated, two thirds of the city had been destroyed, 20,000 houses had disappeared, roughly 6,000 German and 8,000 Soviet soldiers and at least 10,000 civilians (including 3,000 suicides) were dead.[235]

The surrender of the university town of Greifswald without a fight by its military commander Rudolf Petershagen on 30 April was the exception which proved the rule – and saved that town from destruction.[236] The *Volkssturm*, which was supposed to mount the final struggle in the various 'fortress' cities, was incapable of offering significant opposition to the invading Allied armies,[237] and served merely to increase the number of casualties at the behest of a Nazi leadership which had distanced itself increasingly from reality.

With Party radicals in command, the terror of the Nazi regime continued to the very end. Looters were shot and local Nazi Party functionaries were keen to let the public know it, especially where those shot were foreigners.[238] Drum-head courts were introduced, and the results were displayed for all to see – as announced in the headline of the last-ever edition of the *Stargarder Tageblatt* on 17–18 February, which could serve well as an epitaph for the Third Reich: 'On Adolf-Hitler-Square the hanged are swinging in the wind'.[239]

The most terrible treatment was reserved for those who had been enslaved by the Nazi racial state, however. In both eastern and western Europe, the SS closed down its camps as Allied armies approached, and shipped or marched the surviving inmates to concentration camps within the Reich, camps which were ill-equipped to receive a sudden large influx of prisoners. In early 1945, for example, the impending capture of the Auschwitz and Gross Rosen complexes by the Red Army provided the occasion for the most extreme inhumanity imaginable. Weak, desperately ill prisoners were transported in open railway carriages in the middle of winter, and prisoners barely strong enough to walk were forced on to death marches, as the SS evacuated those euphemistically described as 'weak' and 'not capable of work'.[240] Some idea of the grisly consequences can be gained from the account, given shortly after his liberation in 1945, of a prisoner who had been forced to unload the dead and dying from rail cars as they arrived at Mittelbau-Dora in Thuringia:

> These people were evacuated from a camp in Poland before the Russian offensive. They were transported from Poland to central Germany in open goods wagons for 20 days without food. On the way they froze, starved or were shot. Men, women and children of all ages were among them. When we took hold of the dead, arms, legs or heads often came off in our hands, as the corpses were frozen.[241]

Between mid-January and mid-February 1945 the number of prisoners at the main Mittelbau-Dora camp increased by 50 per cent. Housing provision was primitive, death as a result of undernourishment and disease common. And, if that were not enough, the camp administration reacted to the worsening conditions by stepping up its terror: in March 1945 150 prisoners were hanged.[242]

Within German cities, too, the last weeks of war saw the murder of large numbers of foreign prisoners. In the late winter and early spring of 1945 – when controls over foreign labourers were breaking down, when many were starving and when roaming gangs of foreign labourers were committing crimes and looking forward to the imminent defeat of the 'master race' – hundreds of foreign workers who had landed in Gestapo gaols, often for theft of food and for looting, were massacred.[243] In Dortmund alone, more than 230 men and women, most of them Russian workers and prisoners of war, were shot in the back of the neck by the Gestapo. This 'naked terror of the final phase of war' was not a response to orders from the centre. It persisted even beyond the point where there was any direct link with the Nazi regime in Berlin, in regions cut off from the Nazi leadership and the Führer in the Reich capital – for example, in Schleswig-Holstein, which had been cut off from Berlin at the end of March but where the Gestapo and SS continued to execute prisoners.[244] This last orgy of murder was fuelled by prejudice as crime by eastern workers appeared to confirm racist stereotypes, by hatred of people whose countrymen were pounding Germany into the ground, by grudges and thirst for vengeance, and a feeling among Gestapo and SS members who saw little future for themselves in a post-war world that they might as well take as many people down with them as possible. In some respects these crimes paralleled the execution of German 'defeatists' and deserters during the last weeks of the war. Yet they had another, racial dimension: these foreigners – generally from eastern Europe, branded as criminal, often ragged and in ill health, disorderly and constituting a threat to Germans now that the Nazi state was crumbling – were of precisely those groups which the Nazi regime had sought to annihilate. This last escalation of police violence, as Ulrich Herbert has observed, 'can be regarded in many respects as the epitome of National Socialist racial insanity and of the thinking and behaviour of its proponents'.[245]

With the Wehrmacht crumbling, the opportunities for soldiers to make themselves scarce, leave their units and sit out the final stages of the war in relative safety increased, and the number of soldiers who deserted rose accordingly.[246] To prevent this, military police and SS units patrolled behind the lines, in order to catch and kill any soldier who might be suspected of desertion. Any soldier who was apprehended and was unable to provide the necessary identification, or who was suspected of desertion, faced hanging or the firing squad.[247] In January 1945 Himmler had commended the commander of the Fortress Schneidemühl (a German city 200 kilometres east of Berlin) not least because he had shot retreating German soldiers and hung signs from the corpses announcing 'that is what happens to all cowards'.[248] Orders were issued to 'strengthen the front' by capturing deserters, and distributed to the Nazi Party *Gauleiter* on 9 March: all Wehrmacht soldiers who were discovered away from their units and had not been wounded were to be shot.[249] This was no mere rhetoric, as General Wilhelm Wetzel (Deputy Commanding General of the Tenth Army Corps and, in the words of Manfred Messerschmidt, 'an officer of the good old "unpolitical" Reichswehr school') made clear in a proclamation to his troops: 'On 27 March 1945 21 soldiers who the court martial has sentenced to death for desertion were shot in Hamburg. Every shirker and coward will meet the same fate without mercy.'[250]

One may ask what was the sense of such draconian measures at this late date, just weeks before Germany's unconditional surrender. Two answers suggest themselves. First, there was the memory and supposed lessons of the end of the First World War, when 'shirking' behind the lines by hundreds of thousands of soldiers and large-scale desertion accompanied the German collapse in 1918 – when, as Hitler put it in *Mein Kampf*, 'an army of deserters poured into the stations at the rear or returned home'.[251] The remarkable severity with which Wehrmacht 'justice' treated those accused of desertion – some 15,000 of whom were executed, as opposed to just eighteen German soldiers executed for desertion in the First World War[252] – was an expression of the determination that, as Hitler had sworn in September 1939, there would 'never be another November 1918 in German history'. Second, as the end approached, so grew the fixation upon the fantasy of a 'final struggle' in which Germany somehow would emerge triumphant and for which only unconditional commitment and faith in victory was sufficient. Two days after the executions in Hamburg, on 29 March, Field Marshal Walter Model expressed the ideological dementia which had come over a military leadership that, in its saner moments, knew that the war was lost:

> In our struggle for the ideal world of National Socialism against the spiritual wasteland of materialist Bolshevism, we must win with mathematical certainty if we remain unshakeable in our will and faith ... The victory of the National Socialist idea stands beyond doubt, the decision lies in our hands.[253]

With Germany's military position collapsing, all that the generals could offer their troops was faith and annihilation.

The civilian population, too, was placed, literally, in the firing line. On 15 February the radical Reich Justice Minister Otto Georg Thierack issued a decree setting up drum-head courts martial, consisting of a judge, a Nazi Party functionary and a Wehrmacht officer.[254] These courts were to be established in 'defence regions threatened by the enemy', to act 'with the necessary harshness' against all those who out of 'cowardice and self-interest' attempted 'to evade their duties with regard to the general public'. Their jurisdiction extended to any acts 'by which

German fighting strength and determination to fight is endangered',
and they had only three sentences at their disposal: death, acquittal or
handing the accused over to another court. Writing to the Nazi Party
Gauleiter in western Germany, where the British and Americans were
driving forward, Martin Bormann recommended these courts as a
'weapon for the extermination of all parasites to the *Volk* [*Volks-
schädlinge*]', to be used 'as the Führer would have done, ruthlessly
and without regard to person and rank'.[255] As the final collapse drew
near, even the drum-head courts were dispensed with, and on 3 April
Himmler – who by this point himself was seeking to make contacts with
the Allies behind Hitler's back – ordered:

> At the present juncture in the war it all depends on the stubborn,
> unyielding will to hold out. The most drastic measures are to be taken
> against hanging out white flags, opening up anti-tank defences, not
> appearing for service in the *Volkssturm* and similar phenomena.
> Where a white flag appears on a house, all the male persons are to be
> shot.[256]

Vicious and vengeful terror was aimed at 'defeatists' doing little more
than trying to survive the inevitable defeat of the Third Reich in one
piece. At the end of April 1945, the Intelligence Staff of the US Sixth Army
Group, which had occupied large portions of Baden, Württemberg and
western Bavaria, observed that German civilians had to protect their
homes and property not so much against the Allies as against those Nazi
'fanatics' who were unwilling and unable to accept defeat.[257] In the last
days of the Reich, what remained of the Nazi *Volksgemeinschaft* was held
together by terror and murder.

In addition to the escalating terror and the bombing, Germans found
that their country had become the front line. German cities became the
scene of bitter and costly street-fighting, as Allied forces brought massive
firepower to bear on what was left of the German military – most
famously in the battle for Berlin, which began on 16 April and lasted
until 2 May.[258] Wide stretches of the German countryside were laid waste
in the final battles as German military casualties reached their peak.
And while Germany was being turned into a blood-soaked battlefield,
during the last months of the war, as Soviet armies reached territories

settled by Germans, there occurred one of the largest flights of human beings in world history.

Exposed for years to Nazi propaganda which had stressed the supposedly bestial, primitive nature of the 'Asiatic' hordes now streaming into Germany from the east, fearful of the revenge which Soviet troops might exact for what had been done in their country under German occupation, and cognizant of news and rumours about the behaviour of Soviet forces as they arrived in the Reich, Germans fled ahead of the advancing Red Army. Millions of Germans were on the move, taking what belongings they could in suitcases, on trains, on boats, on carts in organized 'treks' moving westwards from one town to the next. The overwhelming majority of the fleeing Germans were women, children and the elderly. Many died along the way in the bitterly cold winter weather, as they left their homes never to return. A racist war which had begun with German forces carrying out mass deportations ended with millions of Germans being uprooted from their homes. By the spring of 1945, the numbers of refugees from the east and evacuees from cities threatened by bombing had reached such proportions – an estimated nineteen million people at the end of March[259] – that one may speak of the widespread destruction of German society. By the end of the war, one quarter of the entire German population had been uprooted, their social networks broken, their economic position destroyed.

In the last months of the war, just about all the once-stable structures of everyday life in Germany disintegrated. The country was literally falling apart, as Allied troops captured ever greater slices of German territory and various parts of the country were cut off from one another. Millions of Germans were fleeing westwards, carrying what was left of their worldly possessions. Bombing and, increasingly, battles on the ground had made an increasing proportion of the German population homeless; and almost everyone had lost friends and relatives. This, no less than the ubiquitous police terror, ensured that there would be no revolution in 1945 as there had been in 1918; it was all Germans could do to survive.

In the end, Hitler was proved right in at least one respect: as he had predicted when the Second World began, 'November 1918' was not repeated. The Wehrmacht did not crack; the more than ten million soldiers in the Wehrmacht in 1944–5 did not follow the example of the imperial German armed forces in 1918, who gave up while still standing on enemy territory. As Andreas Kunz has pointed out in his recent study of the German Army's final months, 'in fact it was the Wehrmacht whose military shield actually made possible the continued existence of the Nazi regime into the spring of 1945'.[260] Before Alfred Jodl signed the unconditional surrender of Germany's armed forces on 7 May 1945 in the American headquarters at Reims, the Wehrmacht had had to be smashed flat and the Soviet flag was flying over the Reichstag. The combination of fear, terror, lack of alternatives and identification with the Nazi regime held that regime together to the bitter end.

The chaos and extreme violence of the last stages of the Second World War was the consequence and culmination of Nazi war: war which had been inspired by a crude Darwinian and racist vision of humanity, which was characterized by a refusal to calculate rationally the likely outcomes of actions, which led to the collapse of normative constraints on civilized behaviour, which opened the vistas for committing mass murder on a hitherto unimaginable scale, and which had turned the continent of Europe into a gigantic prison and a sea of blood. If there was a distillation of Nazism, it lay in the senseless destruction of human life during the final months of the war. In the end, Nazism offered no vision of a 'post-war'; planning for what might come after a German defeat was completely outside the frame of Nazism. In the end, all Nazism had to offer was war and destruction, war without end or an end through war.

Nevertheless, the story of Nazism and war does not end with the horrors of the last months of the war or the German surrender in May 1945. For one thing, and this often is forgotten, the government under Karl Dönitz which succeeded Hitler and continued to function in a manner of speaking until its members were arrested on 23 May was a Nazi government.[261] For another, and far more importantly, the consequences of Nazism and war shaped Germany and Europe for the remainder of the twentieth century. Particular attention has been paid in this book to the last months of the war not only because an appreciation of their horror shifts the commonly received picture of Germany's war (which tends to focus on Barbarossa, Stalingrad and the murder of the Jews in 1941 and 1942) but also because they created the basis for how Nazism and the Second World War were remembered (and forgotten) subsequently. The events of 1944 and 1945 – the experiences of the bombing, of flight westwards ahead of the advancing Russians, of bitter battles fought on German soil with unimaginable numbers of casualties – were so catastrophic for the German people that the shock of this 'final struggle' displaced other, earlier memories of Nazi Germany's war.[262] For many Germans, the Second World War came to mean the terrible suffering they endured during its last months, rather than the comparatively good life they had enjoyed in the early war years or what Germans had inflicted on others. It is hardly surprising that, in the wake of the Second World War, Germans' perceptions of Nazi war differed fundamentally from those of other Europeans, coalesced around a widespread sense of having been victims, and provided a basis for a post-war politics and culture of silence regarding much of what had occurred in the Third Reich.

CHAPTER FOUR

....

THE AFTERMATH OF THE
SECOND WORLD WAR

Deep in his bunker at the Reich Chancellery in the early hours of 29 April 1945, with Soviet troops only a few hundred metres away and just hours before he was to put a bullet through his head, Adolf Hitler dictated his final 'political testament' to his 'most faithful Party comrade' Martin Bormann. The terrible attempt to restructure the racial map of Europe through war had ended in defeat, but not before perhaps fifty million people had lost their lives as a result. Having decided to kill himself, the Nazi dictator looked back over his career. He began where this short history of Nazism began, with the First World War:

> More than thirty years have now passed since in 1914 I made my modest contribution as a volunteer in the First World War that was forced upon the Reich.

After naming his successors to take the reins of what remained of government – with Karl Dönitz as President of the Reich and Joseph Goebbels as Chancellor – he ended with the obsession which lay behind so much of the history of Nazism:

> Above all I adjure the leaders of the nation and those under them to scrupulous observance of the laws of race and to merciless opposition to the universal poisoner of all peoples, International Jewry.

To those he had ruled, all he could offer was death:

I beg the heads of the Army, the Navy, and the Air Force to strengthen by all possible means the spirit of resistance of our soldiers in the National-Socialist sense, especially bearing in mind that I myself also, as founder and creator of the movement, have preferred death to cowardly abdication or even capitulation.

May it become, at some future time, part of the code of honour of the German officer, as it is already in our Navy, that the surrender of a district or of a town is impossible, and that the leaders here above all must march ahead as shining examples, faithfully fulfilling their duty unto death.[1]

This, in a nutshell, is what Nazism had been about: war, race and death. Once the Nazi attempt to build a racist Utopia had gone down in flames, all that remained was to commit suicide.

Hitler's own suicide could hardly have come as a surprise. Hermann Göring stated, while being interrogated in October 1945 in advance of the Nuremberg Trials: 'We always knew that the Fuehrer would kill himself if things were coming to an end. We always knew that [...] he said this only too clearly and too explicitly to different people, and we all know about this exactly.'[2] The Führer was far from the only Nazi leader to kill himself when the Third Reich reached the end of the road. Indeed, one of the most remarkable features of the collapse of Nazi Germany was the large number of suicides which accompanied it or occurred shortly afterwards, and it is revealing that so many people who identified with Nazism chose to kill themselves rather than face life in a post-war world. The eschatological aspect of Nazism was exposed in the most stark manner: for those most committed to its ideology, the end of the Third Reich was the end of the world. Many found it impossible to imagine how Germany or the German *Volk* could survive after the Second World War was lost; many chose to kill themselves rather than face punishment for what they had done during the previous twelve years; and for many, this final act of violence was a last, furious expression of hatred for a *Volk* which had failed them and for a world which had defeated them.[3]

The list of leading Nazis who killed themselves in 1945 and 1946 is a long one. Most famously, it includes Joseph Goebbels, who, after acting as best man at Hitler's macabre wedding party in the bunker on 29 April, followed the example of his Führer by committing suicide together with his wife Magda after they had arranged the murder of their six children. Field Marshal Walter Model, who had been the first troop commander on the eastern front to declare his loyalty to Hitler in the wake of the July 1944 bomb plot, shot himself in a forest near Düsseldorf on 21 April rather than experience surrender. Bernhard Rust, Reich Minister for Education and Science from 1934 until 1945, killed himself in the village of Berne bei Brake/Unterweser on 8 May, the day the Wehrmacht surrendered. Heinrich Himmler killed himself on 23 May 1945 by swallowing a cyanide capsule after having been captured by the British. Konrad Henlein, the leader of the Nazi Sudeten German Party at the time of the Munich crisis of 1938, took his life on 10 May in Plzeň, after having been taken prisoner by the Americans. Odilo Globocnik, who as head of the SS and police in Lublin had played a leading role in the establishment and operation of the extermination camps in occupied Poland, killed himself at the end of May 1945 after having been captured by British troops. Robert Ley, the head of the German Labour Front, hanged himself in his cell on 24 October 1945, before he could be tried at Nuremberg. Hermann Göring managed to kill himself by swallowing cyanide in his cell at Nuremberg on 15 October 1946, just hours before he was due to be hanged. Otto Georg Thierack, the radical Nazi jurist who had become Justice Minister in 1942, followed Göring's example and killed himself in his cell in an internment camp near Paderborn on 23 October 1946. Countless others – local and regional party bosses, minor functionaries, medical practitioners involved in such crimes as the euthanasia campaign, police officials, SS men – followed the example of their Führer and committed suicide. Rarely in modern history has the end of a political system been accompanied by so many of its leaders taking their own lives.

The suicides of prominent figures in the Nazi regime formed only the tip of the iceberg. Already as the war was in its final stages, Nazi voices (including that of Goebbels) had been raised in praise of suicide.[4] Germany in the spring of 1945 was a land full of corpses; throughout the country, people were confronted with the consequences of suicide. After the German military collapse, suicide became a public, almost a mass phenomenon. A sense of helplessness, fear of what the soldiers of the Allied occupying powers, particularly the soldiers of the Red Army, would do (and, particularly, do to women), feelings of impotence and despair at the destruction all round, drove tens of thousands of Germans to take their own lives.[5] At the end of April, a young gymnasium student in Berlin-Friedrichshagen (occupied the week before by the Red Army) described in her diary the waves of suicides around her – the family of the local vicar, a former teacher – and wrote:

On the first day [of the occupation of the district by the Red Army] around a hundred suicides are supposed to have occurred in Friedrichshagen. A blessing that there is no gas, otherwise even more would have taken their lives; we also might perhaps be dead. I was just so desperate! [. . .] My German Fatherland had to come to this, now that we have been handed over, completely without rights, to the power of foreigners.[6]

Perhaps the most extreme case is that of Demmin, a district town in western Pomerania, where roughly 5 per cent of the entire population committed suicide as the Red Army arrived.[7] When the *Landrat*, newly installed by the Soviet occupation authorities, surveyed conditions in Demmin in November 1945, he noted in a matter-of-fact manner: '365 houses, roughly 70 per cent of the city, lay in ruins, over 700 inhabitants had ended their lives through suicide.'[8] In Teterow, a small town in Mecklenburg numbering fewer than ten thousand inhabitants in 1946, the burial register included a 'Continuation of the Appendix for the Suicide Period [*Selbstmordperiode*] Early May 1945' containing details of 120 suicide cases, listing how the act had been carried out: people shot themselves, hanged themselves, drowned themselves, poisoned themselves; reports frequently noted how fathers killed their entire families and then themselves.[9] In the Sudetenland, where Germans now faced extreme violence and expulsion, there also were mass suicides: 'Whole families would dress up in their Sunday finest, surrounded by flowers, crosses, and family albums, and then kill themselves by hanging or poison.'[10] And this wave of suicides did not stop when the deportees arrived in what remained of Germany; according to General Ivan Alexandrovich Serov (head of the Soviet secret police in the Soviet Occupation Zone), in June 1945, 'with their futures ruined and having no hope for anything better, many of them end their lives by suicide, cutting their wrists'.[11] After years of exposure to a political ideology which described the world in the most extreme apocalyptic terms, after the terrible experiences of the last months of the war, and without the vision of a future in which they might rebuild orderly and productive lives, to many Germans death seemed the only way out.

Nevertheless, most Germans did not kill themselves in 1945. Instead, they had to deal with the legacy of Nazism – whether this meant their own involvement with the Nazi regime and its crimes or the enormous physical, social and psychological wreckage which Nazism and war had left in their lives. The story of Nazism therefore does not end in 1945, and the story of Germany's Second World War did not end with the unconditional surrender in 1945, any more than that of Germany's First World War ended with the armistice of 1918.

In late spring 1945, more than eleven million Germans were prisoners of the Allies (roughly 7,745,500 with the western Allies – the majority with the Americans – and 3,349,000 with Soviet forces),[12] the last of whom would not return to Germany from Soviet captivity for more than a decade.[13] Roughly eight million Germans had been evacuated from cities to escape the bombing, and many of them had no homes to return to.[14] Approximately twelve million Germans were uprooted from their homes in territories which fell to Poland, the USSR and Czechoslovakia after the war and, destitute, had to pick up the threads of their lives in a devastated and divided post-war Germany. Millions of women were without husbands and millions of children were without fathers, and many did not know whether the missing men were alive or dead.[15] German cities were piles of rubble and would take years to rebuild. It is difficult to imagine a society more profoundly disrupted than that left behind by Nazism and war.

As the war came to its end, Germans confronted the immediate problems of day-to-day survival in the human and material wreckage left behind by the Third Reich. One example among millions was that of the seventy-year-old blacksmith Robert Nebatz, who experienced the terrible events of 1945 in the city of Cottbus, an important site of armaments production a little over sixty miles south-east of Berlin.

Cottbus had been the target of severe bombing which killed or severely injured thousands of its inhabitants and made thousands more homeless. Declared a fortress city by the Germans, it became a battlefield when the Soviet Army made its final, successful assault and captured the city on 22 April 1945. When the fighting was over, fewer than 8,000 civilians were left in a city which before the war had numbered over 50,000 inhabitants. Over 1,200 German soldiers had been killed in the final, senseless battle for Cottbus, and 187 civilians had taken their own lives.[16] At the end of September Nebatz wrote to his daughter:

> Arnold shot his entire family on the Wednesday before the Russians marched in, and I am living above the forge as caretaker. Lotte has been with me since the 5th of May, as her flat has been confiscated. My old flat and the entire neighbourhood was burnt down on Sunday, the 22nd of April. There was a real drama on the day the Russians marched in. Your flat is half occupied. [...] There are no more pensions. 10 Marks per month support is sufficient to buy what no longer is available. [...] Although I will do everything possible to protect you from hunger, except for fresh eggs there is little in the way of fats. I have, thank God I stayed here, saved 4 of Arnold's hens, from which I have two layers which have 18 chicks.[17]

The combination of catastrophe and everyday concerns, and the need to build on what little remained after the war, were typical of the plight of Germans emerging from Nazism and war. With the country's infrastructure shattered, with one in five dwellings no longer habitable as a result of the bombing,[18] with millions of victorious enemy soldiers having poured into Germany, for many Germans it became a daily struggle to find something to eat and to avoid being assaulted or raped. The one-time master race was reduced to an elementary, everyday struggle for survival.

The fact that German society at the end of the war was largely female heightened Germans' sense of having become victims of forces beyond their control. Women, children and the old made up the vast majority of those who had fled westwards ahead of the Red Army in early 1945;[19] the German population which emerged from the ruins left by Nazism and which now was subjected to Allied occupation was overwhelmingly female;[20] and it was German women who, in their hundreds of thousands, had been raped in late April and early May 1945, primarily (but not solely) by Soviet troops as they entered Germany and Austria (most notably, in Berlin and Vienna).[21] Whether actually raped or not, the women who lived through these frightening weeks often bore psychological scars left by their experiences of hiding in apartments and cellars, afraid to emerge for fear of being assaulted. One young woman described in her diary something of her feelings when hiding in a cellar in Berlin after the Russians arrived:

> Gradually one became more and more stiff, shaking with fear as time passed. [...] I do not know how often I wished in all seriousness to be dead. We now heard constantly when some [Russian soldiers] returned and our people cried in desperation that they had no more watches, that the other comrades already had taken everything away. [...] Mum was afraid most of all. She constantly tried to persuade me that it was just an act of violence that did not change anything in a person.[22]

At the end of their experience of Nazism and war, came a deep sense of fear, of powerlessness, of having been violated, of victimhood (alongside a paradoxical confirmation of their own cultural superiority over the brutish victor from the east who had arrived to 'liberate' them).[23] The fear of rape was ever-present in Germany at the end of the war – even where it did not actually occur[24] and especially in the Soviet Occupation Zone, where it could not be discussed publicly.[25] While not really a topic for public discussion during the 1950s and 1960s – this only really emerged into the public sphere in West Germany during the 1980s – the mass rapes of 1945 remained firmly embedded in popular consciousness and were alluded to constantly in veiled terms. They contributed mightily to a sense of having been overwhelmed by catastrophe, of having been delivered up to violent forces beyond one's control, of being powerless victims. According to Elizabeth Heineman: 'The disproportionately female civilian experience and the almost exclusively female rape experience [...] seem to have been well suited for allowing Germans to consider their nation as a whole an innocent victim of the war.'[26]

Echoing Heineman, Helene Albers, in her recent study of women on the land in Westphalia-Lippe, put it well:

> The topos of rape, especially by supposedly 'barbaric' and 'uncivilized' eastern Europeans, was in this context almost a metaphor for a sub-jugated, suffering Germany which had been made into a victim. The unpleasant memory of the other Germany which had been shaped by male experiences of war, which had attempted brutally and ruthlessly to subjugate other peoples with a powerful military machine and had a genocide of unprecedented dimensions on its conscience, thus could be glossed over.[27]

In the process, memories of Nazism and the war of extermination it launched tended to fade into the background behind memories of rape and suffering.

As a result of the suffering and losses they faced, Germans managed, in the words of Michael Hughes, 'to construct a collective memory of themselves as innocent victims of Nazism and the Second World War – while eliding the role many of them had played in bringing suffering to millions of other Europeans'.[28] The war, as Sabine Behrenbeck observed when examining post-Second World War war memorials, 'became an accident, a tragic fate, a natural catastrophe'.[29] There was no repetition of a public cult of fallen heroes as had been cultivated following the First World War, only a mourning of victims of 'fate'.

The millions of Germans who had suffered material losses due to the war – in West Germany, these amounted to some seventeen million people, or one third of the entire population – sought compensation for the damage which had befallen them, in their eyes, through no fault of their own. In its War Damages Decree of 1940, the Nazi regime had promised full restitution for property losses due to war damage – to be financed essentially by looting a conquered European continent.[30] However, after the bombing had destroyed the homes, businesses and personal property of millions, after flight and expulsion had left millions of refugees with nothing more than they had been able to carry away with them, the claims were vastly greater than could have been imagined in 1940 and Germany was not the master of Europe but instead was conquered, devastated and impoverished. This provided the context for one of the greatest financial redistribution programmes ever seen: the West German *Lastenausgleich* ('Equalization of Burdens') Law of 1952, which regulated a massive transfer of economic resources from those who had not suffered material loss in the war to those who had.[31] In this way, a culture of victimhood underpinned not only the political stability of the Federal Republic but also a sense of community in which Germans bore the costs of the war together (recalling, in a strange sense, the *Volksgemeinschaft* of the recent past).[32]

The post-war community of Germans was fundamentally different from the Nazi 'people's community', however, in that the latter had been a privileged community of conquerers, while the former were a destitute community of the vanquished. The military collapse of the Third Reich, and the imposition of military rule by the Allies, turned a fundamental tenet of Nazism on its head. Between 1933 and 1945 Germany had become, as Klaus Mann had prophesied when Hitler came to power, 'the land of unlimited possibilities'.[33] First within Germany, and then in an even more unrestrained manner throughout Nazi-occupied Europe, representatives of the Nazi regime had been in a position to do anything to anyone. In 1945 they became impotent – something driven home most emphatically by the rape of German women by 'barbaric' and 'uncivilized' eastern Europeans. Germans were humiliated, their moral standards in tatters. Extreme arrogance of power was replaced by a perception that, as Protestant clergy in rural Franconia put it in June 1945, there now was 'human depravity and baseness everywhere', 'girls and women sell themselves for chocolate', and 'disgraceful behaviour by old and young has let us become a laughing stock'.[34] How the mighty had fallen. In May 1945 all political and military power had been removed from German hands; the once all-powerful had become helpless.

In the midst of this, Germans who had survived the war somehow had to carry on with everyday routines. The daily challenges of getting enough to eat, securing shelter, keeping warm, caring for one's family, negotiating the thriving black market and keeping out of harm's way (in a country which, particularly in the Soviet Zone, had become quite dangerous),[35] were overwhelming. With the majority of Germany's young men either dead or in prisoner-of-war camps, it was German women who confronted these challenges.[36] It is more than a bit ironic that Nazism, which had stressed that the woman's world was to be found at home and hearth, as wife and mother of the next generation of the *Volk*, should have left behind a German society in which so many women headed households and had to find their way through life independently of men. After Nazism and war the dominant image of the German woman was not the proud mother of a dozen children but of the *Trümmerfrau*, the woman heroically clearing away the rubble to which Germany's cities had been reduced.

The strikingly low birth rates among German women after the war – in contrast to the baby boom which had followed the First World War – is testimony not only to the absence of millions of potential fathers but also to the disinclination of German women to bear children in the midst of such difficulties. The incidence of abortion soared among German women, in a striking inversion of Nazi pro-natalism.[37] Many shared the conviction of one German woman in Berlin, who asserted after the birth of her younger son in 1947 that 'it was irresponsible in this terrible time of need that I would put another child into the world'.[38] It would take a long time for many Germans – both women who had had to face extreme hardship as the war ended and men who had been taken prisoner and in many cases returned to the Fatherland only years later – to find a path back to 'normal' life through the (re-)establishment of conventional, patriarchal family relationships.[39]

Among the most remarkable features of the history of Nazism after 1945 is that it disappeared so completely from the German landscape. Once Hitler had committed suicide, for many Germans it was almost as if they could awake from the Nazi nightmare and leave their erstwhile beliefs (conveniently) behind. When Hitler died, according to Marlis Steinert, 'the broad mass of the population [...] was too preoccupied with survival [...] to take much notice'. The partial surrender of German forces in the Netherlands, Denmark and Schleswig-Holstein was greeted by a population which was 'in no way dejected'; and the British and American troops arriving to occupy the country were 'seldom still regarded as enemies'.[40] The fact that a political movement and ideology which had attracted more electoral support than any other in German history, which had boasted millions of active members and adherents, which had indoctrinated a generation and which had propelled their country into a world war during which German forces held out against impossible odds to the bitter end, seemingly could disappear almost without trace was indeed remarkable. When they arrived in Germany, the Allies fully expected to face German partisan activity long after formal military surrender, carried out by fanatic guerrilla organizations determined to keep fighting.[41] Yet this did not happen. After Hitler shot himself, Nazism evaporated as a political force. A movement which had mobilized millions of people, and an ideology which had inspired the most terrible outbreak of violence the world had ever seen, vanished after Germany went down to defeat.

Of course, the Allied occupation of Germany (and Austria) meant that any resurrection of the NSDAP itself was out of the question. However, it is noteworthy that Nazism did not stage a successful return in another guise. While it obviously had no public space in which to develop in the Soviet Zone, in post-war West Germany there seemed a substantial potential reservoir of support for revanchist, neo-Nazi politics. In 1950, the Federal Republic contained over ten million expellees and refugees, roughly two million former Reich civil servants, Nazi Party officials and professional soldiers who had lost their jobs, two and a half million war dependants, one and a half million war invalids and their dependants, two million late-returning POWs (*Spätheimkehrer*), and between four and six million people who had been bombed out of their homes – in addition to about one and a half million unemployed.[42] Yet, unlike after the First World War, when the number of Germans who had been affected by the lost war in similar manner was far smaller, defeat was not followed by an upsurge in popular support for political extremism or for the radical right.

In the first post-war Federal German elections, in 1949, the overwhelming majority of voters supported democratic parties favoured by the occupation authorities. Attempts were made in West Germany to attract the former Nazi constituency to nationalistic, right-wing politics, most notably by the Socialist Reich Party (SRP). Formed in 1949, with a party programme which echoed that of the NSDAP, the SRP openly sought the support of former Nazi Party members. However, it achieved only modest successes in regional *Landtag* elections in 1951 and dissolved itself in the face of a ban issued by the Federal Constitutional Court in October 1952.[43] After the Second World War, most Germans were unwilling to associate themselves publicly with Nazi politics. Instead, they either stood back from politics altogether, preferring not to get their fingers burned once again, and tended to their own private concerns, or, if they did get involved in politics, found a home in the approved parties of the post-war German states. In both East and West, it was probably the ruling parties – the Christian Democratic Union and the Free Democratic Party in the Federal Republic, and the Socialist Unity Party in the German Democratic Republic – which proved most successful in integrating former Nazis into the post-war political systems.

Not just the defeat itself but the manner in which Nazi Germany had been defeated contributed mightily to the disappearance of Nazism. Total defeat, symbolized memorably by photos of Russian soldiers planting the Soviet flag on top of the Reichstag and of an American GI giving a mock Nazi salute in front of the huge swastika at the Nuremberg Party rally grounds, and the fact that most of Germany had been occupied by Allied forces before the Wehrmacht surrendered, removed any basis for claiming that the military collapse might have been due to a 'stab in the back'. While it had cost the lives of millions of people, the terrible destruction and bloodletting of the last year of the war also eliminated any room for doubt that Nazi Germany had lost the war to a militarily and economically superior coalition. More than that, defeat fundamentally undermined Nazi racial ideology: the spectacle of Germany being occupied by the 'Mongolian hordes' from the east on the one hand and Afro-American soldiers from the west on the other left little room for an ideology which posited a hierarchy of human worth with Germans at the top. An ideology which had propagated racial war in the end delivered total defeat; a regime which had offered its population participation in violence and plunder in the end left that population helpless and impoverished.

Complete military defeat also meant the end of the Wehrmacht. In contrast with what had occurred after November 1918, when the German armed forces had organized their own demobilization, had maintained their General Staff and had been restricted but not abolished by the Versailles Treaty, after May 1945 the German armed forces were liquid-ated completely. The Potsdam Agreement stipulated:

> All German land, naval and air forces, the SS, SA, SD, and Gestapo, with all their organizations, staffs and institutions, including the General Staff, the Officers' Corps, Reserve Corps, military schools, war veterans' organizations and all other military and semi-military organizations, together with all clubs and associations which serve to keep alive the military tradition in Germany, shall be completely and finally abolished in such manner as permanently to prevent the revival or reorganization of German militarism and Nazism.[44]

It appeared to many – including Theodor Heuss, the man who became the first President of the Federal Republic – that the defeat marked the end of German military history.[45] The use of armed force had so obvi-ously brought catastrophe, and 'militarism' had so obviously led to disaster that popular opinion in post-war Germany took a radical turn away from military values. Even so unlikely an anti-militarist as Franz-Josef Strauss, who had been a Wehrmacht officer during the war and later became (among other things) West German Defence Minister under Konrad Adenauer, was heard to say in 1947, 'whoever once again takes a rifle in his hand, may his hand drop off'.[46]

In a public-opinion survey in West Germany in January 1950, when asked 'Would you think it right to become a soldier again or that your son or your husband again be a soldier?', three-quarters of the respondents answered 'no'.[47] In the autumn of 1951, while a narrow majority of West Germans favoured the formation of a national army, nearly half the population – and more than half of former Wehrmacht soldiers – approved of conscientious objection.[48] Similar sentiments were voiced in the East; police reports on the 'opinion of the population on the creation of the People's Police in Barracks' (the precursor of the East German National People's Army) in the summer of 1952 revealed considerable disquiet about the creation of a new German army. As one farmer (and member of the ruling Socialist Unity Party) near Pasewalk put it: 'Didn't they always say, we want to take no weapons in our hands any more?'[49] No doubt the Social Democratic politician Carlo Schmidt expressed sentiments felt by millions of Germans when he asserted in 1946, 'we never want to send our sons into the barracks again'.[50] During the immediate post-war years, the war experience and, in particular, the shock of the extreme violence of 1944 and 1945, led to a radical shift in German mentalities. A fundamental tenet of Nazism – the belief in the virtue of war, of the military and military values – had been dealt a severe blow.

Of course, Germany did not remain demilitarized for very long. Substantial German armies were formed during the second half of the 1950s on both sides of the East–West border, and if one can speak of a new German anti-militarism following the experience of Nazism and war, this anti-militarism was of a rather peculiar kind. It was a product not only of the shock of the end of the Second World War, but also of the political impotence of a defeated and occupied nation in a world dominated by two superpowers and where the security interests of the two German states ultimately were met by the armed forces of the USA and the USSR. Nazism and the wars it unleashed had effectively destroyed the old Europe in which a medium-sized power could pursue its own military adventures. In the post-war world, both German states sought their future in competing forms of European integration. It was in this context that the pacifist tendency, the 'Count-Me-Out' (*Ohne-Mich*) movement in the Federal Republic of the 1950s, co-existed with a powerful sense of the Soviet threat[51] (one area where the anti-Russian and anti-Bolshevik propaganda of the Nazis found an echo in the attitudes of Germans after 1945). For, if push had come to shove, it was the American armed forces which would have had to deal with the threat from the East. Although until the late 1960s few young men in West Germany took advantage of their constitutional right to avoid military service as conscientious objectors,[52] the idea that it was desirable to sacrifice one's life for the Fatherland played no role.

This is not to say that Germans' perception of the Wehrmacht and the war it fought was essentially negative after 1945. In a curious way, a positive post-war image of the Wehrmacht emerged almost as a counterpoint to a negative assessment of Nazism. Certainly many people had an interest in affirming such an image, which echoed the final report of the Wehrmacht on 9 May 1945, which had spoken of the 'heroic struggle' in which 'in the end the German Wehrmacht lost honourably to a colossal superior force'.[53] Memoir literature published by Wehrmacht generals after the war, for example the memoirs of Erich von Manstein (*Lost Victories*)[54] and of Franz Halder (*Hitler as Military Leader*),[55] stressed the superior fighting ability of the Wehrmacht over the Allied armed forces, which succeeded in vanquishing the Germans thanks to larger quantities of men and materiel, and attributed blame for the defeat to the amateurish military leadership and damaging interference of Hitler. There was no intimation in these accounts that the Wehrmacht had been deeply involved in Nazi crimes, and the Nazi regime was conspicuous by its absence. As Johannes Klotz has observed, 'the swastika on the uniforms [of the Wehrmacht] was subsequently erased'.[56] Politicians no less than former generals subscribed to the idea that the Wehrmacht – in contradistinction to the SS – had fought a clean fight. Political pressure mounted in the late 1940s and early 1950s for a line to be drawn under the past, for an amnesty and an end to raking over the Nazi past. This found its most important expression in the assertion by Konrad Adenauer that the proportion of those 'who are really guilty is so extraordinarily modest and so extraordinarily small that no damage was done to the honour of the German Wehrmacht', and in his famous Declaration of Honour (*Ehrenerklärung*) for the ordinary Wehrmacht soldiers before the Bundestag on 5 April 1951, rejecting 'once and for all' the idea of the 'collective guilt' of former professional soldiers.[57] It was a message which contributed substantially to the political success of the first West German Chancellor after 1949.

Adenauer certainly tapped into the broadly held belief that the Wehrmacht generally had behaved properly in the lands it occupied.[58] The majority of Germans, including those who had been in Wehrmacht uniform, were convinced that the Wehrmacht had acted honourably but had been 'misused' by a criminal Nazi leadership. This 'myth of the clean Wehrmacht' functioned in post-war Germany as an important counterpoint to the condemnation of Nazism and its fanatic representatives in the SS, and allowed people whose own histories had been bound up with the crimes of the Nazi regime to distance themselves from the memory of that regime.

German 'war stories' of the Second World War, both the representations of the war and the Wehrmacht in film and popular literature as well as the stories former soldiers told one another, tended to bracket out Nazism.[59] What thus distinguished the German soldier's war was not that it was a war of imperialist plunder inspired by a racist ideology, but that it had resulted in such terrible German losses. Rather than having fought for a Nazi racial Utopia and, in many cases, having been convinced that this was worth fighting for, German veterans, too, could view themselves as victims who had been compelled to endure terrible hardship while defending their country in a tragic lost cause. The fact that so many millions had been taken prisoner at the end of the war, and that many suffered for years (and that many had died) in Soviet POW camps, reinforced the sense of sacrifice and victimhood. Millions were able to make sense of their time in uniform fighting for the Third Reich by, in effect, removing Nazism from their memories of the war.[60] It was not really until Germany began to emerge from the post-war era that the 'myth of the clean Wehrmacht' was confronted publicly, most notably with the controversial exhibition *Crimes of the Wehrmacht*, which opened in Hamburg in the spring of 1995. Even then, the Wehrmacht exhibition provoked heated emotions, and when it went on nationwide tour in 1997 it met with calls from right-wing circles to boycott this 'attack' on the 'honour of the nation' and with public demonstrations.[61]

The separation in post-war popular memory of the experience of Nazism from the experience of war occurred in other ways as well. During the late 1940s and the 1950s, Germans often looked back positively on the Nazi years – which in their minds did not really include the war years (and particularly not the traumatic final months of the war). In retrospect, the mid- and late 1930s, and even the first half of the war (before the casualties began seriously to mount and before

Allied bombing began seriously to affect life in German cities), appeared in a remarkably sunny light. After the crises and despair of the final Weimar years, the Nazi years were 'good times' in which people were able to find work, establish a family, perhaps travel with the 'Strength through Joy' organization; it was not really until the middle of the war that rising casualties, bombing, fear of death and loss of one's home plunged Germans again into 'bad times' – and this seemed a reflection of the war rather than of Nazism.[62] Long after the bloody demise of the Third Reich, Germans could be heard to extol the benefits of the Nazi regime – the reduction in unemployment, the building of the *Autobahn* network, the enforcement of law and order – as though these were disconnected from the wars and campaigns of genocide pursued by the regime. In so many ways, when Germans looked back upon Nazism and war, they looked back with a divided consciousness.

For millions of Germans, memories of the war – as distinct from memories of the Third Reich – were framed by flight or expulsion from their homes in 1945 and 1946. Defeat had led to the loss to Poland and the USSR of the former German provinces east of the new frontier along the Oder-Neisse (areas whose populations had, before 1933, been most enthusiastic in their support for the Nazi movement, and which comprised roughly one quarter of Reich territory as measured by the borders of 1937). The flight of Germans ahead of the Red Army and then the mass expulsion of Germans from the Sudetenland, East Prussia, Silesia and Pomerania formed one of the largest forced migrations in human history. The first post-war German census, carried out on 29 October 1946 in the four occupation zones, recorded 5,645,000 expellees from the former eastern regions of the Reich (i.e. East Prussia, Pomerania and Silesia), of whom 3,280,000 were in the western occupation zones and 2,273,000 were in the Soviet zone.[63] Altogether, when one adds those expelled from Czechoslovakia (primarily from the Sudetenland), Hungary, Yugoslavia, Romania and the Baltic, and those (relatively few) who went to post-war Austria, the total approaches twelve million. This created a huge reservoir of Germans who, understandably, viewed themselves as victims of Nazism and war, and lost sight of the degree to which, before the catastrophe of 1944 and 1945, they may have profited from the policies of the Nazi regime.

The Potsdam Agreement had stipulated blandly 'that any transfers [of population] that take place should be effected in an orderly and humane manner',[64] but the manner in which the transfer of the German population was carried out by the Poles and the Czechs was anything but humane. Altogether, the expulsions probably led to the deaths of more than a million people. According to rough calculations made by the West German government in the 1950s, as of late 1950 1,390,000 people who had lived in the former eastern regions of Germany were unaccounted for, presumed dead, as a consequence of the fighting in the last months of war, of the deportations carried out by the Soviet authorities, or of the dreadful conditions which had characterized the move westwards.[65] Poles and Czechs who had suffered terribly at the hands of the Nazi occupiers during the war were not inclined to show magnanimity or generosity towards the defeated and helpless Germans in 1945. The cruelty and violence with which the Nazi regime had treated the people of eastern Europe now were echoed in the treatment meted out to the one-time 'master race'. In Czechoslovakia and Poland, Germans were beaten and raped, forced to do humiliating tasks, subjected to sadistic violence in labour camps (sometimes in the same places – as in Theresienstadt – where the Nazis had had their camps), compelled to wear letters on their sleeves identifying their ethnicity, randomly killed, forced on to death marches, and herded on to railway cattle cars for long journeys in the dead of winter.[66] During the 1950s the suffering of the German refugees and expellees – the great majority of whom were women, children and the elderly – was documented with prodigious energy in West Germany,[67] and this dramatic representation of German victimhood occupied a prominent place in post-war public consciousness.

In the preface to the first volume of the Ministry for Refugees' *Dokumentation* of the expulsion, Theodor Schieder, the historian responsible for editing the collection (who, during the war, had authored papers on the removal of Jews and Poles from their homes in occupied Poland to provide 'settlement land' which would be 'a contribution to solving the social question' in Germany),[68] wrote:

The expulsion of the Germans from the East is an event whose full historical importance is still beyond a judgement today. One may regard it as the final act of a war in which the written and unwritten

laws of relations between nations and states were broken thousands
of times and the extermination of entire peoples was not only
preached as a goal but in fact was begun; or one may view it as the
final phase of an ever more bitter struggle between nationalities
which has been raging for almost a century and a half in the
ethnically heterogeneous zone of Europe; in any case the familiar
yardsticks of European history leave us in the lurch.[69]

The calamity which befell millions of Germans from the east was
described not as a consequence of Nazism but as the 'final act' of a
terrible war and as the 'final phase' of an 'ever more bitter struggle
of nationalities'. Schieder employs the passive voice, neatly gliding
over the question of agency. It was not Nazi Germany's brutal and
murderous occupation of most of the European continent which
provided the images which the war left behind for millions of
Germans, but memories of the 'treks' of destitute people streaming
westwards ahead of the Red Army, of families cruelly expelled from
their homes at a few hours' notice never to return, of women raped,
of towns destroyed, of personal possessions and *Heimat* lost. The
terrible, traumatic accounts of the expulsion collected during the
1950s almost always begin in 1945, when the refugees' and expellees'
world collapsed as the Red Army approached their homes. Germans
are portrayed as victims; personal tragedy stands at the centre of the
accounts; Nazism and the Nazi regime are themes conspicuous by their
absence. Nazism and war in effect are de-coupled in the narratives. Not
the crimes of Nazism but suffering and a sense of victimhood shaped
the post-war German imagination.

At the same time, the occupation and subsequent division of
Germany, and the arrival of the American and Soviet powers in
central Europe, left no possibility for a new German politics of
territorial revision. This time there would be no revision of an eastern
'bleeding frontier'. In West Germany during the 1950s and 1960s,
organizations of Germans uprooted from the east – the *Lands-*
mannschaften – kept the lost eastern territories in public consciousness
and may have appeared to be a powerful political force, and for years
the fiction was maintained that the former Prussian provinces east of
the Oder-Neisse were merely 'under Polish administration'. However,

there was nothing that the Germans could do to change the situation. In the German Democratic Republic, which actually bordered Poland, the subject was effectively banned from public discussion. Early attempts by German politicians in the Soviet Occupation Zone (in particular by the leadership of the CDU) to raise the issue of the Oder-Neisse border were quashed by the Soviet military authorities.[70] The history of German settlements east of the new border became largely a taboo subject. Expellees and refugees could not be described as such publicly and instead were designated 'resettlers'; and the 'Oder-Neisse Peace Border' was celebrated as the permanent frontier between the German Democratic Republic and the People's Republic of Poland.

The defeat of Nazi Germany also meant the reversal of the *Anschluss* of Austria. This had been one of the points agreed at Potsdam in the summer of 1945 and, as had been the case after the First World War, German-speaking Austria was prohibited from joining a future German state. However, unlike after the First World War, after the Second there was little desire in Austria for union with Germany. Indeed, separation from Germany proved very convenient for the Austrians, who were able to distance themselves from blame for what had occurred between 1938 and 1945, were not burdened with reparations demands, and did not have their country divided into separate states as a result of Allied occupation. Although the leader of the Third Reich had been an Austrian and although the *Anschluss* in 1938 had been greeted with enthusiasm by the majority of the Austrian population, after the war Austrians ceased to identify with Germany. Nazism and war effectively purged Austria of pan-Germanism and made possible a viable Austrian national consciousness separate and distinct from being German. The shock of the war losses and of defeat, of the destruction and violence which accompanied the collapse of the Third Reich of which Austria had been a part – for Austrian cities, too, had been bombed; Austrians, too, had been killed and wounded while in Wehrmacht uniform; and thousands of Viennese women had been raped by Soviet soldiers in 1945 as had their counterparts in Berlin – destroyed the appeal of a Greater Germany. It also allowed the cultivation of a convenient historical amnesia, whereby Austrians could view their country not as part and parcel of the Third Reich and intimately bound up with the history and crimes of Nazism, but instead as the first country to fall victim to Nazi aggression.

The most difficult legacy of Nazism arose from the campaigns of mass murder which the Nazi regime had unleashed. While the overwhelming majority of the Jews who had lived in Germany when Hitler captured power had either emigrated or had been murdered, and while very few of the Jews who had emigrated from Nazi Germany chose to return after the war,[71] Germany was not a country without Jews after May 1945. Some 15,000 German Jews had managed to survive in the Third Reich and about 50,000 Jews had been freed from slave-labour camps or death marches during the last two months of the war.[72] After the war, roughly a quarter of a million Jewish survivors, who more often than not had lost all members of their families, found themselves in the 'waiting room' of displaced-persons (DP) camps in the American and British occupation zones, desperately hoping to emigrate to the United States or to Palestine. As Michael Brenner has noted (echoing the comments of many contemporary observers), 'it belonged to the ironies of history that Germany, of all places, became under the occupation of the Allied powers a sheltering haven for several hundred thousand Jews'.[73] Largely from eastern Europe and concentrated particularly in the American Occupation Zone in Bavaria, these Jewish survivors embodied the most terrible consequences of Nazism and war.

Yet, among Germans, preoccupied with their own everyday concerns, they were often perceived rather differently, if indeed they were perceived at all. The concentration of traumatized and impoverished eastern European Jews in DP camps in Germany, the inevitable participation of some camp residents in the thriving post-war black market and the perception that Jews were being privileged by the occupation authorities served to reinforce long-standing prejudices that had been cultivated by the Nazi regime. Despite German responsibility for the murder of some six million European Jews, there remained a substantial residue of anti-semitic prejudice which would take some time to dissipate.[74] Just as race prejudice did not originate with Nazism, nor did it end with Nazism either, although the defeat of the Nazi regime and the exposure of the deeds it perpetrated largely removed overt antisemitism from the political stage – at least in western Europe.

Jewish survivors comprised only a small proportion of the 'displaced persons' in Germany when the Third Reich collapsed. They were far outnumbered by the millions of workers the Nazi regime had drafted to work in the German war economy. As the war came to an end, as production collapsed and German control over foreign labourers dissipated, these workers posed a tremendous public-order problem. Not only were they now ill-inclined to be meek and law-abiding, and often served to confirm the negative stereotypes which had been a daily diet served up by Goebbels's propaganda; they also needed to be returned to their native lands as quickly as possible, from a country where food was in short supply and transport facilities severely disrupted. In the British Occupation Zone (which included the Ruhr industrial region) alone, there were about two million 'displaced persons' in June 1945.[75] They were repatriated remarkably quickly – by November, the number of DPs in the British Zone had fallen to 540,000. Alongside Germans' own tribulations, the liberation of the foreigners who had slaved for the Third Reich underlined how the world of Nazism was turned upside-down.

For prominent figures in the Nazi regime who had not chosen to kill themselves, life also changed fundamentally after 1945. Suddenly the hunters became the hunted, and Allied victory was followed for many by flight, hiding, internment, interrogation, trial, imprisonment and, in some cases, execution. Those who had the bad luck to be brought to trial in eastern Europe or were brought to trial early tended to be treated harshly. Not only were eleven (twelve, if one includes Martin Bormann, who was tried *in absentia*) of the eighteen defendants found guilty at the Trial of the Major War Criminals before the International Military Tribunal at Nuremberg in 1945–6 sentenced to death, but the same was true for many lesser figures of the regime who were brought to justice soon after the war. One such was Kurt Daluege, appointed commander of the German 'Order Police' in 1936, charged with Hitler's personal security during the war and, in the wake of the assassination of Reinhard Heydrich in 1942, responsible for the murder of the entire male population of the Czech town of Lidice. Daluege was arrested in 1945 and extradited to Czechoslovakia in 1946, where he was put on trial and hanged.

Those not brought to trial until the late 1940s or early 1950s (when the Cold War rather than the Second World War dominated public discussion) tended to receive lighter sentences, which often were served only in part. For example, Alfred Franz Six, the wartime head of the Office VII ('ideological research') of the Reich Security Main Office and Commander of the 'Advance Commando Moscow' of the *Einsatzgruppe B* during the summer of 1941, received a twenty-year prison sentence from a US military court in 1948, but was released four years later. Some, like Gertrud Scholtz-Klink, spent months or years in hiding, under assumed names, before being found out. Scholtz-Klink, who had been Leader of the Nazi Women's Organization and of the *Deutsches Frauenwerk* and who at least nominally had been the most powerful woman in the Third Reich, spent a short period in 1945 in a Soviet prisoner-of-war camp, from which she managed to flee. She then lived for three years with her husband near Tübingen under an assumed name before being found out, arrested and sentenced first to eighteen months' imprisonment for falsifying documents and later to thirty months in a labour camp for her activities before 1945. An example of someone less lucky is Richard Drauz, the brutal Nazi Party *Kreisleiter* in Heilbronn (the 'butcher of Heilbronn'), who initially escaped capture by the Allies by seeking refuge in a monastery under an assumed name. He was found out in June 1945 by the American intelligence service, arrested, tried as a war criminal for his part in the shooting of an American pilot whose plane had crashed in March 1945, sentenced to death in December 1945 and hanged in December 1946.[76]

Most former Nazis, of course, did not face trial. Tens of thousands were dismissed from their posts in government and public administration once the Allied occupation armies arrived; hundreds of thousands (in particular, former members of the SS and political officials of the NSDAP) were interned by the Allied military governments in 1945 and 1946;[77] and millions of former Nazis faced uncertainty during the post-war years as a consequence of 'denazification'. The victorious Allies arrived in Germany with an expressed determination to wipe out all traces of Nazism, a determination which had been confirmed when

Churchill, Roosevelt and Stalin met at Yalta in February 1945. After Germany surrendered, the Nazi Party and all its various subdivisions were banned, Nazi racial laws repealed, Nazi textbooks removed from schools and Nazi monuments demolished. At Potsdam in the summer of 1945, the leaders of the United Kingdom, the United States and the Soviet Union also agreed that:

All members of the Nazi Party who have been more than nominal participants in its activities and all other persons hostile to Allied purposes shall be removed from public and semi-public office, and from positions of responsibility in important private undertakings. Such persons shall be replaced by persons who, by their political and moral qualities, are deemed capable of assisting in developing genuine democratic institutions in Germany.[78]

The result was an Allied offensive against the Nazi political élite, who were removed from their positions with the arrival of the occupation troops and many of whom received punishment. This involved not just the Trial of the Major War Criminals at Nuremberg which began in the autumn of 1945 and the various successor trials; it also involved the prosecution of thousands of former members of the SS and Wehrmacht, as well as of local Nazi Party bosses, local-government officials and businessmen. Large numbers of people had been arrested by the Allies upon their arrival in Germany; at the peak just after the war, the Allies held a quarter of a million such Germans prisoner, and at the end of 1946 the number of those interned was still over 90,000.[79] In the years that followed, tens of thousands of Germans were brought to trial, first in Allied courts and then in the courts of the two post-war German states. Between May 1945 and the mid-1980s, in the West roughly 90,000 people were brought before Allied and then West German courts, accused of war crimes and crimes against humanity, 6,479 of whom were convicted (most between 1945 and 1951). In the Soviet Occupation Zone, some 12,500 people were convicted of war crimes.[80] In both German states, the number of prosecutions tailed off rapidly during the 1950s, as each sought in its own way to draw a line under the past, leaving many thousands of people who probably should have been charged with murder neither indicted nor punished. Nevertheless, the campaign eradicated Nazism as a political force. No one who had been prominent in the Nazi regime would be able to continue a political career in either of the two German post-war successor states (or in Austria, for that matter) – although the same was not the case for other functional élites (such as doctors, lawyers, journalists, businessmen, civil servants and academics), who were remarkably successful in picking up the pieces of their careers in post-war West Germany.[81]

However, beyond those who had obviously held leading positions in the state and police apparatus before May 1945 and were purged from post-war public life, it was not necessarily clear who had been 'more than nominal participants' in the activities of the Nazi regime. Millions of Germans had been members of the NSDAP and other Nazi organizations between 1933 and 1945. How was their participation to be assessed and dealt with? To cope with this, the Allies instituted programmes of 'denazification', involving the screening of millions of Germans in order to evaluate the degree of their complicity and, where this complicity was deemed sufficiently serious, to have them dismissed from positions of leadership and responsibility in public office or in the economy. Fairly soon – in the American Zone this had occurred already in March 1946 – the task of screening defendants was transferred to German committees and tribunals. Millions of Germans – some six million altogether – were compelled to fill out lengthy questionnaires, from which tribunals were to determine the extent of their involvement in the Nazi regime. In the American Occupation Zone, where (initially at least) this process was carried out with the greatest rigour, a bureaucracy employing 20,000 people was set up to run tribunals which placed those brought before them in one of five categories: 1. Major Offenders (*Hauptschuldige*); 2. Offenders (*Belastete*); 3. Lesser Offenders (*Minderbelastete*); 4. Followers (*Mitläufer*); and 5. Exonerated Persons (*Entlastete*).[82] Those placed in the first two categories were liable to terms in labour camps, the expropriation of their property and the loss of state pensions; those placed in the third category faced the prospect of a period of up to three years during which they were not permitted to occupy any leading positions and moderate financial penalties (e.g. reduction in salary or pension); and the *Mitläufer* faced only moderate financial penalties.[83]

*

The predictable result of the denazification process was that, leaving aside the overall majority who were exonerated completely, the vast majority were classified as 'followers'.[84] This meant that, in effect, the denazification machinery functioned as what has been described as a *Mitläuferfabrik* – a 'followers factory' – from which the vast majority of those deemed to have been implicated in the Nazi regime emerged as passive participants.[85] However, as preoccupation with the Cold War and reconstruction displaced preoccupation with the defunct Nazi regime, the denazification process was soon brought to an end – in the American Zone, the military administration ended it in May 1948. Generally, the greater the delay before a case was examined, the less rigorous was the examination, and those whose cases were still to be decided when the curtain fell on denazification did not have to face the music at all. (In Austria, too, the denazification process largely ceased in 1948, with the Amnesty Law agreed by the *Nationalrat* in April; this ended denazification proceedings for the 487,067 Austrians – more than 90 per cent of all the registered former National Socialists – who had been classified as 'less incriminated', *minderbelastet.*)[86]

Denazification served two purposes, and served them both well. The first was the political purge, which effectively prevented those prominent in the Nazi regime from acquiring any further position of political importance. The political purge was necessary not only to satisfy the Allies that Germany and Austria could be trusted again to run their own affairs, but also to respect the large numbers of people, Germans and Austrians included, who had suffered as a consequence of Nazism. The second purpose was the reintegration into post-war societies of the large numbers of 'followers' who otherwise might have become a reservoir feeding a right-wing politics of resentment. This was necessary not only for political stability but also for economic recovery (for it made little sense to exclude a substantial minority of the adult population from full economic activity) and the social reintegration of many former Nazis.[87] After the terrible experiences of the final stages of the war, and after the suffering and hardship which accompanied the occupation in 1945, the end of denazification allowed people to feel that they finally would be left in peace.

The denazification process had two important and interrelated consequences for the ways in which Germans looked back on Nazism and their involvement in it. First, it reinforced the common and convenient belief that most former Nazis had been mere 'followers', who in a totalitarian system had had little choice but to go along with the regime. Writing in the journal *Die Wandlung* in August 1947, Karl Heinrich Knappstein (a former editor of the *Frankfurter Zeitung* and after the war a senior civil servant in Hesse before entering the diplomatic service) expressed the widespread perception:

> Denazification is called upon to hold those responsible for the National Socialist regime to account and to remove them and keep them removed from important positions in the democratic community. Who now was the leadership stratum of National Socialism? In the US Zone was it really 3.3 million people? Have we forgotten that National Socialism was a total dictatorship, culminating in one single – admittedly crazy – head, that its leadership stratum, in contrast to the élite of other state structures, consisted of a small centralized clique that tried to solve the problem of ruling the masses in its fashion with the especially sophisticated use of means of indoctrination which are unknown elsewhere? [...] In any event, it was not hundreds of thousands of people who were responsible for the system of terror, and certainly not millions.[88]

The idea that most Germans were at worst 'followers' made it easier to overlook the broad involvement in the crimes of the Nazi regime and the degree to which large numbers of 'ordinary' Germans had profited from it, at least until catastrophe overwhelmed them at the end of the war.

Second, the way denazification was carried through left Germans with a strong sense that the process had been unfair and unjust, and this helped to buttress the widespread perception among the German population that they had emerged from Nazism and war as victims. Opinion polls taken by the American Military Government indicate that initially, in late 1945 and early 1946, denazification met with considerable popular approval. However, by 1949 only a small minority among the German public expressed satisfaction at the way in which it had been carried out.[89] By the time the two German successor states were established in 1949, there was widespread popular support for drawing a line under the past, for declaring an amnesty so that those perhaps with a chequered Nazi past – in a country whose population included millions of former members of the NSDAP – would not constantly have to worry about whether that past would catch up with them. This 'politics of the past' was signalled clearly by Konrad Adenauer in his first 'government declaration' on 29 September 1949, when he stated to the Bundestag:

> Much distress and much harm was caused by denazification. Those truly guilty of the crimes which were committed during the National Socialist period and the war should be punished with all severity. Otherwise, however, we must no longer differentiate between two classes of people in Germany: those who are politically blameless and those who are not blameless. This differentiation must disappear as soon as possible.[90]

The way was clear for the reintegration of former Nazis into West German society, and a significant number of people who had prospered and advanced under the Nazis were able to do so again in West Germany during the 1950s. In November 1946, speaking to the German heads of the *Länder* and provinces in the British Occupation Zone, General Gerald Templer had noted that 'the question of denazification' was 'a problem which for you as well as us presents very real difficulties', and that 'the disease can only be cured by the Germans themselves'. He expected 'key positions' would be held 'not only by non-Nazis but by positive non-Nazis'.[91] However, as it turned out the 'disease' was not 'cured' as Templer had envisaged. Instead, after a decent interval, many former Nazis found their way back into positions of influence and responsibility, at least in West Germany. During the 1950s, businessmen, journalists, academics, jurists, officers and doctors who had been deeply involved in the Nazi regime were able to pick up the threads of their old careers and prosper.[92] For those who managed to escape the noose during the immediate post-war years, and for those who had not been members of what the Allies declared criminal organizations (the SS and its Security Service, the Gestapo and the Reich Security Main Office), life after Nazism often did not turn out all that badly.

In the east, in the Soviet Occupation Zone and the German

Democratic Republic, the process of denazification and the consequences of it unfolded rather differently.[93] When the denazification
process began in the Soviet Zone, it was conducted with a rigour equal
to that witnessed in the American Zone, but with quite different intent.
In the Soviet Zone the denazification process was used deliberately to
achieve structural change in the economy and society – not merely to
remove former Nazis from positions of political influence or administrative power but also to strip economic and social élites of their power
and property. It also was conducted against the background of the
activities of the Soviet Secret Police and the Soviet Special Camps dotted
across the Soviet Zone. The denazification process in the East also
differed from that in the West in that it ended sooner and less ambigu-
ously. In August 1947 the Soviet Military Administration issued its Order
201, which opened the way for the rehabilitation of nominal former
Nazi Party members (who thereby were restored their civil and political
rights); and on 26 February 1948 the Soviet Military Administration
declared denazification in the Soviet Zone officially at an end. A line
was indeed drawn under the past, but unlike what occurred in the West
there was no return of ex-Nazis to positions of influence in the civil
service or the economy. Instead, the denazification process was used to
promote a social, political and economic revolution of far-reaching
proportions. Former Nazi Party members, insofar as they were not
found guilty of war crimes and had not died in Soviet internment,[94]
could integrate themselves into the new 'antifascist-democratic' and
then 'real-existing socialist' order. However, there was no question of a
public discussion of possible injustices committed in the denazification
process, and no question of a return by former Nazis to positions of
influence and authority.

With hindsight, one might argue that in the West the reintegration
of former Nazis may have been necessary. In a democratic political
system, it would have been problematical to exclude hundreds of thousands, perhaps millions, of people from participation in public life for
the rest of their lives because of their possibly chequered past. At the
same time, the fact that the foundations of the West German state were
laid while those who had identified with the Nazi regime remained
excluded from public office and influence may have allowed their reintegration to occur without endangering West German democracy.[95]

However, this also meant that it was not until the end of the 1960s and the decades which followed that confronting the Nazi past assumed a prominent place in (West) German public discussion. For decades, the extreme violence of the war, and especially of the last year of the war, overshadowed memories of Nazism, and this allowed the separation of Nazism and war in popular memory. This separation served an important political function in the post-war years, and may have contributed to the stability of German democracy. By not really confronting the past, Germans could avoid deeply disturbing and divisive issues while they were still raw.

Reporting on her first visit to Germany after the Second World War, between November 1949 and March 1950, Hannah Arendt famously expressed her incredulity at the attitudes she found. Amidst the ubiquitous evidence of wartime destruction, the Germans she met displayed what to her eyes seemed an absence of mourning for the dead, indifference to the fate of the refugees in their midst and a deep-rooted and stubborn refusal to come to terms with what had happened.[96] Instead, according to Arendt, Germans had become overcome with self-pity and preoccupied with their own fate, which precluded probing their own responsibility for what had occurred. To the 'average German', in her view, the war was not a consequence of Nazism but an expression of innate human nature as it had existed since Adam and Eve were driven from the Garden of Eden.

Arendt's observations were not simply the product of the very different perspectives of, on the one hand, a German-Jewish intellectual who had emigrated in 1933 and, on the other, of Germans who had remained in Germany. They also highlight a key element of how Germans viewed Nazism after its demise: the critical importance of Germans' wartime experiences, in particular the shock of the extreme violence of 1944 and 1945, for sweeping consideration of Nazism into the background. For Hannah Arendt, as for most people (including most Germans) today, Nazism was linked inextricably with violence and genocide. It was, as Ian Kershaw has written, 'an assault on the roots of civilisation',[97] an assault which makes questions of guilt and responsibility unavoidable. However, immediately after their terrible experiences as the war came to a close, Germans were preoccupied with rather different concerns. In Germany after 1945, Nazism was buried in a double sense: it was buried as a political movement and an ideology capable of mobilizing mass support, and it was buried in public memory. Through the horrors of 1944–5, Nazi Germany was transformed into *armes Deutschland* – 'poor Germany' – to be pitied rather than reviled. In their own eyes, Germans emerged as victims of war, not perpetrators of Nazism. It would take at least a generation before this perception could be challenged effectively.

NOTES

Introduction

1 Adolf Hitler, *Mein Kampf*, translated by James Murphy (London, 1939), p. 150.

2 See, especially, the fine synthesis by Mark Mazower, *Dark Continent: Europe's Twentieth Century* (London, 1998).

3 This perhaps can best be gauged by the recent impressive, mammoth three-volume collection, edited by John K. Roth, Elisabeth Maxwell, Margot Levy and Wendy Whitworth, *Remembering for the Future. The Holocaust in an Age of Genocide* (Basingstoke and New York, 2001).

4 Dieter Pohl, *Nationalsozialistische Judenverfolgung in Ostgalizien 1941– 1944. Organisation und Durchführung eines staatlichen Massenverbrechens* (Munich, 1996); Thomas Sandkühler, '*Endlösung' in Galizien. Der Judenmord in Ostpolen und die Rettungsinitiativen von Bertold Beitz 1941– 1944* (Bonn, 1996); Bernhard Chiari, *Alltag hinter der Front. Besatzung, Kollaboration und Widerstand in Weissrussland 1941–1944* (Düsseldorf, 1998); Christian Gerlach, *Kalkulierte Mörde. Die deutsche Wirtschafts- und Vernichtungspolitik in Weissrussland 1941 bis 1944* (Hamburg, 1999); Ulrich Herbert (ed.), *National Socialist Extermination Policies. Contemporary German Perspectives and Controversies* (New York and Oxford, 2000).

5 Yaacov Lozowick, *Hitler's Bureaucrats. The Nazi Security Police and the Banality of Evil* (London and New York, 2000); Michael Wildt, *Generation des Unbedingten. Das Führungskorps des Reichssicherheitshauptamtes* (Hamburg, 2002).

6 Gabriele Czarnowski, *Das kontrollierte Paar. Ehe- und Sexualpolitik im Nationalsozialismus* (Weinheim, 1991); Lisa Pine, *Nazi Family Policy 1933– 1945* (Oxford and New York, 1997).

7 Michael Zimmermann, *Rassenutopie und Genozid. Eine nationalsozialistische 'Lösung der Zigeunerfrage'* (Hamburg, 1996); Gunter Lewy, *The Nazi Persecution of the Gypsies* (New York, 2000).

8 Wolfgang Ayass, *'Asoziale' im Nationalsozialismus* (Stuttgart, 1995).

9 Patrick Wagner, *Volksgemeinschaft ohne Verbrecher. Konzeption und Praxis der Kriminalopolizei der Weimarer Republik und des Nationalsozialismus* (Hamburg, 1996); Patrick Wagner, *Hitlers Kriminalisten. Die deutsche Kriminalpolizei und der Nationalsozialismus* (Munich, 2002).

10 Rolf-Dieter Müller, *Hitlers Ostkrieg und die deutsche Siedlungspolitik. Die Zusammenarbeit von Wehrmacht, Wirtschaft und SS* (Frankfurt am Main, 1991).

11 Jan Erik Schulte, *Zwangsarbeit und Vernichtung: Das Wirtschaftsimperium der SS. Oswald Pohl und das SS-Wirtschafts-Verwaltungshauptamt 1933–1945* (Paderborn, 2001); Michael Thad Allen, *The Business of Genocide. The SS, Slave Labor, and the Concentration Camps* (Chapel Hill, 2002).

12 Ernst Klee, *'Euthanasie' im NS-Staat. Die 'Vernichtung lebensunwerten Lebens'* (Frankfurt am Main, 1985); Paul Weindling, *Health, Race and German Politics between National Unification and Nazism 1870–1945* (Cambridge, 1989); Michael Burleigh, *Death and Deliverance. 'Euthanasia' in Germany* (Cambridge, 2000); Michael Burleigh, *Ethics and Extermination. Reflections on Nazi Genocide* (Cambridge, 1997).

13 Michael Burleigh and Wolfgang Wippermann, *The Racial State. Germany 1933–1945* (Cambridge, 1991), p. 306.

14 See Götz Aly, *Rasse und Klasse. Nachforschungen zum deutschen Wesen* (Frankfurt am Main, 2003), pp. 230–4.

15 Aly, *Rasse und Klasse*, p. 81.

1 The Aftermath of the First World War and the Rise of Nazism

1 Adolf Hitler, *Mein Kampf,* translated by James Murphy (London, 1939), p. 178.

2 Hitler, *Mein Kampf,* pp. 182–4.

3 See Ian Kershaw, *Hitler 1889–1936: Hubris* (London, 1998), pp. 96–7.

4 See Jeffrey Verhey, *The Spirit of 1914. Militarism, Myth and Mobilization in Germany* (Cambridge, 2000).

5 See Wilhelm Deist, 'The Military Collapse of the German Empire: The Reality Behind the Stab-in-the-Back Myth', in *War in History,* vol. 3, no. 2 (1996), pp. 186–207.

6 Between 1919 and 1923, criminal convictions more than doubled, from 348,247 to 823,902. Nikolaus Wachsmann, 'From Confinemant to Extermination. "Habitual Criminals" in the Third Reich', in Robert Gellately

and Nathan Stoltzfus (eds), *Social Outsiders in Nazi Germany* (Princeton and Oxford, 2001), p. 171.

7 Wolfgang Homering (ed.), *Zeitzeugen des Jahrhunderts. Norbert Elias. Im Gespräch mit Hans Christian Huf* (Berlin, 1999), p. 25.

8 Stadtarchiv Heidelberg, 212a, 7: Kriegsministerium to the Ober-kommando in den Marken, sämtl. stellv. Gen. Kdos., an sämtl. Gar-nisonkommandos (ausser Elsass-Lothringen), Berlin, 16. Nov. 1918.

9 Gerhard A. Ritter and Susanne Miller (eds), *Die deutsche Revolution 1918–1919* (Frankfurt am Main, 1983), pp. 139–41.

10 See Andreas Dorpalen, *Hindenburg and the Weimar Republic* (Princeton, 1964), pp. 51–2. Roger Chickering, *Imperial Germany and the Great War, 1914–1918* (Cambridge, 1998), p. 190. The assertion about 'an English general' seems to have stemmed from a misreading of an article published in the *Neue Züricher Zeitung* in December 1918. See Friedrich Frhr. Hiller von Gaertringen, '"Dolchstoss"-Diskussion und "Dolchstosslegende" im Wandel von vier Jahrzehnten', in Waldemar Besson and Friedrich Frhr. Hiller von Gaertringen (eds), *Geschichte und Gegenwartsbewusstsein. Historische Betrachtungen und Untersuchungen. Festschrift für Hans Rothfels zum 70. Geburtstag* (Göttingen, 1963), pp. 127–8.

11 George L. Mosse, *Fallen Soldiers: Reshaping the Memory of the World Wars* (New York and Oxford, 1990), p. 7.

12 Hitler, *Mein Kampf*, p. 182.

13 Kershaw, *Hitler 1889–1936*, pp. 109–28.

14 See Robert G. L. Waite's pioneering study, *Vanguard of Nazism. The Free Corps Movement in Postwar Germany 1918–1933* (Cambridge, Mass., 1952).

15 Hagen Schulze, *Freikorps und Republik 1918–1920* (Boppard am Rhein, 1969), pp. 36–7.

16 See Ulrich Herbert, '"Generation der Sachlichkeit". Die völkische Stu-dentenbewegung der früheren zwanziger Jahren in Deutschland', in Frank Bajohr, Werner Johe and Uwe Lohalm (eds), *Zivilisation und Barbarei. Die widersprüchlichen Potentiale der Moderne* (Hamburg, 1991), pp. 115–20; Michael Wildt, *Generation des Unbedingten. Das Führungskorps des Reichssicherheitshauptamtes* (Hamburg, 2002), pp. 46–52.

17 Sebastian Haffner, *Defying Hitler. A Memoir* (London, 2002), p. 16.

18 On this theme, see the revealing account by Dirk Walter, *Antisemitische Kriminalität und Gewalt. Judenfeindschaft in der Weimarer Republik* (Bonn, 1999), which documents the widespread nature of antisemitic violence in Weimar Germany.

19 Thus Hitler in his 'Basic Guidelines for the Reconstitution of the National Socialist German Workers Party', published in the *Völkischer Beobachter*

on 26 February 1925, p. 2. (Text in Albrecht Tyrell, *Führer befiehl ...
Selbstzeugnisse aus der 'Kampfzeit' der NSDAP* [Düsseldorf, 1969], pp. 105–7.)

20 On this process in Lower Saxony, see Jeremy Noakes, *The Nazi Party in
Lower Saxony 1921–1933* (Oxford, 1971), pp. 89–107; on this process in
eastern Germany, see Richard Bessel, *Political Violence and the Rise of
Nazism. The Storm Troopers in Eastern Germany 1925–1934* (New Haven
and London, 1984), pp. 13–14; on this process in Thuringia, see Donald R.
Tracey, 'Der Aufstieg der NSDAP bis 1930', in Detlev Heiden and Gunther
Mai (eds), *Nationalsozialismus in Thüringen* (Weimar, Cologne and
Vienna, 1995), pp. 53–67.

21 The figure for 1928 claimed during the 1930s was 108,717. See *Schlag nach!
Wissenswerte Tatsachen aus allen Gebieten* (2nd edn, Leipzig, 1939), p. 220.
In fact, the number was slightly lower: Michael Kater gives it as 96,918.
See Michael Kater, *The Nazi Party. A Social Profile of Members and Leaders,
1919–1945* (Oxford, 1983), p. 263.

22 According to Michael Kater, 'half of the entire German student body may
have joined the Nazis by 1930'. See Kater, *The Nazi Party*, p. 44.

23 Quoted in Thomas Childers, 'The Limits of National Socialist Mobil-
isation: The Elections of 6 November 1932 and the Fragmentation of the
Nazi Constituency' in Thomas Childers (ed.), *The Formation of the Nazi
Constituency 1919–1933* (London and Sydney, 1986), p. 232.

24 Proclamation of the Stahlhelm-Landesverband Brandenburg from 2 February 1928, quoted in Wolfram Wette, 'Ideologien, Propaganda und
Innenpolitik als Voraussetzungen der Kriegspolitik des Dritten Reiches',
in Wilhelm Deist, Manfred Messerschmidt, Hans-Erich Volksmann and
Wolfram Wette, *Ursachen und Voraussetzungen der deutschen Kriegspolitik*
(*Das Deutsche Reich und der Zweite Weltkrieg*, Band I) (Stuttgart, 1979),
p. 41.

25 Analysing patterns of electoral support, Jürgen Falter has described the
voter coalition behind Hindenburg in 1925 as 'the harbinger of the electoral triumphs of the NSDAP of 1932 and 1933'. Jürgen W. Falter, 'The
Two Hindenburg Elections of 1925 and 1932: A Total Reversal of Voter
Coalitions', *Central European History*, vol. 23, no. 2/3 (1990), p. 239. See
also Peter Fritzsche, 'Presidential Victory and Popular Festivity in Weimar
Germany: Hindenburg's 1925 Election', *Central European History*, vol. 23,
no. 2/3 (1990), pp. 205–24.

26 See Bernd Weisbrod, 'Gewalt in der Politik. Zur politischen Kultur der
Gewalt in Deutschland zwischen den beiden Weltkriegen', *Geschichte in
Wissenschaft und Unterricht*, vol. 43 (1992), pp. 391–404; Bernd Weisbrod,

'The Crisis of Bourgeois Society in Interwar Germany', in Richard Bessel (ed.), *Fascist Italy and Nazi Germany. Comparisons and Contrasts* (Cambridge, 1996), pp. 34–7; Dirk Schumann, *Politische Gewalt in der Weimarer Republik 1918–1933. Kampf um die Strasse und Furcht vor dem Bürgerkrieg* (Essen, 2001).

27 Wilhelm Deist, *Militär, Staat und Gesellschaft. Studien zur preussisch-deutschen Militärgeschichte* (Munich, 1991), p. 390.

28 Michael Geyer, *Aufrüstung der Sicherheit. Die Reichswehr in der Krise der Machtpolitik 1924–1936* (Wiesbaden, 1980), pp. 23–7, 80–2.

29 'Denkschrift des Reichswehrministers Groener zur wehrpolitischen Lage des Deutschen Reiches Ende 1928', in Otto Ernst Schüddekopf, *Das Heer und die Republik. Quellen zur Politik der Reichswehrführung 1918–1933* (Hannover and Frankfurt am Main, 1955), pp. 251–4.

30 See Michael Geyer, 'Professionals and Junkers: German Rearmament and Politics in the Weimar Republic', in Richard Bessel and E. J. Feuchtwanger (eds), *Social Change and Political Development in Weimar Germany* (London, 1981), pp. 77–133.

31 F. L. Carsten, *The Reichswehr and Politics, 1918–1933* (Oxford, 1966), pp. 351–6.

32 Bessel, *Political Violence and the Rise of Nazism*, pp. 67–74.

33 Albert Grzesinski, *Inside Germany* (New York, 1939), p. 135.

34 Quoted in Christian Streit, *Keine Kameraden. Die Wehrmacht und die sowjetischen Kriegsgefangenen 1941–1945* (Stuttgart, 1978), p. 115.

35 Bessel, *Political Violence and the Rise of Nazism*, p. 48.

36 Bundesarchiv, NS 23/274, ff. 105175–7: The Führer der Untergruppe Mittelschlesien Süd to the Oberste SA-Führung, Reichenbach (Eulengeb.), 26 Sept. 1932.

37 Kershaw, *Hitler 1889–1936*, pp. 337–8.

38 Richard Bessel, 'The Potempa Murder', *Central European History*, vol. 10 (1977), pp. 241–54; Kershaw, *Hitler 1889–1936*, pp. 381–2.

39 Joseph Goebbels, *Kampf um Berlin* (9th edn, Munich, 1936), p. 30.

40 See Eve Rosenhaft, *Beating the Fascists? The German Communists and Political Violence 1929–1933* (Cambridge, 1983).

41 Bessel, *Political Violence and the Rise of Nazism*, pp. 87–92.

42 See Conan Fischer, *Stormtroopers. A Social, Economic and Ideological Analysis, 1929–1935* (London, 1983), pp. 179–205; Bessel, *Political Violence and the Rise of Nazism*, pp. 97–118; Eric G. Reiche, *The Development of the SA in Nurnberg, 1922–1934* (Cambridge, 1986), pp. 173–86; Peter Longerich, *Die braunen Bataillone. Geschichte der SA* (Munich, 1989), pp. 165–79.

43 Walter, *Antisemitische Kriminalität und Gewalt*, pp. 211–21.

44 Esra Bennathan, 'Die demographische und wirtschaftliche Struktur der Juden', in Werner E. Mosse and Arnold Paucker (eds), *Entscheidungsjahr 1932. Zur Judenfrage in der Endphase der Weimarer Republik* (Tübingen, 1966), pp. 88–131; Donald L. Niewyck, *The Jews in Weimar Germany* (Baton Rouge and London, 1980), pp. 11–19.

45 See, for example, Peter H. Merkl, *Political Violence under the Swastika. 581 Early Nazis* (Princeton, 1975), pp. 498–517; Peter H. Merkl, *The Making of a Stormtrooper* (Princeton, 1980), pp. 222–8.

46 'Central-Verein deutscher Staatsbürger jüdischen Glaubens. Ortsgruppe Köln', Cologne, November 1930, printed in Arnold Paucker, *Der jüdische Abwehrkampf gegen Antisemitismus und Nationalsozialismus in den letzten Jahren der Weimarer Republik* (2nd edn, Hamburg, 1968), p. 194.

47 Thomas Childers, *The Nazi Voter. The Social Foundations of Fascism in Germany, 1919–1933* (Chapel Hill and London, 1983), p. 268.

48 See Richard F. Hamilton, *Who Voted for Hitler?* (Princeton, 1982); Childers, *The Nazi Voter*; Jürgen W. Falter, *Hitlers Wähler* (Munich, 1991).

49 Richard Bessel, *Germany after the First World War* (Oxford, 1993), pp. 270–1.

50 Wolfram Wette, 'From Kellogg to Hitler (1928–1933). German Public Opinion Concerning the Rejection or Glorification of War', in Wilhelm Deist (ed.), *The German Military in the Age of Total War* (Leamington Spa, 1985), pp. 79.

51 Against the wave of literature glorifying the war, Erich Maria Remarque's best-selling *All Quiet on the Western Front* remained an isolated – and controversial – exception. For a perceptive discussion of the reception and success of Remarque's famous book, see Modris Eksteins, *Rites of Spring. The Great War and the Birth of the Modern Age* (London, 2000), pp. 274–99.

52 For the classic statement of this thesis, see Tim Mason, 'The Legacy of 1918 for National Socialism', in Anthony Nicholls and Erich Matthias (eds), *German Democracy and the Triumph of Hitler. Essays in Recent German History* (London, 1971), pp. 215–39.

2 The Nazi Regime and the Path to War

1 Reinhard Müller, 'Hitlers Rede vor der Reichswehrführung 1933. Eine neue Moskauer Überlieferung', *Mittelweg 36* (1/2001), pp. 73–90. This version, which recently surfaced in Moscow, offers a fuller and more

detailed record of Hitler's speech than do the notes taken at the meeting by General Kurt Liebmann – which hitherto have been quoted frequently in accounts of the establishment of the Nazi government. For the Liebmann notes, see Thilo Vogelsang, 'Neue Dokumente zur Geschichte der Reichswehr 1930–1933', *Vierteljahrshefte für Zeitgeschichte*, vol. II (1954), doc. nr. 8, pp. 434–5. For an English translation of the Liebmann notes, see J. Noakes and G. Pridham (eds), *Nazism 1919–1945. Volume 3: Foreign Policy, War and Racial Extermination. A Documentary Reader* (Exeter, 2001), pp. 20–1.

2 Müller, 'Hitlers Rede vor der Reichswehrführung 1933', pp. 76–9.

3 Cited in Müller, 'Hitlers Rede vor der Reichswehrführung 1933', p. 73.

4 Quoted in Klaus-Jürgen Müller, *Das Heer und Hitler. Armee und national-sozialistisches Regime 1933–1940* (Stuttgart, 1969), p. 63.

5 Müller, *Das Heer und Hitler*, pp. 37–9.

6 Wilhelm Deist, *The Wehrmacht and German Rearmament* (London, 1981), p. 104.

7 Wolfram Wette, *Die Wehrmacht. Feindbilder, Vernichtungskrieg, Legenden* (Frankfurt am Main, 2002), pp. 151–3.

8 Henry Ashby Turner, Jr., *Hitler's Thirty Days to Power. January 1933* (Reading, Mass., 1996), pp. 144–5; Ian Kershaw, *Hitler 1889–1936: Hubris* (London, 1998), p. 420.

9 Kershaw, *Hitler 1889–1936*, p. 421. See also Larry Eugene Jones, '"The Greatest Stupidity of My Life". Alfred Hugenberg and the Formation of the Hitler Cabinet, January 1933', *Journal of Contemporary History*, vol. 27 (1992), pp. 63–87.

10 Quoted in J. Noakes and G. Pridham (eds), *Nazism 1919–1945. Volume 1: The Rise to Power 1919–1934. A Documentary Reader* (Exeter, 1983), pp. 134–5.

11 Quoted in Michael Wildt, *Generation des Unbedingten. Das Führungskorps des Reichssicherheitshauptamtes* (Hamburg, 2002), p. 143.

12 Richard Bessel, *Political Violence and the Rise of Nazism. The Storm Troopers in Eastern Germany 1925–1934* (New Haven and London, 1984), pp. 98–9.

13 Archiwum Panstwowe w Wroclawiu, Rejencja Opolska I/1797, f. 1: The Pr. Minister des Innern to the Ober- und Regierungspräsidenten and the Polizeipräsident in Berlin, Berlin, 15 Feb. 1933.

14 See Karl Dietrich Bracher, Wolfgang Sauer and Gerhard Schultz, *Die nationalsozialistische Machtergreifung. Studien zur Errichtung des totalitären Herrschaftssystems in Deutschland 1933/34* (2nd edn., Cologne and Opladen, 1962), pp. 72–3, 864–5.

15 Bracher/Sauer/Schulz, *Die nationalsozialistische Machtergreifung*, p. 66; Bessel, *Political Violence and the Rise of Nazism*, pp. 112–14.

16 *Reichsgesetzblatt*, 1933, I, p. 35: Verordnung des Reichspräsidenten zum Schutz des Deutschen Volkes vom 4. Februar 1933.

17 *Reichsgesetzblatt*, 1933, I, p. 83: Verordnung des Reichspräsidenten zum Schutz von Volk und Staat vom 28. Februar 1933.

18 Heinrich Uhlig, *Die Warenhäuser im Dritten Reich* (Cologne and Opladen, 1956), pp. 77–85.

19 Kurt Pätzold, *Faschismus Rassenwahn Judenverfolgung. Eine Studie zur politischen Strategie und Taktik des faschistischen deutschen Imperialismus (1933–1945)* (Berlin, 1975), p. 40.

20 For example, in Pasewalk: Archiwum Panstwowe w Szczecinie, Regierung Stettin – Präsidial Abteilung Polizei, Nr. 36, f. 141: The Bürgermeister to the Landrat in Uekermünde, Pasewalk, 13 March 1933.

21 Bessel, *Political Violence and the Rise of Nazism*, pp. 105–6. Generally, see also Eric Johnson, *The Nazi Terror. The Gestapo, Jews and Ordinary Germans* (London, 1999), pp. 88–90; Michael Wildt, 'Violence against Jews in Germany, 1933–1939', in David Bankier (ed.), *Probing the Depths of German Antisemitism. German Society and the Persecution of the Jews, 1933–1941* (Oxford and Jerusalem, 2000), pp. 191–4; Dirk Schumann, *Politische Gewalt in der Weimarer Republik 1918–1933. Kampf um die Strasse und Furcht vor dem Bürgerkrieg* (Essen, 2001), pp. 331–4.

22 See Bessel, *Political Violence and the Rise of Nazism*, pp. 105–9; Saul Friedländer, *Nazi Germany and the Jews. The Years of Persecution 1933–1939* (London, 1997), pp. 21–3.

23 See Helmut Genschel, *Die Verdrängung der Juden aus der Wirtschaft im Dritten Reich* (Göttingen, 1966); Avraham Barkai, *From Boycott to Annihilation: The Economic Struggle of German Jews, 1933–1943* (Hanover, NH, 1989).

24 Bundesarchiv, R 43 II/1195, f. 61: 'Aufruf Adolf Hitlers an SA und SS', Berlin, 10 March 1933.

25 Bessel, *Political Violence and the Rise of Nazism*, pp. 122–5.

26 *Die Tagebücher von Joseph Goebbels. Sämtliche Fragmente* (ed. Elke Fröhlich), *Teil I. Aufzeichnungen 1924–1941. Band 2 1.1.1931–31–12–1936* (Munich, New York, London and Paris, 1987), p. 398 (entry for 27 March 1933).

27 Kershaw, *Hitler 1889–1936*, p. 502.

28 Ian Kershaw, *The 'Hitler Myth'. Image and Reality in the Third Reich* (Oxford, 1987), pp. 54–6.

29 *Reichsgesetzblatt*, 1933, I, p. 141 : Gesetz zur Behebung der Not von Volk und Reich (Ermächtigungsgesetz) vom 24. März 1933.

30 *Reichsgesetzblatt,* 1933, I, p. 479: Gesetz gegen die Neubildung von Parteien vom 14. Juli 1933.

31 'Ausführungen des Reichswehrministers von Blomberg vor den Gruppen- und Wehrkreisbefehlshabern im Reichswehrministerium. Hand- schriftliche Aufzeichnungen des Gen.Lt. Liebmann'. Printed in Thilo Vogelsang, 'Neue Dokumente zur Geschichte der Reichswehr 1930–1933', *Vierteljahrshefte für Zeitgeschichte,* vol. 2 (1954), doc. nr. 7, p. 432.

32 'Lagebericht der Staatsopolizeistelle Stettin an das Geheime Staats- polizeiamt über den Monat Juli', 4 Aug. 1934, printed in Robert Thévoz, Hans Branig and Cécile Lowenthal-Hensel (eds), *Pommern 1934/35 im Spiegel von Gestapo-Lageberichten und Sachakten (Quellen)* (Cologne and Berlin, 1974), p. 31.

33 'Halbmonatsbericht des Bezirkamts Ebermannstadt', 14 July 1934, in Martin Broszat, Elke Fröhlich and Falk Wiesemann (eds), *Bayern in der NS-Zeit. Soziale Lage und politisches Verhalten der Bevölkerung im Spiegel vertraulicher Berichte* (Munich, 1977), p. 71.

34 See Kershaw, *The 'Hitler Myth',* pp. 84–95.

35 Hitler's Reichstag speech of 13 July 1934, in Erhard Klöss (eds), *Reden des Führers. Politik und Propaganda Adolf Hitlers* (Munich, 1967), p. 146. On the army's reaction to the 'Röhm affair', see Müller, *Das Heer und Hitler,* pp. 125–33.

36 R. J. Overy, *War and Economy in the Third Reich* (Oxford, 1994), p. 78.

37 Martin Kornrumpf, *HAFRABA e.V. Deutsche Autobahn-Planung 1926– 1934* (Bonn, 1990); Franz W. Siedler, 'Fritz Todt – Vom Autobahnbauer zum Reichsminister', in Ronald Smelser and Rainer Zitelmann (eds), *Die braune Elite* (Darmstadt, 1989), pp. 299–312; Erhard Schütz and Eckhard Gruber, *Mythos Reichsautobahn. Bau und Inszenierung der 'Strassen des Führers' 1933–1941* (Berlin, 1996).

38 Overy, *War and Economy in the Third Reich,* p. 85.

39 James D. Shand, 'The Reichsautobahnen. Symbol for the Third Reich', *Journal of Contemporary History,* vol. 19 (1984), pp. 189–200.

40 At the peak in March 1934, some 630,000 people were employed in work- creation schemes. See Overy, *War and Economy in the Third Reich,* p. 53.

41 Overy, *War and Economy in the Third Reich,* p. 39.

42 Overy, *War and Economy in the Third Reich,* p. 196. See also Ulrich Herbert, *Geschichte der Ausländerbeschäftigung in Deutschland 1880 bis 1980. Sai- sonarbeiter, Zwangsarbeiter, Gastarbeiter* (Bonn, 1986), pp. 120–4.

43 Between 1933 and 1939, the average number of hours worked by industrial workers increased from 42.9 to 48.7 per week. See Rüdiger Hachtmann, *Industriearbeit im 'Dritten Reich'. Untersuchungen zu den Lohn- und*

Arbeitsbedingungen in Deutschland 1933–1945 (Göttingen, 1989), p. 51.

44 See Götz Aly, *Rasse und Klasse. Nachforschungen zum deutschen Wesen* (Frankfurt am Main, 2003), pp. 230–44.

45 R. J. Overy, *Goering. The 'Iron Man'* (London, 1984), pp. 64–8.

46 Overy, *War and Economy in the Third Reich*, p. 87.

47 Norbert Frei, *National Socialist Rule in Germany, The Führer State 1933–1945* (Oxford and Cambridge, Mass., 1993), p. 82; Hans Mommsen and Manfred Grieder, *Das Volkswagenwerk und seine Arbeiter im Dritten Reich* (Düsseldorf, 1996), pp. 189–202. The number of savings contracts signed for the 'Strength through Joy' cars stood at 270,000 at the end of 1939; a further 70,000 people had signed up by the spring of 1945.

48 Ian Kershaw chose 1936 as the dividing point for his recent two-volume biography of Hitler, the time when the Nazi dictator 'became the foremost believer in his own Führer cult' and nemesis took over from hubris. See Kershaw, *Hitler 1889–1936*, p. 591.

49 While War Minister von Blomberg remained worried, Foreign Minister von Neurath was convinced on the basis of intelligence that the French would not take military action. See Zach Shore, 'Hitler, Intelligence and the Decision to Remilitarize the Rhine', *Journal of Contemporary History*, vol. 34, no. 1 (Jan. 1999), pp. 5–18. According to Stephen Schuker, it is doubtful whether, after having made substantial cuts in military budgets, the French were capable of resisting the remilitarization. See Stephen A. Schuker, 'France and the Remilitarization of the Rhineland, 1936', *French Historical Studies*, vol. 14, no. 3. (Spring, 1986), pp. 299–338.

50 Michael Geyer, 'The Dynamics of Military Revisionism in the Interwar Years. Military Politics between Rearmament and Diplomacy', in Wilhelm Deist (ed.), *The German Military in the Age of Total War* (Leamington Spa, 1985), p. 130.

51 Quoted in Kershaw, *Hitler 1889–1936*, p. 591.

52 Quoted in Overy, *War and Economy in the Third Reich*, p. 189.

53 Wilhelm Treue, 'Hitlers Denkschrift zum Vierjahresplan 1936', *Vierteljahrshefte für Zeitgeschichte*, vol. 3. (1955), pp. 204–6.

54 Treue, 'Hitlers Denkschrift zum Vierjahresplan 1936', p. 210.

55 Wilhelm Deist, *The Wehrmacht and German Rearmament* (London, 1981), p. 53.

56 Wilhelm Deist, *Militär, Staat und Gesellschaft. Studien zur preussisch-deutschen Militärgeschichte* (Munich, 1991), pp. 410–13. The Anglo-German Naval Agreement of July 1935, which foresaw a German Navy 35 per cent that of the British, was regarded by the naval leadership as only 'provisional'.

57 Charles S. Thomas, *The German Navy in the Nazi Era* (London, 1990), p. 141; Jost Düllfer, *Weimar, Hitler und die Marine. Realpolitik und Flottenbau 1920–1939* (Düsseldorf, 1973), pp. 457–8. During the Wilhelmine period, the most under construction an any one time had been 200,000 tonnes.

58 See Klaus-Jürgen Müller, *Armee und Drittes Reich 1933–1939. Darstellung und Dokumentation* (Paderborn, 1987), pp. 100–1.

59 In fact the army had reached a strength of 2,758,000 when war was launched on 1 September 1939. See Deist, *The Wehrmacht and German Rearmament*, p. 89.

60 Müller, *Armee und Drittes Reich 1933–1939*, p. 101.

61 Deist, *Militär, Staat und Gesellschaft*, pp. 413–14.

62 See Overy, *Goering. The 'Iron Man'*, p. 68.

63 Printed in Klaus-Jürgen Müller, *Armee und Drittes Reich 1933–1939*, pp. 311–16. Quotation from p. 311.

64 Willi A Boelcke, *Die Kosten von Hitlers Krieg. Kriegsfinanzierung und finanzielles Kriegserbe in Deutschland 1933–1948* (Paderborn, 1985), p. 51; Overy, *War and Economy in the Third Reich*, p. 20.

65 Overy, *War and Economy in the Third Reich*, p. 21.

66 'Ausarbeitung des Allgemeinen Heeresamtes über den Aufbau des Friedens- und Kriegsheeres vom 1 August 1936', in Müller, *Armee und Drittes Reich 1933–1939*, pp. 304–8.

67 Quoted in Müller, *Armee und Drittes Reich 1933–1939*, p. 102.

68 This was the title of an article published by Herbert Backe in the *NS-Landpost* on 7 July 1942. Extract in Gustavo Corni and Horst Gies, *"Blut und Boden". Rassenideologie und Agrarpolitik im Staat Hitlers* (Idstein, 1994), p. 207.

69 Herbert Backe, 'Die russische Getreidewirtschaft als Grundlage der Land- und Volkswirtschaft Russlands'. I wish to thank Adam Tooze for bringing this to my attention.

70 See Gustavo Corni and Horst Gies, *Brot, Butter Kanonen. Die Ernährungswirtschaft in Deutschland unter der Diktatur Hitlers* (Berlin 1997), pp. 399–409.

71 Ian Kershaw, *Popular Opinion and Political Dissent in the Third Reich: Bavaria 1933–1945* (Oxford, 1983), p. 83. The problem was described extensively, for example, in the SPD report of August 1935, in which comparison was made to conditions during the First World War. See *Deutschland-Berichte der Sozialdemokratischen Partei Deutschlands (Sopade) 1934–1940. Zweiter Jahrgang 1935* (Frankfurt am Main, 1980), pp. 951–60 (here, p. 960).

72 This greatly agitated War Minister von Blomberg. See the letter of the

Reichskriegsministers und Oberbefehlshabers der Wehrmacht of 5 August 1937 to the Reichsarbeitsminister zur Landarbeiterfrage, in Corni and Gies, "*Blut und Boden*", pp. 167–8.

73 Thus, for example, the race-theorist Hans Friedrich Karl Günther, then Director of the Institute for Racial Studies, Biology of Peoples and Rural Sociology (*Anstalt für Rassenkunde, Völkerbiologie und Ländliche Soziologie*) at the University of Berlin, in a speech at the ceremony celebrating the 126th anniversary of the founding of the Berlin University in November 1936. See Elvira Weisenburger, 'Der "Rassepabst". Hans Friedrich Karl Günther, Professor für Rassenkunde', in Michael Kissner and Joachim Scholtyseck (eds), *Die Führer der Provinz. NS-Biographien aus Baden und Württemberg* (Konstanz, 1997), p. 189.

74 Hans Land, 'Die Bekämpfung der Schwarzarbeit, des Doppelverdienertums und der Frauenarbeit im Rahmen der deutschen Konjunkturpolitik' (Diss. Marburg, 1937), p. 45. Quoted in Dorothee Klinksiek, *Die Frau im NS-Staat* (Stuttgart, 1982), p. 100.

75 *Reichsgesetzblatt*, 1933, I, pp. 326–29: Gesetz zur Verminderung der Arbeitslosigkeit vom 1. Juni 1933, Abschitt V: Förderung der Eheschliessungen; *Reichsgesetzblatt*, 1933, I, pp. 377–9: Durchführungsverordnung über die Gewährung von Ehestandsdarlehen (ED-DVO) vom 20. Juni 1933. Loans of up to 1,000 RM, in the form of vouchers for particular household goods, were made available to women who gave up work to marry; 25 per cent of the amount to be repaid was dropped with the birth of each child. See also Klinksiek, *Die Frau im NS-Staat*, p. 102; Gabriele Czarnowski, *Das kontrollierte Paar. Ehe- und Sexualpolitik im Nationalsozialismus* (Wiesbaden, 1991), pp. 101–35; Gabriele Czarnowski, '"The Value of Marriage for the *Volksgemeinschaft*". Policies towards Women and Marriage under National Socialism', in Richard Bessel (ed.), *Fascist Italy and Nazi Germany. Comparisons and Contrasts* (Cambridge, 1996), pp. 100–1; and Elizabeth D. Heineman, *What Difference Does a Husband Make? Women and Marital Status in Nazi and Postwar Germany* (Berkeley, Los Angeles and London, 1999), p. 22. In 1938 two-fifths of couples who married received marriage loans; altogether between 1933 and 1944 roughly two million such loans had been granted.

76 'Wortprotokoll der 5. Tagung der Reichsarbeitskammer vom 24. November 1936 in Berlin', printed in Timothy W. Mason, *Arbeiterklasse und Volksgemeinschaft. Dokumente und Materialien zur deutschen Arbeiterpolitik 1936–1939* (Opladen, 1975), pp. 170–91 (here p. 185).

77 Klinksiek, *Die Frau im NS-Staat*, p. 105; Rüdiger Hachtmann, *Industriearbeit im "Dritten Reich"*, pp. 39–41.

78 Lisa Pine, *Nazi Family Policy, 1933–1945* (Oxford and New York, 1997), p. 109. By 1941 1.1 million families had received such one off-grants.

79 *Reichsgesetzblatt*, 1933, I, pp. 529–31: Gesetz zur Verhütung erbkranken Nachwuchses vom 14. Juli 1933.

80 Gisela Bock, *Zwangssterilisation im Nationalsozialismus. Studien zur Rassenpolitik und Frauenpolitik* (Opladen, 1986), p. 232. See also Annette Feldmann and Horst-Pierre Bothien, 'Zwangssterilisation in Bonn. Zur Arbeit des Erbsgesundheitsgerichts Bonn (1934–1944)', in Annette Kuhn (ed.), *Frauenleben im NS-Alltag. Bonner Studien zur Frauengeschichte* (Pfaffenweiler, 1994), pp. 248–9.

81 Bock, *Zwangssterilisation im Nationalsozialismus*, p. 372.

82 Reiner Pommerin, *Sterilisierung der Rheinlandbastarde. Das Schicksal einer farbigen deutschen Minderheit 1918–1937* (Düsseldorf, 1979), pp. 77–84.

83 *Reichsgesetzblatt*, 1935, I, p. 1246: Gesetz zum Schutze der Erbsgesundkeit des deutschen Volkes (Ehegesundheitsgesetz) vom 18. Oktober 1935. See also Heineman, *What Difference Does a Husband Make?*, pp. 23–5.

84 Walter Schnell, *Die öffentliche Gesundheitspflege* (Leipzig, Stuttgart and Berlin, 1938), p. 66. Quoted in Ernst Klee, *Deutsche Medizin im Dritten Reich. Karrieren vor und nach 1945* (Frankfurt am Main, 2001), p. 63.

85 Klinksiek, *Die Frau im NS-Staat*, pp. 80–1.

86 See Ulrich Herbert, 'Good Times, Bad Times: Memories of the Third Reich', in Richard Bessel (ed.), *Life in the Third Reich* (revised edition, Oxford, 2001), pp. 97–110.

87 Statistisches Reichsamt (ed.), *Statistisches Jahrbuch für das Deutsche Reich 1936* (Berlin, 1936), p. 35.

88 Detlev J. K. Peukert, *Inside Nazi Germany. Conformity, Opposition and Racism in Everyday Life* (London, 1987), p. 76.

89 Klinksiek, *Die Frau im NS-Staat*, pp. 120–2; Ute Benz, 'Einleitung. Frauen im Nationalsozialismus', in Ute Benz (ed.), *Frauen im Nationalsozialismus. Dokumente und Zeugnisse* (Munich, 1993), pp. 14–15. At the end of 1938 the *Deutsches Frauenwerk* numbered almost 1.8 million members, with an additional four million 'corporate members', in the 'Altreich'.

90 *Deutschland-Berichte der Sozialdemokratischen Partei Deutschlands (Sopade) 1934–1940. Erster Jahrgang 1934* (Frankfurt am Main, 1980), p. 117.

91 Michael Schneider, *Unterm Hakenkreuz. Arbeiter und Arbeiterbewegung 1933 bis 1939* (Bonn, 1999), p. 178.

92 Schneider, *Unterm Hakenkreuz*, pp. 168–243.

93 Frei, *National Socialist Rule in Germany*, p. 82; Schneider, *Unterm Hakenkreuz*, pp. 230–1.

94 *Deutschland-Berichte der Sozialdemokratischen Partei Deutschlands (Sopade) 1934–1940. Zweiter Jahrgang 1935* (Frankfurt am Main, 1980), p. 410: report for April 1933.

95 *Deutschland-Berichte der Sozialdemokratischen Partei Deutschlands (Sopade) 1934–1940. Zweiter Jahrgang 1935* (Frankfurt am Main, 1980), p. 412: report for April 1935. Similar reactions were reported a little over a year later, in the summer of 1936, when the period of compulsory military service was extended from one to two years. See *Deutschland-Berichte der Sozialdemokratischen Partei Deutschlands (Sopade) 1934–1940. Dritter Jahrgang 1936* (Frankfurt am Main, 1980), pp. 1097–1103: report for September 1936. Generally, see Ute Frevert, *Die kasernierte Nation. Militärdienst und Zivilgesellschaft in Deutschland* (Munich, 2001), pp. 317–19.

96 *Deutschland-Berichte der Sozialdemokratischen Partei Deutschlands (Sopade) 1934–1940. Zweiter Jahrgang 1935* (Frankfurt am Main, 1980), p. 412: report for April 1935.

97 *Deutschland-Berichte der Sozialdemokratischen Partei Deutschlands (Sopade) 1934–1940. Dritter Jahrgang 1936* (Frankfurt am Main, 1980), p. 304: report for March 1936.

98 *Deutschland-Berichte der Sozialdemokratischen Partei Deutschlands (Sopade) 1934–1940. Dritter Jahrgang 1936* (Frankfurt am Main, 1980), p. 301: report for March 1936.

99 Wolfgang Ribbe (ed.), *Die Lageberichte der Geheimen Staatspolizei über die Provinz Brandenberg und die Reichshauptstadt Berlin 1933 bis 1936. Teilband I. Der Regierungsbezirk Potsdam* (Weimar and Vienna, 1998), p. 251: Lagebericht der Staatspolizeistelle Potsdam für April 1935. On corruption in the 'Third Reich' generally, Frank Bajohr, 'Nationalsozialismus und Korruption', *Mittelweg* 36, no. 1 (1998), pp. 57–77; Frank Bajohr, *Parvenüs und Profiteure. Korruption in der NS-Zeit* (Frankfurt am Main, 2001).

100 *Deutschland-Berichte der Sozialdemokratischen Partei Deutschlands (Sopade) 1934–1940. Dritter Jahrgang 1936* (Frankfurt am Main, 1980), p. 829: report for July 1936.

101 Text printed in Müller, *Armee und Drittes Reich 1933–1939*, pp. 316–23 (Dok. 145). Quotation from p. 316.

102 For a careful description of the complicated events of January–February 1938, see Ian Kershaw, *Hitler 1936–1945. Nemesis* (London, 2000), pp. 52–60.

103 Quoted in Overy, *War and Economy in the Third Reich*, p. 185.

104 Beck's 'Betrachtungen zur gegenwärtigen militärpolitischen Lage Deutschlands', in Müller, *Armee und Drittes Reich 1933–1939*, pp. 326–9.

105 Carola Sachse, et al., *Angst, Belohnung, Zucht und Ordnung. Herrschaftsmechanismen im Nationalsozialismus* (Opladen, 1982).

106 Robert Gellately, *The Gestapo and German Society. Enforcing Racial Policy 1933–1945* (Oxford, 1990); Klaus-Michael Mallmann and Gerhard Paul, *Herrschaft und Alltag. Ein Industrierevier im Dritten Reich* (Bonn, 1991); Klaus-Michael Mallmann and Gerhard Paul, 'Allwissend, allmächtig, allgegenwärtig? Gestapo, Gesellschaft und Widerstand', *Zeitschrift für Geschichtswissenschaft*, vol. 41 (1993); Gerhard Paul and Klaus-Michael Mallmann (eds), *Die Gestapo. Mythos und Realität* (Darmstadt, 1995).

107 Robert Gellately, *Backing Hitler. Consent and Coercion in Nazi Germany* (Oxford, 2001).

108 Mallmann and Paul, *Herrschaft und Alltag*, p. 249.

109 Wildt, *Generation des Unbedingten*.

110 Andreas Seeger, *'Gestapo Müller'. Die Karriere eines Schreibtischtäters* (Berlin, 1996), pp. 28–52.

111 Quoted in Seeger, *'Gestapo Müller'*, p. 39.

112 Reinhard Heydrich, 'Die Bekämpfung der Staatsfeinde', in *Deutsches Recht*, vol. 6, no. 7/8 (15 April 1936), pp. 121–3 (here, 121). Quoted in Wildt, *Generation des Unbedingten*, p. 13.

113 *Reichsgesetzblatt*, 1933, I, p. 175: Gesetz zur Wiederherstellung des Berufsbeamtentums vom 7. April 1933.

114 *Reichsgesetzblatt*, 1935, I, p. 1146: Reichsbürgergesetz vom 15. September 1935; *Reichsgesetzblatt*, 1935, I, pp. 1146–7: Gesetz zum Schutze des deutschen Blutes und der deutschen Ehre vom 15. September 1935. On the Nuremberg Laws, see Hans Mommsen, *Auschwitz, 17. Juli 1942. Der Weg zur europäischen "Endlösung des Judenfrage"* (Munich, 2002), pp. 41–55; and, especially, Cornelie Essner, *Die "Nürnberger Gesetze" oder Die Verwaltung des Rassenwahns 1933–1945* (Paderborn, 2002), pp. 76–173. At the beginning of 1936 Gypsies and non-whites were included in the terms of the law 'for the protection of German blood'.

115 *Reichsgesetzblatt*, 1935, I, pp. 1333–4: Erste Verordnung zum Reichsbürgergesetz vom 14. November 1935.

116 *Reichsgesetzblatt*, 1935, I, p. 700: Verordnung über die Musterung und Aushebung 1935 vom 29. Mai 1935. According to this decree, which stipulated that 'Aryan descent is a precondition for active military service', a 'Non-Aryan' was defined as 'whoever is a descendent of Non-Aryans, especially of Jewish parents or grandparents. It suffices if one

parent or grandparent is Non-Aryan. This is to be assumed especially if a parent or grandparent is of the Jewish religion.'

117 Essner, *Die "Nürnberger Gesetze"*, p. 445.

118 Peter Longerich, *Politik der Vernichtung. Eine Gesamtdarstellung der nationalsozialistischen Judenverfolgung* (Munich and Zurich, 1998), pp. 106–11.

119 *Deutschland-Berichte der Sozialdemokratischen Partei Deutschlands (Sopade) 1934–1940. Dritter Jahrgang 1936* (Frankfurt am Main, 1980), p. 27: report for January 1936.

120 See, for example, Wolfgang Ribbe (ed.), *Die Lageberichte der Geheimen Staatspolizei über die Provinz Brandenberg und die Reichshauptstadt Berlin 1933 bis 1936. Teilband I. Der Regierungsbezirk Potsdam* (Weimar and Vienna, 1998), p. 366: Lagebericht der Staatspolizeistelle Potsdam für September 1935.

121 By the spring of 1938, between 60 per cent and 70 per cent of all Jewish-owned businesses operating in Germany in January 1933 had either ceased trading or else were in the hands of 'Aryans'. See Avraham Barkai, '"Schicksalsjahr 1938". Kontinuität und Verschärfung der wirtschaftlichen Ausplünderung der deutschen Juden', in Walter H. Pehle (ed.), *Der Judenpogrom 1938. Von der 'Reichskristallnacht' zum Völkermord* (Frankfurt am Main, 1994), p. 96.

122 This occurred, for example, in the Osnabrück region in the summer of 1935. See Gerd Steinwascher (ed.), *Gestapo Osnabrück meldet ... Polizei- und Regierungsberichte aus dem Regierungsbezirk Osnabrück aus den Jahren 1933 bis 1936* (Osnabrück, 1995), pp. 249–52: Dokument 39: 'Lagebericht der Staatspolizeistelle Osnabrück an das Geheime Staatspolizeiamt für den Monat August 1935 vom 4. September 1935'.

123 See, especially, Marion Kaplan, *Between Dignity and Despair: Jewish Life in Nazi Germany* (New York and Oxford, 1998).

124 Steinwascher (ed.), *Gestapo Osnabrück meldet ...*, p. 166: 'Lagebericht der Staatspolizeistelle Osnabrück an das Geheime Staatspolizeiamt für die Monate März und April 1935 vom 4. Mai 1935'.

125 Avraham Barkai, "Schicksalsjahr 1938", p. 96.

126 Marion Kaplan, 'When the Ordinary Became Extraordinary. German Jews Reacting to Nazi Persecution, 1933–1939', in Robert Gellately and Nathan Stoltzfus (eds), *Social Outsiders in Nazi Germany* (Princeton and Oxford, 2001), p. 90.

127 Konrad Kwiet, 'Gehen oder bleiben? Die deutschen Juden am Wendepunkt', in Pehle (ed.), *Der Judenpogrom 1938*, p. 139.

128 Shortly thereafter, Mussolini discovered that he personally and the Ital-

ians generally were 'Aryans' too, and at the beginning of August Fascist Italy began to enact its own antisemitic laws. See R. J. B. Bosworth, *Mussolini* (London, 2002), pp. 334–44.

129 On the delirious welcome received by the Wehrmacht and by Hitler in Austria, see Evan Burr Bukey, *Hitler's Austria. Popular Sentiment in the Nazi Era 1938–1945* (Chapel Hill and London, 2000), pp. 28–33.

130 Franz von Papen, *Memoirs* (London, 1952), p. 438. Quoted in Kershaw, *Hitler 1936–1945*, p. 83.

131 Hans Witek, '"Arisierung" in Wien. Aspekte nationalsozialistischer Enteignungspolitik 1938–1940', in Emmerich Talos, Ernst Hanisch and Wolfgang Neugebauer (eds.), *NS-Herrschaft in Österreich 1938–1945* (Vienna, 1988), pp. 199–216; Hans Safrian, *Eichmann und seine Gehilfen* (Frankfurt am Main, 1995), pp. 23–67.

132 Karl A. Schleunes, *The Twisted Road to Auschwitz. Nazi Policy Toward German Jews 1933–39* (London, 1971).

133 Trude Maurer, 'Abschiebung und Attentat. Die Ausweisung der polnischen Juden und der Vorwand für die "Kristallnacht"', in Pehle (ed.), *Der Judenpogrom 1938*, pp. 52–73.

134 Uwe Dietrich Adam, 'Wie spontan war der Pogrom?', in Pehle (ed.), *Der Judenpogrom 1938*, p. 76–80.

135 See Heinz Lauber, *Judenpogrom: 'Reichskristallnacht' November 1938 in Grossdeutschland. Daten, Fakten, Dokumente, Quellentexte, Thesen und Bewertungen* (Gerlingen, 1981), pp. 123–4.

136 *Reichsgesetzblatt*, 1938, I, p. 1579: Reichsverordnung über eine Sühneleistung der Juden deutscher Staatsangehörigkeit vom 12. November 1938.

137 *Deutschland-Berichte der Sozialdemokratischen Partei Deutschlands (Sopade) 1934–1940. Fünfter Jahrgang 1938* (Frankfurt am Main, 1980), pp. 1204–5: report Nr. 11, 'Abgeschlossen am 10. Dezember 1938'. See also William Sheridan Allen, 'Die deutsche Bevölkerung und die "Reichskristallnacht". Konflikte zwischen Werthierarchie und Propaganda im Dritten Reich', in Detlev Peukert and Jürgen Reulecke (eds.), *Die Reihen fast geschlossen. Beiträge zur Geschichte des Alltags unterm Nationalsozialismus* (Wuppertal, 1980), pp. 397–412.

138 From March 1939 a similar measure was applied to the Sinti and Roma, who were identified in their passports as 'gypsies' (*Zigeuner*).

139 See Saul Friedländer, *Nazi Germany and the Jews. The Years of Persecution 1933–39* (London, 1997), pp. 280–8.

140 On Nazi Germany's critical shortage of foreign exchange in early 1938, see Albrecht Ritschl, 'Die deutsche Zahlungsbilanz 1936–1941 und das

Problem des Devisenmangels vor Kriegsbeginn', *Vierteljahrshefte für Zeitgeschichte*, vol. 39, no. 1 (1991), pp. 103–23.

141 Müller, *Armee und Drittes Reich 1933–1939*, p. 118; Kershaw, *Hitler 1936–1945*, pp. 163–5.

142 Müller, *Armee und Drittes Reich 1933–1939*, p. 359: Weisung Hitlers vom 21. Oktober 1938.

143 Wilhelm Treue, 'Rede Hitlers vor der deutschen Presse (10. November 1938)', *Vierteljahrshefte für Zeitgeschichte*, vol. 6, no. 2 (1958), pp. 175–91.

144 Hitler, *Mein Kampf*, pp. 540–2: 'National Socialism [...] must teach our people not to fix their attention on the little things but rather on the great things, not to exhaust their energies on secondary objects and not to forget that the object we shall have to fight for one day is the bare existence of our people.'

145 *Deutschland-Berichte der Sozialdemokratischen Partei Deutschlands (Sopade) 1934–1940. Fünfter Jahrgang 1938* (Frankfurt am Main, 1980), p. 944: report Nr. 9, 'Abgeschlossen am 10. Oktober 1938'.

146 Treue, 'Rede Hitlers vor der deutschen Presse', pp. 184–5. Translation in J. Noakes and G. Pridham (eds), *Nazism 1919–1945. Volume 3: Foreign Policy, War and Racial Extermination* (Exeter, 2001), pp. 113–16.

147 Treue, 'Rede Hitlers vor der deutschen Presse', p. 185.

148 See Müller, *Armee und Drittes Reich 1933–1939*, p. 119.

149 Müller, *Armee und Drittes Reich 1933–1939*, p. 370: Rede Hitlers am 10. Februar 1939 vor Truppenkommandeuren in Berlin.

150 Müller, *Armee und Drittes Reich 1933–1939*, pp. 373–4: Rede Hitlers am 10. Februar 1939 vor Truppenkommandeuren in Berlin.

151 Müller, *Armee und Drittes Reich 1933–1939*, pp. 123–4.

152 Michael Geyer, 'The Dynamics of Military Revisionism in the Interwar Years. Military Politics between Rearmament and Diplomacy', in Wilhelm Deist (ed.), *The German Military in the Age of Total War* (Leamington Spa, 1985), p. 147.

153 Deist, *The Wehrmacht and German Rearmament*, pp. 88–9. This helped to compensate for production shortfalls in Germany and came in very handy once war broke out. Three armoured divisions were equipped with Czechoslovak combat vehicles for the campaign against France.

154 Müller, *Armee und Drittes Reich 1933–1939*, p. 377: Weisung des Chefs des Oberkommando der Wehrmacht, Generaloberst Keitel, vom 3. April 1939.

155 Müller, *Armee und Drittes Reich 1933–1939*, pp. 375–6: Vermerk über Mitteilungen Hitlers an General von Brauchitsch vom 25. März 1939 betreffend künftige politische und militärishe Pläne.

156 Müller, *Armee und Drittes Reich 1933–1939*, p. 380: Niederschrift des Oberstleutnants Schmundt über die Besprechung in der Reichskanzlei am 23. Mai 1939. Bericht über die Besprechung Hitlers am 23.5.1939.

157 Müller, *Armee und Drittes Reich 1933–1939*, p. 385: Ausführungen Hitlers vor dem Oberbefehlshaber des Heeres und dem Chef des Generalstabes am 17. August 1939.

158 Müller, *Armee und Drittes Reich 1933–1939*, p. 385.

3. Nazism and the Second World War

1 J. Noakes and G. Pridharn (eds), *Nazism 1919–1945. Volume 3: Foreign Policy, War and Racial Extermination* (Exeter, 2001), p. 1049.

2 Hans Mommsen, 'The Realization of the Unthinkable: The "Final Solution of the Jewish Question" in the Third Reich', in Gerhard Hirschfeld (ed.), *The Policies of Genocide. Jews and Soviet Prisoners of War in Nazi Germany* (London, 1986), pp. 93–144.

3 This was discussed more than a quarter of a century ago with remarkable clarity by Andreas Hiligruber, 'Die "Endlösung" und das deutsche Ostimperium als Kernstück des rassenideologischen Programms des Nationalsozialismus', in Manfred Funke (ed.), *Hitler, Deutschland und die Mächte. Materialien zur Aussenpolitik des Dritten Reiches* (Düsseldorf, 1978), pp. 94–114.

4 See Gabriele Schneider, *Mussolini in Afrika. Die faschistische Rassenpolitik in den italienischen Kolonien 1936–1941* (Cologne, 2000), p. 143.

5 Gerhard L. Weinberg, *A World at Arms. A Global History of World War II* (Cambridge, 1994), pp. 322, 862–63.

6 Hitler's Reichstag speech of 1 September 1939, printed in Erhard Klöss (ed.), *Reden des Führers. Politik und Propaganda Adolf Hitlers 1922–1945* (Munich, 1967), p. 215.

7 See Rüdiger Overmans, *Deutsche militärische Verluste im Zweiten Weltkrieg* (Munich, 1999), p. 239.

8 Weinberg, *A World at Arms*, p. 57.

9 Peter Longerich estimates that the conquest of Poland in 1939 brought roughly 1.7 million Jews under German control. See Peter Longerich, *Politik der Vernichtung. Eine Gesamtdarstellung der nationalsozialistischen Judenverfolgung* (Munich and Zurich, 1998), p. 252.

10 *Die Tagebücher von Joseph Goebbels. Sämtliche Fragmente, Teil I. Aufzeichnungen 1924–1941. Band 3. 1.1.1937–31.12.1939* (ed. Elke Fröhlich)(Munich, New York, London and Paris, 1987), p. 628: entry for 2 Nov. 1939.

11 Generaloberst (Franz) Halder, *Kriegstagebuch. Bd. 1. Vom Polenfeldzug bis zum Ende der Westoffensive (14.8.1939–30.6.1940)* (ed. Hans-Adolf Jacobsen) (Stuttgart, 1962), pp. 183–4: entry from 5 Feb. 1940. See also Rolf-Dieter Müller, *Hitlers Ostkrieg und die deutsche Siedlungspolitik* (Frankfurt am Main, 1991), pp. 20–2; Christopher R. Browning, *Nazi Policy, Jewish Workers, German Killers* (Cambridge, 2000), p. 61.

12 Otto Dietrich, *Auf den Strassen des Sieges. Erlebnisse mit dem Führer in Polen* (Munich, 1940), p. 180.

13 Martin Broszat, *Nationalsozialistische Polenpolitik 1939–1945* (Stuttgart, 1961), pp. 85–6; Ian Kershaw, *Hitler 1936–1945. Nemesis* (London, 2000), p. 318.

14 The numbers of Poles thus expelled has been estimated at between 365,000 as of mid-March 1941 (Broszat, *Nationalsozialistische Polenpolitik*, pp. 100–101) to more than 800,000 by the end of 1941 (Götz Aly and Susanne Heim, *Vordenker der Vernichtung. Auschwitz und die deutschen Plane für eine neue europäische Ordnung* (Frankfurt am Main, 1993), p. 160; Jost Düllfer, *Nazi Germany 1933–1945. Faith and Annihilation* (London, 1996), p. 156).

15 Düllfer, *Nazi Germany 1933–1945*, p. 156; Aly and Heim, *Vordenker der Vernichtung*, p. 153.

16 Götz Aly, *'Final Solution'. Nazi Population Policy and the Murder of the Jews* (London, 1999), pp. 113–19.

17 See Longerich, *Politik der Vernichtung*, pp. 251–70.

18 See Aly and Heim, *Vordenker der Vernichtung*, pp. 257–65; Longerich, *Politik der Vernichtung*, pp. 273–85.

19 Michael Wildt, *Generation des Unbedingten. Das Führungskorps des Reichssicherheitshauptamtes* (Hamburg, 2002), pp. 421–8.

20 Michael Wildt, 'Radikalisierung und Seibstradikalisierung 1939. Die Geburt des Reichssicherheitshauptamtes aus dem Geist des völkischen Massenmords', in Gerhard Paul and Klaus-Michael Mallniann (eds), *Die Gestapo im Zweiten Weltkrieg. 'Heimatfront' und besetztes Europa* (Darmstadt, 2000), pp. 22–3.

21 See Wlodzimierrz Borodziej, *Terror und Politik. Die deutsche Polizei und die polnische Widerstandsbewegung im Generalgouvernement 1939–1944* (Mainz, 1999), p. 26.

22 Wildt, *Generation des Unbedingten*, pp. 428–73.

23 Quoted in Wildt, 'Radikalisierung und Seibstradikalisierung', p. 30. See also Longerich, *Politik der Vernichtung*, p. 243.

24 Generaloberst (Franz) Halder, *Kriegstagebuch. Bd. 1. Vom Polenfeldzug bis zum Ende der Westoffensive (14.8.1939–30.6.1940)*, ed. Hans-Adolf Jacobsen

(Stuttgart, 1962), pp. 81–2: entry from 20 Sept. 1939.

25 Hans Mommsen, *Auschwitz, 17. Juli 1942. Der Weg zur europäischen 'Endlösung der Judenfrage'* (Munich, 2002), p. 97.

26 Longerich, *Politik der Vernichtung*, pp. 256–60.

27 Christian Jansen and Arno Weckbecker, *Der 'Volksdeutsche Selbstschutz' in Polen 1939/40* (Munich, 1992), p. 155. See also Borodziej, *Terror und Politik*, p. 29; Wildt, 'Radikalisierung und Selbstradikalisierung', p. 36.

28 Generaloberst (Franz) Halder, *Kriegstagebuch. Bd. 1. Vom Polenfeldzug bis zum Ende der Westoffensive (14.8.1939–30.6.1940)*, ed. Hans-Adolf Jacobsen (Stuttgart, 1962), p. 107: entry for 18 Oct. 1939.

29 *Die Tagebucher von Joseph Goebbels. Sämtliche Fragmente, Teil I. Aufzeichnungen 1924–1941. Band 3. 1.1.1937–31.12.1939*, ed. Elke Fröhlich (Munich, New York, London and Paris, 1987), p. 604: entry for 10 Oct. 1939.

30 Uwe Dietrich Adam, *Judenpolitik im Dritten Reich* (Düsseldorf, 1972), p. 255; Longerich, *Politik der Vernichtung*, p. 270.

31 For a description of some of the massacres committed between the autumn of 1939 and the spring of 1940, see Longerich, *Politik der Vernichtung*, pp. 245–46.

32 Helmuth Groscurth, *Tagebücher eines Abwehroffiziers 1938–1940* (Stuttgart, 1970), S. 438–40: General der Artillerie [Walter] Petzel, [Befehlshaber] Wehrkreiskommando XXI to BdE [Befehlshaber des Ersatzheeres], Posen, 23.11.1939.

33 Wildt, 'Radikalisierung und Seibstradikalisierung', p. 41.

34 Ernst Klee, *'Euthanasie' im NS-Staat. Die 'Vernichtung lebensunwerten Lebens'* (Frankfurt am Main, 1985), pp. 95–8; Longerich, *Politik der Vernichtung*, pp. 236–7.

35 Detlev J.K. Peukert, 'Rassismus und "Endlösungs"-Utopie. Thesen zur Entwicklung und Struktur der nationalsozialistischen Vernichtungspolitik', in Christoph Klessmann (ed.), *Nicht nur Hitlers Krieg. Der Zweite Weltkrieg und die Deutschen* (Düsseldorf, 1989), p. 71.

36 Klee, *'Euthanasie' im NS-Staat*, p. 417.

37 Nikolaus Wachsmann, 'From Indefinite Confinement to Extermination. "Habitual Criminals" in the Third Reich', in Robert Gellately and Nathan Stoltzfus (eds), *Social Outsiders in Nazi Germany* (Princeton, 2001), p. 177. The number of offences punishable by death rose from three in 1933 to forty-six by the end of the war.

38 Wolfgang Ayass, *'Asoziale' im Nationalsozialismus* (Stuttgart, 1995); Patrick Wagner, *Volksgemeinschaft ohne Verbrecher. Konzeption und Praxis der Kriminalpolizei in der Zeit der Weimarer Republik und des Nationalsozialismus* (Hamburg, 1996); Patrick Wagner, *Hitlers Kriminalisten. Die*

deutsche Kriminalpolizei und der Nationalsozialismus (Munich, 2002); Nikolaus Wachsmann, 'From Indefinite Confinement to Extermination', pp. 165–91.

39 Wagner, *Hitlers Kriminalisten*, p. 11.

40 Patrick Wagner, *Volksgemeinschaft ohne Verbrecher. Konzeption und Praxis der Kriminalpolizei in der Zeit der Weimarer Republik und des Nationalsozialismus* (Hamburg, 1996), p. 374.

41 Elizabeth D. Heineman, *What Difference Does a Husband Make? Women and Marital Status in Nazi and Postwar Germany* (Berkeley, Los Angeles and London, 1999), pp. 46–7.

42 See John Keegan, *The Mask of Command* (New York, 1987), pp. 274–5.

43 It is worth noting in this context that even in August 1941, as German casualties in Russia were mounting, Armed Forces Chief of Staff Franz Halder was drawing favourable comparisons with the vastly higher German losses during the first two years of the First World War. See Generaloberst (Franz) Halder, *Kriegstagebuch,. Bd. III Der Russlandfeldzug bis zum Marsch auf Stalingrad (22.6.1941–24.9.1942)*, ed. Hans-Adolf Jacobsen (Stuttgart, 1964), p. 190: entry for 21 Aug. 1941.

44 See Omer Bartov, 'From Blitzkrieg to Total War: Controversial Links between Image and Reality', in Ian Kershaw and Moshe Levin (eds), *Stalinism and Nazism: Dictatorship in Comparison* (Cambridge, 1997), pp. 160–5.

45 Cited in Hans-Erich Volkmann, 'Von Blomberg zu Keitel – Die Wehrmachtführung und die Demontage des Rechtsstaates', in Rolf-Dieter Müller and Hans-Erich Volkmann (eds), *Die Wehrmacht. Mythos und Realität* (Munich, 1999), p. 63.

46 *Meldungen aus dem Reich. Die geheimen Lageberichte des Sicherheitsdienstes der SS 1938–1945* (ed. by Heinz Boberach), vol. 4 (Herrsching, 1984), p. 1218: 'Meldungen aus dem Reich (nr. 94) 6. Juni 1940'.

47 Generaloberst (Franz) Halder, *Kriegstagebuch,. Bd. II. Von der geplanten Landung in England bis zum Beginn des Ostfeldzuges (1.7.1940–21.6.1941)*, ed. Hans-Adolf Jacobsen (Stuttgart, 1963), p. 455: entry for 14 June 1941. Wilhelm Deist, *Militär, Staat und Gesellschaft. Studien zur preussisch-deutschen Militärgeschichte* (Munich, 1991), pp. 371–12.

48 Andreas Hillgruber, *Hitlers Strategie. Politik und Kriegführung 1940–1941* (Frankfurt am Main, 1965), pp. 506–7; Weinberg, *A World at Arms*, p. 204.

49 Walter Manoschek, ' "Gehst mit Juden erschiessen?" Die Vernichtung der Juden in Serbien', in Hannes Heer und Klaus Naumann (eds), *Vernichtungskrieg. Verbrechen der Wehrmacht 1941 bis 1944* (Hamburg, 1995), pp. 39–56.

50 Walter Manoschek, 'Serbien ist judenfrei'. Militärische Besatzungspolitik und Judenvernichtung in Serbien 1941/42 (Munich, 1993), p. 31: Korpsbefehl nr. 9 von General v. Kortzfleisch, Generalkommando XI. Armeekorps, 27.4.1941.

51 Manoschek, 'Serbien ist judenfrei', p. 31.

52 Manoschek, 'Serbien ist judenfrei', p. 32: Befehl des Oberbefehlshabers der 2. Armee, Weichs, 28.4.1941.

53 Mark Mazower, Inside Hitler's Greece. The Experience of Occupation, 1941–1944 (New Haven and London, 1993), pp. 238–44; <motlc.wiesenthal.com/text/x29/xr2934.html>.

54 Generaloberst (Franz) Halder, Kriegstagebuch,. Bd. II. Von der geplanten Landung in England bis zum Beginn des Ostfeldzuges (1.7.1940–21.6.1941), ed. Hans-Adolf Jacobsen (Stuttgart, 1963), p. 464, Anlage 2: Oberkommando des Heeres, H.Qu.OKH, den 31. Januar 1941, 'Aufmarschanweisung Barbarossa'.

55 It often is overlooked that the Germans overran many of the same 'desolate, dirty and war-ravaged lands' in the east during the First World War as they were to do in the Second, and that the earlier experience of occupation greatly affected how Germans viewed the East in the 1940s. See the important study by Vejas Gabriel Liulevicius, War Land on the Eastern Front. Culture, National Identity and German Occupation in World War I (Cambridge, 2000). Liulevicius also points out the extent to which the idea of Lebensraum took shape in the German experience of the east in the First World War (pp. 247–77).

56 Andreas Hillgruber, 'Das Russland-Bild der führenden deutschen Militärs vor Beginn des Angriffs auf die Sowjetunion', in Alexander Fischer, Günter Moltmann and Klaus Schwabe (eds), Russland-Deutschland-Amerika. Festschrift für Fritz T. Epstein zum 80. Geburtstag (Wiesbaden, 1978), pp. 296–310, here p. 306.

57 Deist, Militär, Staat und Gesellschaft, p. 371. Wilhelm Deist points out, however, that the size of the force which invaded the Soviet Union was not greater than that which had attacked in the West the year before; what was far greater was the length of the front, which in June 1941 was more than twice that in May 1940.

58 Generaloberst (Franz) Halder, Kriegstagebuch,. Bd. II. Von der geplanten Landung in England bis zum Beginn des Ostfeldzuges (1.7.1940–21.6.1941), ed. Hans-Adolf Jacobsen (Stuttgart, 1963), p. 320: entry for 17 Mar. 1941.

59 Generaloberst (Franz) Halder, Kriegstagebuch,. Bd. II. Von der geplanten Landung in England bis zum Beginn des Ostfeldzuges (1.7.1940–21.6.1941), ed Hans-Adolf Jacobsen (Stuttgart, 1963), pp. 336–7: entry for 30 Mar.

1941. Generally, see Christian Streit, *Keine Kameraden. Die Wehrmacht und die sowjetischen Kriegsgefangenen 1941–1945* (Stuttgart, 1978), pp. 34–5; Reinhard Otto, *Wehrmacht, Gestapo und sowjetische Kriegsgefangene im deutschen Reichsgebiet 1941/42* (Munich, 1998), pp. 49–57.

60 Deist, *Militär, Staat und Gesellschaft*, p. 381.

61 Generaloberst (Franz) Halder, *Kriegstagebuch,. Bd. II. Von der geplanten Landung in England bis zum Beginn des Ostfeldzuges (1.7.1940–21.6.1941)*, ed. Hans-Adolf Jacobsen (Stuttgart, 1963), p. 337: entry for 30 Mar. 1941.

62 Deist, *Militär, Staat und Gesellschaft*, pp. 381–2.

63 Deist, *Militär, Staat und Gesellschaft*, pp. 382–3; Mommsen, *Auschwitz*, p. 114.

64 Quoted in Jürgen Förster, 'Das Unternehmen "Barbarossa" als Eroberungs- und Vernichtungskrieg' in Horst Boog et al., *Der Angriff auf die Sowjetunion* (Frankfurt am Main, 1991), p. 531. Hoepner was the tank commander who in December 1941 came closest to Moscow and then, in January 1942, was dismissed by Hitler for ordering the tactical withdrawal of his troops to avoid unnecessary losses. Hoepner was hanged in August 1944 in Berlin-Ploetzensee for his role in the July bomb plot.

65 Generaloberst (Franz) Halder, *Kriegstagebuch,. Bd. III. Der Russlandfeldzug bis zum Marsch auf Stalingrad (22.6.1941–24.9.1942)*, ed. Hans-Adolf Jacobsen (Stuttgart 1964), p. 53: entry for 8 July 1941.

66 Quoted in Andreas Hillgruber, 'Die "Endlösung" und das deutsche Ostimperium als Kernstück des rassenideologischen Programms des Nationalsozialismus', in Manfred Funke (ed.), *Hitler, Deutschland und die Mächte. Materialien zur Aussenpolitik des Dritten Reiches* (Düsseldorf, 1978), p. 107. See also Streit, *Keine Kameraden*, p. 115.

67 Quoted in Hillgruber, 'Die "Endlösung" und das deutsche Ostimperium', pp. 107–8.

68 Streit, *Keine Kameraden*, p. 36; Michael Burleigh, *The Third Reich. A New History* (London 2000), p. 513; Pavel Polian, 'Sowjetische Staatsangehörige im "Dritten Reich" während des Zweiten Weltkriegs. Gruppen und Zahlen', in Babette Quinkert (ed.), *'Wir sind die Herren dieses Landes'. Ursachen, Verlauf und Folgen des deutschen Überfalls auf die Sowjetunion* (Hamburg, 2002), pp. 140–1.

69 Generaloberst (Franz) Halder, *Kriegstagebuch,. Bd. III. Der Russlandfeldzug bis zum Marsch auf Stalingrad (22.6.1941–24.9.1942)*, ed. Hans-Adolf Jacobsen (Stuttgart, 1964), p. 29: entry for 30 June 1941.

70 Generaloberst (Franz) Halder, *Kriegstagebuch,. Bd. III. Der Russlandfeldzug bis zum Marsch auf Stalingrad (22.6.1941–24.9.1942)*, ed. Hans-Adolf Jacobsen (Stuttgart, 1964), p. 117: entry for 25 July 1941.

71 Overmans, *Deutsche militärische Verluste*, pp. 238–9.

72 Generaloberst (Franz) Halder, *Kriegstagebuch,. Bd. III. Der Russland-feldzug bis zum Marsch auf Stalingrad (22.6.1941–24.9.1942)*, ed. Hans-Adolf Jacobsen (Stuttgart, 1964), p 374: entry for 5 Jan. 1942.

73 Generaloberst (Franz) Halder, *Kriegstagebuch,. Bd III. Der Russlandfeldzug bis zum Marsch auf Stalingrad (22.6.1941–24.9.1942)*, ed. Hans-Adolf Jacobsen (Stuttgart, 1964), p. 170: entry for 11 Aug. 1941.

74 Deist, *Militär, Staat und Gesellschaft*, pp. 376–8.

75 Generaloberst (Franz) Halder, *Kriegstagebuch,. Bd III. Der Russlandfeldzug bis zum Marsch auf Stalingrad (22.6.1941–24.9.1942)*, ed. Hans-Adolf Jacobsen (Stuttgart, 1964), p. 336: entry for 9 Dec. 1941.

76 According to the order by General von Brauchitsch of 28 April 1941 outlining the agreement between the OKH and the SS, the *Einsatzgruppen* were assigned to Army groups 'with regard to marching, equipment and provisioning' but carried out their duties independently. See Hans-Adolf Jacobsen, 'Kommissarbefehl und Massenexekutionen sowjetischer Kriegsgefangener', in Hans Buchheim, Martin Broszat, Hans-Adolf Jacobsen and Helmut Krausnick, *Anatomie des SS-Staates*, vol. II (Munich, 1967), pp. 171–3.

77 Helmut Krausnick and Hans-Heinrich Wilhelm, *Die Truppe des Welt-anschauungskrieges. Die Einsatzgruppen der Sicherheitspolizei und des SD 1938–1942* (Stuttgart, 1981), p. 140.

78 Andrei Angrick, Martina Voigt, Silke Ammerschubert and Peter Klein, '"Da hätte man schon ein Tagebuch führen müssen". Das Polizeibataillon 322 und die Judenmorde im Bereich der Heeresgruppe Mitte während des Sommers und Herbstes 1941', in Helge Grabitz, Klaus Bästlein and Johannes Tuchel (eds), *Die Normalität des Verbrechens. Bilanz und Perspektiven der Forschung zu den nationalsozialistischen Gewaltverbrechen* (Berlin, 1994), pp. 325–85; Christian Gerlach, 'Die Wannsee-Konferenz, das Schicksal der deutschen Juden und Hitlers politische Grundsatzentscheidung, alle Juden Europas zu ermodern', *WerkstattGeschichte*, vol. 6, no. 18 (1997), p. 9.

79 Krausnick and Wilhelm, *Die Truppe des Weltanschauungskrieges*, pp. 145–47; Mommsen, *Auschwitz*, pp. 115–17.

80 Quoted in Krausnick and Wilhelm, *Die Truppe des Weltanschauungskrieges*, p. 157.

81 Cited in Krausnick and Wilhelm, *Die Truppe des Weltanschauungskrieges*, p.158.

82 Mommsen, *Auschwitz*, pp. 115–17.

83 Cited in Krausnick and Wilhelm, *Die Truppe des Weltanschauungskrieges*, p. 158.

84 See Christopher Browning, *Fateful Months. Essays on the Emergence of the Final Solution* (New York and London, 1991), pp. 39–56; Manoschek, *'Serbien ist Judenfrei'*, pp. 55–108; Longerich, *Politik der Vernichtung*, pp. 458–60.

85 See Dieter Pohl, *Nationalsozialistische Judenverfolgung in Ostgalizien 1941–1944. Organisation und Durchfuhrung eines staatlichen Massenverbrechens* (Munich, 1996), pp. 139–54; Thomas Sandkühler, *'Endlösung' in Galizien. Der Judenmord in Ostpolen und die Rettungsinitiativen von Bertold Beitz 1941–1944* (Bonn, 1996), pp. 148–55.

86 Streit, *Keine Kameraden*, p. 220. Roughly 1,000 were gassed; others were put to work building the new 'Birkenau' camp on the other side of the railway tracks.

87 See Wolfgang Scheffler and Helge Grabitz, 'Die Wannsee-Konferenz. Ihre Bedeutung in der Geschichte des nationalsozialistischen Völkermords', in *Studia nad Faszyzmem i Zbrodniami Hitlerowskimi*, vol. XVIII (Wroclaw, 1995), pp. 197–218; Christian Gerlach, 'Die Wannsee-Konferenz'; Peter Longerich, *Die Wannsee-Konferenz vom 20. Januar 1942. Planung und Beginn des Genozids an den europäischen Juden* (Berlin, 1998); Longerich, *Politik der Vernichtung*, pp. 466–72; Mark Roseman, *The Villa, the Lake, the Meeting: Wannsee and the Final Solution* (London, 2003). The minutes of the Wannsee Conference are available on the internet (both as facsimile and as text) at <http://www.ghwk.de>.

88 Quoted in Evan Burr Bukey, *Hitler's Austria. Popular Sentiment in the Nazi Era 1938–1945* (Chapel Hill and London, 2000), p. 164.

89 Ian Kershaw, *Popular Opinion and Political Dissent in the Third Reich: Bavaria 1933–1945* (Oxford, 1983), pp. 361–2. According the the SD's report from 9 October 1941: 'The decree on the identification of the Jews was welcomed by the overwhelming majority of the population and received with satisfaction, especially since such an identification had been expected by many for a long time already.' See *Meldungen aus dem Reich. Die geheimen Lageberichte des Sicherheitsdienstes der SS 1938–1945* (ed. Heinz Boberach), vol. 8 (Herrsching, 1984), p. 2849: 'Meldungen aus dem Reich (Nr. 227) 9. Oktober 1941'.

90 See Michael Zimmermann, *Rassenutopie und Genozid. Die national-sozialistische 'Lösung der Zigeunerfrage'* (Hamburg, 1996); Guenter Lewy, *The Nazi Persecution of the Gypsies* (New York, 2000); Sybil H. Milton, ' "Gypsies" as Social Outsiders in Nazi Germany', in Gellately and Stoltzfus (eds.), *Social Outsiders in Nazi Germany*, pp. 212–32.

91 Rolf-Dieter Müller, *Hitlers Ostkrieg und die deutsche Siedlungspolitik. Die Zusammenarbeit von Wehrmacht, Wirtschaft und SS* (Frankfurt am Main, 1991), pp. 40–8.

92 'Richtlinien Görings für die Wirtschaftspolitik im Osten, vom 8.11.1941', quoted in Müller, *Hitlers Ostkrieg und die deutsche Siedlungspolitik*, p. 43.

93 Quoted in Götz Aly, *Rasse und Klasse. Nachforschungen zum deutschen Wesen* (Frankfurt am Main, 2003), p. 234.

94 This from the minutes of a meeting, held on 2 May 1941, of the Permanent Secretaries of the General Council of the Four-Year Plan Authority, quoted in Aly and Heim, *Vordenker der Vernichtung*, p. 372.

95 Quoted in Aly and Heim, *Vordenker der Vernichtung*, pp. 372–3. Also cited in Düllfer, *Nazi Germany 1933–1945*, p. 158.

96 The General Council of the Four-Year Plan Authority, of which Backe was a member, reckoned with roughly 30 million dead. See Aly and Heim, *Vordenker der Vernichtung*, p. 369.

97 Quoted in Aly and Heim, *Vordenker der Vernichtung*, p. 376.

98 John Erickson, *The Road to Stalingrad. Stalin's War with Germany. Volume 1* (London, 1975), p. 241.

99 Quoted in Hillgruber, 'Die "Endlösung" und das deutsche Ostimperium', p. 106; Peter Klein, 'Zwischen den Fronten. Die Zivilbevölkerung Weissrusslands und der Krieg der Wehrmacht gegen die Partisanen', in Quinkert (ed.), *'Wir sind die Herren dieses Landes'*, pp. 84–5.

100 This from a letter home from a German soldier on 15 September 1941, quoted in Klaus Latzel, *Deutsche Soldaten – nationalsozialistischer Krieg? Kriegserlebnis – Kriegserfahrung – 1939–1945* (Paderborn, 2000), pp. 54–5.

101 Quoted in Edgar M. Howell, *The Soviet Partisan Movement 1941–1944* (Washington, 1956), p. 59.

102 Bernhard Chiari, *Alltag hinter der Front. Besatzung, Kollaboration und Widerstand in Weissrussland 1941–1944* (Düsseldorf, 1998), p. 175.

103 Theo Schulte, *The German Army and Nazi Policies in Occupied Russia* (Providence, 1989), pp. 139–40. See also Jonathan E. Gumz, 'Wehrmacht Perceptions of Mass Violence in Croatia, 1941–1942', *The Historical Journal*, vol. 44, no. 4 (2001), pp. 1035–37.

104 Cited in Ben Shepherd, 'The Continuum of Brutality: Wehrmacht Security Divisions in Central Russia, 1942', in *German History*, vol. 21, no. 1 (2003), p. 63.

105 Cited in Shepherd, 'The Continuum of Brutality', p. 63.

106 Ben Shepherd has focused on one security division (the 221st) which in the summer of 1942 was both poorly trained and equipped and 'responsible, with well below 7,000 combat strength, for an area of 30,000 square kilometers, 2,560 villages and over 1,300,000 inhabitants'. In

September 1942 they were outnumbered by the partisans by nearly two to one. See Shepherd, 'The Continuum of Brutality', p. 72.

107 Bernd Wegner, 'Der Krieg gegen die Sowjetunion 1942/43', in Horst Boog et al., *Der Globale Krieg. Die Ausweitung zum Weltkrieg und der Wechsel der Initiative 1941–1943* (Stuttgart, 1990), p. 911.

108 Wegner, 'Der Krieg gegen die Sowjetunion 1942/43', p. 917.

109 Norbert Müller (ed.), *Okkupation Raub Vernichtung. Dokumente zur Besatzungspolitik der faschistischen Wehrmacht auf sowjetischem Territorium 1941 bis 1944* (Berlin, 1980), pp. 139–40; Shepherd, 'The Continuum of Brutality', p. 53. See also Christian Gerlach, *Kalkulierte Mörde. Die deutsche Wirtschafts- und Vernichtungspolitik in Weissrussland 1941–1944* (Hamburg, 1999), pp. 884–1036.

110 Wolfgang Benz, Konrad Kwiet and Jürgen Matthäus (eds.), *Einsatz im 'Reichskommissariat Ostland'. Dokumente zum Völkermord im Baltikum und in Weissrussland 1941–1944* (Berlin, 1998), pp. 237–9: Auszüge aus dem Bericht (des RKO) 'Zentralinformation I/lb' über die Entwicklung der Partisanenbewegung vom 1. Juli 1942 bis zum 30. April 1943.

111 Benz, Kwiet and Matthäus (eds), *Einsatz im 'Reichskommissariat Ostland'*, pp. 239–42: Auszüge aus dem Abschlussbericht des HSSPF Ostland (Jeckeln) an den Kommandostab RFSS vom 6. November 1942 betr. "Unternehmen Sumpffieber".

112 For this last argument, see Jonathan E. Gumz, 'Wehrmacht Perceptions of Mass Violence in Croatia, 1941–1942', *The Historical Journal*, vol. 44, no. 4 (2001), p. 1035.

113 Sarah Farmer, *Martyred Village. Commemorating the 1944 Massacre at Oradour-sur-Glane* (Berkeley, Los Angeles and London, 1999), pp. 20–8.

114 Lutz Klinkhammer, 'Der Partisanenkrieg der Wehrmacht 1941–1944', in Rolf-Dieter Müller and Hans-Erich Volkmann, *Die Wehrmacht. Mythos und Realität* (Munich, 1999), pp. 833–6. Mark Mazower, 'Military Violence and National Socialist Values: The Wehrmacht in Greece 1941–1944', *Past & Present*, no. 134 (1992), 129–58; Michael Geyer, ' "Es muss daher mit schnellen und drakonischen Massnehmen durchgegriffen werden". Civitella in Val di Chiana am 29. Juni 1944', in Hannes Heer und Klaus Naumann (eds), *Vernichtungskrieg. Verbrechen der Wehrmacht 1941 bis 1944* (Hamburg, 1995), pp. 208–37.

115 See, especially, Omer Bartov, *The Eastern Front, 1941–45. German Troops and the Barbarisation of Warfare* (London, 1985); and Omer Bartov, *Hitler's Army. Soldiers, Nazis, and War in the Third Reich* (New York and Oxford, 1992). For an account which, unlike Bartov's, focuses on the

troops stationed in the rear and which places less emphasis on the role of Nazi ideology, see Schulte, *The German Army and Nazi Policies in Occupied Russia*.

116 Quoted in Bartov, *Hitler's Army*, pp. 158, 163.

117 Quoted in Bartov, *Hitler's Army*, p. 163.

118 Quoted in Bartov, *Hitler's Army*, p. 161.

119 See Bartov, *Hitler's Army*, pp. 163–5.

120 Generaloberst (Franz) Halder, *Kriegstagebuch,. Bd. III. Der Russlandfeldzug bis zum Marsch auf Stalingrad (22.6.1941–24.9.1942)*, ed. Hans-Adolf Jacobsen (Stuttgart, 1964), p. 348: entry from 15 Dec. 1941.

121 Hitler remained Supreme Commander of the Army until his death; he was succeeded, from 30 April until Germany's unconditional surrender on 8 May 1945, by Field Marshal Ferdinand Schörner.

122 Quoted in Andreas Hillgruber and Gerhard Hümmeichen, *Chronik des Zweiten Weltkrieges* (Frankfurt am Main, 1966), p. 57.

123 Max Domarus, *Hitler. Reden und Proklamationen 1932–1945. Kommentiert von einem deutschen Zeitgenossen. Band II Untergang, Zweiter Halbband 1941–1945* (Wiesbaden, 1973), p. 1814.

124 Generaloberst (Franz) Halder, *Kriegstagebuch,. Bd. III. Der Russlandfeldzug bis zum Marsch auf Stalingrad (22.6.1941–24.9.1942)*, ed. Hans-Adolf Jacobsen (Stuttgart, 1964), p. 371: entry for 2 Jan. 1942.

125 Generaloberst (Franz) Halder, *Kriegstagebuch,. Bd. III. Der Russlandfeldzug bis zum Marsch auf Stalingrad (22.6.1941–24.9.1942)*, ed. Hans-Adolf Jacobsen (Stuttgart, 1964), p. 356: entry for 20 Dec. 1941.

126 Willi A. Boelcke (ed.), *Deutschlands Rüstung im Zweiten Weltkrieg. Hitlers Konferenzen mit Albert Speer 1942–1945* (Frankfurt am Main, 1969), p. 127: meeting on 24 May 1942 at the *Führerhauptquartier*.

127 Richard Muck, *Kampfgruppe Scherer. 105 Tage eingeschlossen* (Oldenburg, 1943).

128 Generaloberst (Franz) Halder, *Kriegstagebuch,. Bd. III Der Russlandfeldzug bis zum Marsch auf Stalingrad (22.6.1941–24.9.1942)*, ed. Hans-Adolf Jacobsen (Stuttgart, 1964), pp. 430–2: entry for 21 Apr. 1942.

129 MacGregor Knox, '1 October 1942: Adolf Hitler, Wehrmacht Officer Policy, and Social Revolution', *The Historical Journal*, vol. 43, no. 3 (2000), pp. 801, 823.

130 Gerd R. Ueberschär, 'Stalingrad – eine Schlacht des Zweiten Weltkrieges', in Wolfram Wette and Gerd R. Ueberschär (eds), *Stalingrad. Mythos und Wirklichkeit einer Schlacht* (Frankfurt am Main, 1993), p. 19.

131 Heinz Boberach, 'Stimmungsumschwung in der deutschen Bevölkerung', in Wolfram Wette and Gerd R. Ueberschär (eds), *Stalingrad.*

Mythos und Wirklichkeit einer Schlacht (Frankfurt am Main, 1993), pp. 61–6.

132 See Ulrich Herbert, *Hitler's Foreign Workers. Enforced Foreign Labor in Germany under the Third Reich* (Cambridge, 1997), pp. 258–9.

133 Helmut Heiber (ed.), *Goebbels Reden 1932–1945, vol 2: 1939–1945* (Düsseldorf, 1972), pp. 172–208. An English translation of Goebbels' 'total war' speech may be found on the internet at <http://www.calvin.edu/academic/cas/gpa/goeb36.htm>.

134 *Meldungen aus dem Reich. Die geheimen Lageberichte des Sicherheitsdienstes der SS 1938–1945* (ed. Heinz Boberach), vol. 12 (Herrsching, 1984), p. 4831: 'Meldungen aus dem Reich (Nr. 361) 22. Februar 1943'.

135 *Meldungen aus dem Reich. Die geheimen Lageberichte des Sicherheitsdienstes der SS 1938–1945* (ed. Heinz Boberach), vol. 12 (Herrsching, 1984), p. 4831: 'Meldungen aus dem Reich (Nr. 361) 22. Februar 1943'.

136 *Meldungen aus dem Reich. Die geheimen Lageberichte des Sicherheitsdienstes der SS 1938–1945* (ed. Heinz Boberach), vol. 13 (Herrsching, 1984), p. 4945: 'Meldungen aus dem Reich (Nr. 367) 15. März 1943'.

137 Bernd Wegner, 'Krieg ohne Zukunft: Anmerkungen zu Deutschlands politisch-strategischer Lage 1942/43', in Stefan Martens and Maurise Vaïsse (eds), *Frankreich und Deutschland im Krieg (November 1942– Herbst 1944). Okkupation, Kollaboration, Résistance* (Bonn, 2000), p. 26. See also Bernd Wegner, 'Defensive ohne Strategie. Die Wehrmacht und das Jahr 1943', in Rolf-Dieter Müller and Hans-Erich Volkmann (eds), *Die Wehrmacht. Mythos und Realität* (Munich, 1999), pp. 197–209.

138 In October 1943, the Germans were keeping 1,370,000 military personnel in western Europe, as opposed to 3,900,000 on the eastern front. See Wegner, 'Defensive ohne Strategie', p. 203.

139 Wegner, 'Krieg ohne Zukunft', p. 26.

140 Williamson Murray, 'Betrachtungen zur deutschen Strategie im Zweiten Weltkrieg', in Rolf-Dieter Müller and Hans-Erich Volkmann (eds), *Die Wehrmacht. Mythos und Realität* (Munich, 1999), p. 318.

141 Cited in Wegner, 'Defensive ohne Strategie', pp. 205–6.

142 See Martin Kitchen, *The Silent Dictatorship. The Politics of the German High Command under Hindenburg and Ludendorff 1916–1918* (London, 1976), pp. 247–70.

143 Wegner, 'Defensive ohne Strategie', p. 207.

144 *Meldungen aus dem Reich. Die geheimen Lageberichie des Sicherheitsdienstes der SS 1938–1945* (ed. Heinz Boberach), vol. 13 (Herrsching, 1984), p. 4966: 'Meldungen aus dem Reich (Nr. 368) 18. März 1943'.

145 Weinberg, *A World at Arms*, p. 602.

146 For a perceptive account of the battle, see Richard Overy, *Why the Allies Won* (London. 1995), pp. 91–8. Most recently, and taking a critical look at the losses suffered by German and Soviet forces respectively, Roman Töppel, 'Legendenbildung in der Geschichtsschreibung – Die Schlacht bei Kursk', in *Militärgeschichtliche Zeitschrft*, 61 (2002), no. 2, pp. 369–401.

147 Overy, *Why the Allies Won*, p. 96.

148 Aly, *Rasse und Klasse*, p. 242.

149 A particularly good description of this is provided by an SD report from November 1943 on morale among German women. See *Meldungen aus dem Reich. Die geheimen Lageberichte des Sicherheitsdienstes der SS 1938– 1945* (ed. Heinz Boberach), vol. 15 (Herrsching, 1984), pp. 6025–33: 'SD-Berichte zu Inlandsfragen vom 18. November 1943'.

150 Carl-Ludwig Holtfrerich, 'Die Deutsche Bank vom Zweiten Weltkrieg über die Besatzungsherrschaft zur Rekonstruktion 1945–1957', in Lothar Gall et al., *Die Deutsche Bank 1870–1995* (Munich, 1995), p. 418. The main concern, as became increasingly clear in late 1944 and 1945, was what should be done in the 'Ivan Case' (*Iwanfall*), i.e. a Soviet occupation of that part of Germany where the bank had its headquarters.

151 Neil Gregor, *Daimler-Benz in the Third Reich* (New Haven and London, 1998), pp. 240–2. By way of contrast, however, Peter Hayes asserts that 'within IG Farben, there was little evidence ... of efforts to ride out the gathering catastrophe' during the second half of the war. See Peter Hayes, *Industry and ideology. IG Farben in the Nazi Years* (Cambridge and New York, 1987), p. 375.

152 See Overmans, *Deutsche militärische Verluste*, pp. 238–9.

153 See Rudolf Absolon (ed.), *Die Wehrmacht im Dritten Reich* (Band 6: 19. Dezember bis 9. Mai 1945) (Boppard am Rhein, 1995), p. 586.

154 See Rudolf Absolon (ed.), *Die Wehrmacht im Dritten Reich* (Band 6: 19. Dezember bis 9. Mai 1945) (Boppard am Rhein, 1995), p. 587. The text of the decree was published in the *Völkischer Beobachter*, 26 July 1944. See also Hermann Jung, *Die Ardennen-Offensive 1944/45* (Zürich and Frankfurt am Main, 1971), p. 64.

155 Jung, *Die Ardennen-Offensive 1944/45*, pp. 74–5.

156 *Meldungen aus dem Reich. Die geheimen Lageberichte des Sicherheitsdienstes der SS 1938–1945* (ed. Heinz Boberach), vol. 17 (Herrsching, 1984), p. 6686: 'Meldungen über die Entwicklung in den öffentlichen Meinungsbildung vom 28. Juli 1944'.

157 See Wildt, *Generation des Unbedingten*, p. 343. For the Hitler's Directive on the 'Reorganisation of the Administration of Prisoners of War' of 25

Sept. 1944, see Martin Moll (ed.), 'Führer-Erlasse' 1939–1945. Edition
sämtlicher überlieferter, nicht im Reichsgesetzblatt abgedrückter, von Hitler
während des Zweiten Weltkrieges schriftlich erteilter Direktiven aus den
Bereichen Staat, Partei, Wirtschaft, Besatzungspolitik und Militär-
verwaltung (Stuttgart, 1997), pp. 460–1. The decree naming Himmler as
Commander of the Replacement Army on 20 July 1944 is printed in Moll
(ed.), 'Führer-Erlasse' 1939–1945, p. 433.

158 Jung, Die Ardennen-Offensive 1944/45, p. 12; Bernd Wegner, Hitlers politische Soldaten: Die Waffen-SS 1933–1945. Studien zu Leitbild, Struktur
und Funktion einer nationalsozialistischen Elite (Paderborn, 1982), p. 210.

159 Jung, Die Ardennen-Offensive 1944/45, p. 12. On 22 November American
forces had taken Metz and, on 23 November, Strasbourg.

160 See Christian Gerlach and Götz Aly, Das letzte Kapitel. Realpolitik, Ideo-
logie und der Mord an den ungarischen Juden 1944/1945 (Stuttgart, 2002).

161 Overmans, Deutsche militärische Verluste, pp. 238–9.

162 Quoted in Kunz, 'Die Wehrmacht in der Agonie der nationalsozialistischen Herrschaft', p. 108.

163 Reichsgesetzblatt 1944, I, p. 253 (20 October 1944); also published in
Völkischer Beobachter, 20 Oct. 1944. See Jung, Die Ardennen-Offensive
1944/45, pp. 78–79. Hitler's Decree creating the Volkssturm was dated 25
Sept. 1944, but for propaganda purposes was not made public until the
anniversary of the 'Battle of the Nations' in October. Generally, see Rolf-
Dieter Müller and Gerd R. Ueberschär, Kriegsende 1945. Die Zerstörung
des Deutschen Reiches (Frankfurt am Main, 1994), pp. 42–47.

164 See Roland Müller, Stuttgart zur Zeit des Nationalsozialismus (Stuttgart,
1988), pp. 519–20. By this point, Germans were far from enthusiastic to
become cannon fodder for an obviously lost cause, and it was not
uncommon for men to seek to avoid being organized into the Volkssturm.

165 On corruption under the Nazis, see Frank Bajohr, Parvenüs und Pro-
fiteure. Korruption in der NS-Staat (Frankfurt am Main, 2001); Gerd R.
Ueberschär and Winfried Vogel, Dienen und Verdienen. Hitlers Geschenke
an seine Eliten (Frankfurt am Main, 1999); Norman J.W. Goda, 'Hitler's
Bribery of His Senior Officers during World War II', The Journal of
Modern History, vol. 72 (2000), pp. 413–52.

166 R. J. Overy, Goering. The 'Iron Man' (London, 1984), pp. 111, 128.

167 Michael Thad Allen, The Business of Genocide. The SS, Slave Labor,
and the Concentration Camps (Chapel Hill and London, 2002), pp. 108,
137.

168 See Rolf-Dieter Müller, 'Albert Speer und die Rüstungspolitik im totalen
Krieg', in Bernhard Kroener, Rolf-Dieter Müller and Hans Umbreit,

Organisation und Mobilisierung des deutschen Machtbereichs. Band 5/1. Kriegsverwaltung, Wirtschaft und personelle Ressourcen 1942–1944/45 (Stuttgart, 1999), pp. 275–325.

169 R. J. Overy, *War and Economy in the Third Reich* (Oxford, 1994), pp. 278, 312. Overy has done more than just about anyone to strip away myths about the Nazi economy at war.

170 Overy, *War and Economy in the Third Reich*, p. 273.

171 See Willi A. Boelcke, *Die Kosten von Hitlers Krieg. Kriegsfinanzierung und finanzielles Kriegserbe in Deutschland 1933–1948* (Paderborn, 1985), pp. 98–108.

172 Overy, *War and Economy in the Third Reich*, pp. 270–1.

173 Overy, *War and Economy in the Third Reich*, pp. 268-9.

174 Overy, *War and Economy in the Third Reich*, p. 289.

175 Overy, *War and Economy in the Third Reich*, p. 312.

176 See Overy, *War and Economy in the Third Reich*, pp. 343–75.

177 Boelcke, *Deutschlands Rüstung im Zweiten Weltkrieg*, pp. 22–5.

178 For a balanced, careful and detailed study of this complicated story, see Harold James, *The Deutsche Bank and the Economic War against the Jews* (Cambridge, 2001).

179 Frank Bajohr, *'Arisierung' in Hamburg. Die Verdrängung der jüdischen Unternehmer 1933–1945* (Hamburg, 1997), p. 333.

180 Rolf-Dieter Müller, 'Das Scheitern der wirtschaftlichen "Blitzkriegsstrategie"', in Horst Boog et al., *Der Angriff auf die Sowjetunion* (Frankfurt am Main, 1991), p. 1187.

181 Müller, 'Das Scheitern der wirtschaftlichen "Blitzkriegsstrategie"', p. 1187.

182 Figures in Jung, *Die Ardennen-Offensive 1944/45*, p. 293.

183 Heineman, *What Difference Does a Husband Make?*, p. 63.

184 Ulrich Herbert, *Hitler's Foreign Workers. Enforced Foreign Labor in Germany under the Third Reich* (Cambridge, 1997), p. 167.

185 Figures in Herbert, *Hitler's Foreign Workers*, pp. 296–8.

186 Quoted in Jens-Christian Wagner, *Produktion des Todes. Das KZ Mittelbau-Dora* (Göttingen, 2001), p. 173.

187 Herbert, *Hitler's Foreign Workers*, pp. 132–3, 166; Heineman, *What Difference Does a Husband Make?*, p. 59.

188 See Andreas Heusler, *Ausländereinsatz. Zwangsarbeit für die Münchner Kriegswirtschaft 1939–1945* (Munich, 1996), pp. 212–22; Herbert, *Hitler's Foreign Workers*, pp. 130–1, 219–20; Wagner, *Produktion des Todes*, pp. 175–6.

189 See Wagner, *Produktion des Todes*.

190 Wagner, *Produktion des Todes*, pp. 423–6.

191 Gerhard Schreiber, *Deutsche Kriegsverbrechen in Italien. Täter – Opfer – Strafverfolgung* (Munich, 1996), p. 40. Generally, see Gerhard Schreiber, *Die italienischen Militärinternierten im deutschen Machtbereich 1943 bis 1945: verraten – verachtet – vergessen* (Munich, 1990).

192 Schreiber, *Deutsche Kriegsverbrechen in Italien*, pp. 214–15.

193 See Geyer, "'Es muss daher mit schnellen und drakonischen Massnahmen durchgegriffen werden", pp. 208–38. There is also evidence of increasing hatred among German civilians for Italians during the later phases of the war. See, for example, *Meldungen aus dem Reich. Die geheimen Lageberichte des Sicherheitsdienstes der SS 1938–1945* (ed. by Heinz Boberach), vol. 17 (Herrsching, 1984), p. 6705: 'Meldungen aus den SD-Abschnittsberichten vom 10. August 1944'.

194 See Michael Krause, *Flucht vor dem Bombenkrieg. 'Umquartierungen' im Zweiten Weltkrieg und die Wiedereingliederung der Evakuierten in Deutschland 1943–1963* (Düssedorf, 1997); Jörg Friedrich, *Der Brand. Deutschland in Bombenkrieg 1940–1945* (Munich, 2002); Neil Gregor, 'A *Schicksalsgemeinschaft*? Allied Bombing, Civilian Morale, and Social Dissolution in Nuremburg, 1942–1945', *The Historical Journal*, vol. 43, no. 5 (2000), p. 1070.

195 This sense of victimhood is echoed in the recent best-selling history of the bombing campaign by Jörg Friedrich, *Der Brand. Deutschland im Bombenkrieg 1940–1945* (Munich, 2002).

196 Sir Charles Webster and Noble Frankland, *The Strategic Air Offensive against Germany 1939–1945*, vol. I (London, 1961), p. 393.

197 This follows Krause, *Flucht vor dem Bombenkrieg*, pp. 28–9. See also Martin Middlebrook, *The Battle of Hamburg. Allied Bomber Forces against a German City in 1943* (London, 1980); Friedrich, *Der Brand*, pp. 192–5.

198 Boelcke, *Deutschlands Rüstung im Zweiten Weltkrieg*, p. 35.

199 Over half the total tonnage of bombs dropped by the Allies during the war was dropped in 1944, and one quarter was dropped from January to April 1945 alone; in the first four months of 1945 nearly one and a half times as many tonnes were dropped as in the four years 1940 through 1943 put together.

BOMBS DROPPED BY BRITISH AND AMERICAN AIR FORCES ON
GERMANY AND THE OCCUPIED TERRITORIES IN THE WEST,
1940–5 (IN TONNES)

| 1940: 14,631 | 1942: 53,755 | 1944: 1,118,577 |
| 1941: 35,509 | 1943: 226,513 | 1945: 477,051 |

Source: Bundesminister für Vertriebene, Flüchtlinge und Kriegs-
beschädigte (ed.), *Dokumente Deutscher Kriegsschäden. Evakuierte –
Kriegsgeschädigte – Währungsgeschädigte. Die geschichtliche und rechtliche
Entwicklung*, vol. 1 (Bonn, 1958), p. 46. See also Krause, *Flucht vor dem
Bombenkrieg*, p. 34.

200 Adolf Klein, *Köln im Dritten Reich. Stadtgeschichte der Jahre 1933–1945*
(Cologne, 1983), p. 280; Bernd-A. Rusinek, *Gesellschaft in der Katastrophe. Terror, Illegalität, Widerstand – Köln 1944/45* (Essen, 1989), p.
102.

201 Bundesminister für Vertriebene, Flüchtlinge und Kriegsbeschädigte
(ed.), *Dokumente Deutscher Kriegsschäden*, pp. 51–3.

202 Wagner, *Produktion des Todes*, p. 280.

203 Bundesminister für Vertriebene, Flüchtlinge und Kriegsbeschädigte
(ed.), *Dokumente Deutscher Kriegsschäden*, pp. 58–62; Krause, *Flucht vor
dem Bombenkrieg*, pp. 36–7; Friedrich, *Der Brand*, p. 168.

204 Neil Gregor, 'A *Schicksalsgemeinschaft*?', p. 1070.

205 Rusinek, *Gesellschaft in der Katastrophe*, p. 94.

206 Matthias Menzel, *Die Stadt ohne Tod. Berliner Tagebuch 1943/45* (Berlin,
1946), pp. 48–50. Quoted in Hans Dieter Schäfer, *Berlin im Zweiten
Weltkrieg. Der Untergang der Reichshauptstadt in Augenzeugenberichten*
(Munich and Zürich, 1985), p. 268.

207 See Friedrich Blumenstock, *Der Einmarsch der Amerikaner und Franzosen im nördlichen Wurttemberg im April 1945* (Stuttgart, 1957), pp. 17–
20.

208 Manfred Uschner, *Die zweite Etage. Funktionsweise eines Machtapparates*
(Berlin, 1993), p. 29.

209 Quoted in Manfried Rauchensteiner, *Der Krieg in Österreich 1945* (2nd
edn, Vienna, 1984), p. 25.

210 Tim Mason, 'The Legacy of 1918 for National Socialism', in Anthony
Nicholls and Erich Matthias (eds), *German Democracy and the Triumph
of Hitler. Essays in Recent German History* (London, 1971), pp. 215–40.

211 Quoted in Schäfer, *Berlin im Zweiten Weltkrieg*, p. 309: 'Bericht über den
"Sondereinsatz Berlin" für die Zeit vom 30.3.–7.4.1945', dated 10. April
1945.

212 See Overmans, *Deutsche militärische Verluste im Zweiten Weltkrieg*, p.
238. See also the suggestive comments in Andreas Kunz, 'Die Wehrmacht
in der Agonie der nationalsozialistischen Herrschaft 1944/45. Eine Ge-
dankenskizze', in Jörg Hillmann and John Zimmermann (eds), *Kriegsende 1945 in Deutschland* (Munich, 2002), p. 107.

213 Printed in Walther Hubatsch (ed.), *Hitlers Weisungen für die Krieg-*

führung 1939–1945. Dokumente des Oberkommandos der Wehrmacht (Frankfurt am Main, 1962), p. 299.

214 Quoted in Jung, *Die Ardennen-Offensive 1944/45*, p. 21.

215 Quoted in Heinrich Schwendenmann, "'Deutsche Menschen vor der Vernichtung durch den Bolschewismus zu retten': Das Programm der Regierung Dönitz und der Beginn einer Legendenbildung', in Jörg Hillmann and John Zimmermann (eds), *Kriegsende 1945 in Deutschland* (Munich, 2002), p. 9.

216 Marlis Steinert, *Hitler's War and the Germans. Public Mood and Attitude during the Second World War* (Athens, Ohio, 1977), p. 287. Also note the ZDF television programme, 'Die Wahrheit über Nemmersdorf', broadcast on 25.11.2001: <http://www.zdf.de/ZDFde/inhalt/ 0,1872,2004695 ,oo.html>.

217 Text of this 'Aufruf an die Soldaten der Ostfront' from 15 April 1945 in *Kriegstagebuch des Oberkommandos der Wehrmacht (Wehrmacht-führungsstab), Band IV: 1. Januar 1944–22 Mai 1945* (ed. Percy Ernst Schramm) (Frankfurt am Main, 1961), pp. 1589–90.

218 Cited in Steinert, *Hitler's War and the Germans*, p. 288.

219 See John Zimmermann, 'Die Kämpfe gegen die Westalliierten 1945 – Ein Kampf bis zum Ende oder die Kreierung einer Legende?', in Jörg Hillmann and John Zimmermann (eds), *Kriegsende 1945 in Deutschland* (Munich, 2002), pp. 115–33.

220 Quoted in Christoph Studt, *Das Dritte Reich in Daten* (Munich, 2002), p. 244.

221 MacGregor Knox, *Common Destiny. Dictatorship, Foreign Policy, and War in Fascist Italy and Nazi Germany* (Cambridge, 2000), pp. 237–8.

222 See Klaus-Dietmar Henke, *Die amerikanische Besetzung Deutschlands* (Munich, 1995), p. 422.

223 See Alfred C. Mierzejewski, 'When Did Albert Speer Give Up?', *The Historical Journal*, vol. 31, no. 2 (1988), p. 392.

224 Text of this 'Führerbefehl' in *Kriegstagebuch des Oberkommandos der Wehrmacht (Wehrmachtführungsstab), Band IV: 1. Januar 1944–22. Mai 1945* (ed. Percy Ernst Schramm) (Frankfurt am Main, 1961), pp. 1580–1.

225 On this, and with a critical view of Speer's motives, see Mierzejwski, 'When Did Albert Speer Give Up?'; Henke, *Die amerikavnische Besetzung Deutschlands*, pp. 427–35.

226 Boelcke, *Deutschlands Rustung im Zweiten Weltkrieg*, p. 21.

227 The text of this letter from Speer to Hitler on 29 March 1945 is published in *Kriegstagebuch des Oberkommandos der Wehrmacht (Wehrmachtführungsstab), Band IV: 1. Januar 1944–22. Mai 1945* (ed.

Percy Ernst Schramm) (Frankfurt am Main, 1961), pp. 1581–4.

228 Albert Speer, *Inside the Third Reich* (London, 1975), pp. 607–8.

229 See Dietrich Eichholtz, *Geschichte der deutschen Kriegswirtschaft 1939–1945. Band III: 1943–1945* (Berlin, 1996), pp. 663–8.

230 Walther Hubatsch (ed.), *Hitlers Weisungen für die Kriegführung 1939–1945. Dokumente des Oberkommandos der Wehrmacht* (Frankfurt am Main, 1962), pp. 256–58: Erlass des Führers über die Befehlsgewalt in einem Operationsgebiet innerhalb des Reiches vom 13. Juli 1944; pp. 259–60: Erlass des Führers über die Zusammenarbeit von Partei und Wehrmacht in einem Operationsgebiet innerhalb des Reiches vom 13. Juli 1944; pp. 260–4: Befehl des Chefs OKW betr. Vorbereitungen für die Verteidigung des Reichs, Der Chef des Oberkommandos der Wehrmacht, F.H.Qu., den 19.7.1944; pp. 294–5: Zweiter Erlass des Führers über die Zusammenarbeit von Partei und Wehrmacht in einem Operationsgebiet innerhalb des Reichs vom 19. September 1944; pp. 295–7: Zweiter Erlass des Führers über die Befehlsgewalt in einem Operationsgebiet innerhalb des Reiches vom 20. September 1944. See generally Kunz, 'Wehrmacht in der Agonie der nationalsozialistischen Herrschaft', pp. 103–4.

231 See David Keith Yelton, '"Ein Volk steht auf". The German Volkssturm and Nazi Strategy 1944–1945', *The Journal of Military History*, vol. 64 (2000), p. 1066–7.

232 Quoted in Yelton, "Ein Volk steht auf", p. 1069.

233 For thoughts along these lines, see Yelton, "Ein Volk steht auf", pp. 1068–70. See also Gerhard L. Weinberg, 'German Plans for Victory, 1944–1945', in his *Germany, Hitler and World War II. Essays in Modern German and World History* (Cambridge, 1994), pp. 274–86.

234 Himmler's Decree of 12 April 1945, printed in Rolf-Dieter Müller and Gerd R. Ueberschär, *Kriegsende 1945. Die Zerstörung des Deutschen Reiches* (Frankfurt am Main, 1994), p. 171.

235 For an account of the siege of Breslau, see Norman Davies and Roger Moorhouse, *Microcosm, Portrait of a Central European City* (London, 2003), pp. 13–37.

236 Erich Murawski, *Die Eroberung Pommerns durch die Rote Armee* (Boppard, 1969), pp. 341–2.

237 For one example, see Friedrich Blumenstock, *Der Einmarsch der Amerikaner und Franzosen im nördlichen Württemberg im April 1945* (Stuttgart, 1957), pp. 21–5.

238 'Mitteilungsblatt' of the NSDAP Kreisleitung in Küstrin, 5. Feb. 1945, reproduced in Hermann Thrams, *Küstrin 1945. Tagebuch einer Festung* (Berlin, 1992), p. 47.

239 Quoted in Hans-Martin Stimpel, *Widersinn 1945. Aufstellung, Einsatz und Untergang eines militärischen Verbandes* (Göttingen, 1998), p. 68.

240 Wagner, *Produktion des Todes*, p. 268.

241 Quoted in Wagner, *Produktion des Todes*, p. 332. Mittelbau-Dora received roughly 4,000 prisoners from Auschwitz in early 1945, followed by more than 10,000 from Gross-Rosen. See Wagner, *Produktion des Todes*, pp. 269–70.

242 Wagner, *Produktion des Todes*, pp. 272–3.

243 On this practice in the cities of the Ruhr region, where a large number of foreign workers had been employed in industry, see Herbert, *Hitler's Foreign Workers*, pp. 370–4.

244 See Gerhard Paul, *Landunter. Schleswig-Holstein und das Hakenkreuz* (Münster 2001), pp. 298–300.

245 Herbert, *Hitler's Foreign Workers*, p. 374.

246 Manfred Messerschmidt and Fritz Wüllner, *Die Wehrmachtjustiz im Dienste des Nationalsozialismus. Zerstörung einer Legende* (Baden-Baden, 1987), p. 131.

247 See, for example, Blumenstock, *Der Einmarsch der Amerikaner und Franzosen*, pp. 28–34.

248 Details in Kunz, 'Wehrmacht in der Agonie der nationalsozialistischen Herrschaft', p. 103, fn. 26.

249 Quoted in Rudolf Absolon (ed.), *Die Wehrmacht im Dritten Reich* (Band 6: 19. Dezember bis 9. Mai 1945) (Boppard am Rhein, 1995), p. 604.

250 Quoted in Messerschmidt and Wüllner, *Die Wehrmachtjustiz*, p. 117.

251 Hitler, *Mein Kampf*, p. 449. Hitler had been adamant that 'the deserter must be given to understand that his desertion will bring upon him just the very thing that he is flying from. At the front a man *may* die, but the deserter *must* die. Only this draconian threat against every attempt to desert the flag can have a terrifying effect, not merely on the individual but also on the mass.' See also Wette, *Die Wehrmacht*, p. 165.

252 By contrast, only one American soldier and no British soldiers were executed for desertion during the Second World War. See Steven R. Welch, '"Harsh but Just"? German Military Justice in the Second World War: A Comparative Study of the Court-Martialling of German and US Deserters', *German History*, vol. 17, no. 3 (1999), p. 389.

253 Quoted in Messerschmidt and Wüllner, *Die Wehrmachtjustiz*, p. 118.

254 *Reichsgesetzblatt* 1945, I, p. 30: Verordnung über die Errichtung von Standgerichten vom 15. Februar 1945.

255 Quoted in Henke, *Die amerikanische Besetzung Deutschlands*, p. 845.

256 Quoted in Absolon (ed.), *Die Wehrmacht im Dritten Reich*, p. 604.

257 Sixth Army Group, G-2, Weekly Intelligence Summary Nr. 32, 28 April 1945. Quoted in Henke, *Die amerikanische Besetzung Deutschlands*, p. 853.

258 See Antony Beevor, *Berlin. The Downfall 1945* (London, 2002).

259 See Dietrich Eichholtz, *Geschichte der deutschen Kriegswirtschaft 1939–1945. Band III: 1943–1945* (Berlin, 1996), pp. 632–4.

260 Andreas Kunz, 'Zweierlei Untergang: Das Militär in der Schlussphase der nationalsozialistischen Herrschaft zwischen Sommer 1944 und Frühjahr 1945' (Phil. Diss., Universität der Bundeswehr Hamburg, 2003), p. 4.

261 For a good, concise discussion of the Dönitz government, see Martin Kitchen, *Nazi Germany at War* (London, 1995), pp. 288–301.

262 This can be seen in German women's subsequent recollections of the war which, as Elizabeth Heineman has pointed out, 'focus on the events which most dramatically affected their lives: bombing raids, evacuation, flight, widowhood, rape and hunger.' See Heineman, *What Difference Does a Husband Make?*, p. 79.

4. The Aftermath of the Second World War

1 Text in Jeremy Noakes (ed.), *Nazism 1919–1945. Volume 4. The German Home Front in World War II* (Exeter, 1998), pp. 667–71.

2 Interrogation of Hermann Goering taken at Nuremberg on 3 October 1945 by Colonel J. H. Amen, in Richard Overy, *Interrogations. The Nazi Elite in Allied Hands, 1945* (London, 2002), p. 312.

3 On this theme, see Richard Bessel, 'Hatred after War', in Alon Confino (ed.), *Thinking of Twentieth-Century Germany* (forthcoming).

4 Marlis Steinert, *Hitler's War and the Germans. Public Mood and Attitude during the Second World War* (Athens, Ohio, 1977), p. 288.

5 In Berlin alone more than 7,000 Germans took their own lives in 1945, nearly 4,000 of them women. See Ursula Baumann, *Vom Recht auf den eigenen Tod. Die Geschichte des Suizids vom 18. bis zum 20. Jahrhundert* (Weimar, 2001), p. 377.

6 Quoted in Susanne zur Nieden, *Alltag im Ausnahmezustand. Frauentagebücher im zerstörten Deutschland 1943 bis 1945* (Berlin, 1993), p. 160.

7 Baumann, *Vom Recht auf den eigenen Tod*, p. 376.

8 Mecklenburgisches Landeshauptarchiv Schwerin, Kreistag/Rat des Kreises Demmin, Nr. 46, ff. 62–64: [Der Landrat] des Kreises Demmin to the Präsidenten des Landes Mecklenburg-Vorpommern, Abteilung Innere Verwaltung, 'Tätigkeitsbericht', [Demmin], 21 Nov. 1945.

9 Quoted in Damian van Melis, *Entnazifizierung in Mecklenburg-Vorpommern. Herrschaft und Verwaltung 1945–1948* (Munich, 1999), pp. 23–4.

10 Norman M. Naimark, *Fires of Hatred. Ethnic Cleansing in Twentieth-Century Europe* (Cambridge, Mass., and London, 2001), p. 117.

11 Letter of General Serov to Beria, 8 June 1945, quoted in Naimark, *Fires of Hatred*, p. 117.

12 Arthur L. Smith, *Heimkehr aus dem Zweiten Weltkrieg. Die Entlassung der deutschen Kriegsgefangenen* (Stuttgart, 1985), p. 11.

13 Andreas Hilger, *Deutsche Kriegsgefangene in der Sowjetunion, 1941–1956. Kriegsgefangenenpolitik, Lageralitag und Erinnerung* (Essen, 2000), pp. 314–67. The last of the 'Heimkehrer' from Soviet POW camps arrived in the Federal Republic and the GDR in January 1956.

14 In November 1944 the number of evacuated people registered throughout the Reich stood at 7,769,880, with an additional 460,648 who had been transferred when the factories in which they worked were moved. See Katja Klee, *Im 'Luftschutzkeller des Reiches'. Evakuierte in Bayern: Politik, soziale Lage, Erfahrungen* (Munich, 1999), p. 175.

15 In West Germany in 1950 there were still over a million men listed as 'missing'. See Elizabeth D. Heineman, *What Difference Does a Husband Make? Women and Marital Status in Nazi and Postwar Germany* (Berkeley, Los Angeles and London, 1999), p. 118.

16 Heinz Petzold, 'Cottbus zwischen Januar und Mai 1945', in Werner Stang and Kurt Arlt (eds.), *Brandenburg im Jahr 1945. Studien* (Potsdam 1995), pp. 124–5.

17 Quoted in Petzold, 'Cottbus zwischen Januar und Mai 1945', p. 125.

18 Marie-Luise Recker, 'Wohnen und Bombardierung im Zweiten Weltkrieg', in Lutz Niethammer (ed.), *Wohnen im Wandel. Beiträge zur Geschichte des Alltags in der bürgerlichen Gesellschaft* (Wuppertal, 1979), p. 410.

19 See, for example, Andreas Hofmann, *Nachkriegszeit in Schlesien. Gesellschafis- und Bevölkerungspolitik in den polnischen Siedlungsgebieten 1945–1948* (Cologne, Weimar and Vienna, 2000), pp. 21–2.

20 According to the first postwar census, there were 126 females to 100 males; in Berlin, the ratio was 146 females to 100 males. See Robert G. Moeller, *Protecting Motherhood. Women and the Family in the Politics of Postwar West Germany* (Berkeley and Los Angeles, 1993), p. 27.

21 Norman Naimark, *The Russians in Germany. A History of the Soviet Zone of Occupation, 1945–1949* (Cambridge, Mass., 1995), pp. 69–140; Atina Grossmann, 'A Question of Silence: The Rape of German Women by Occupation Soldiers', in Robert G. Moeller (ed.), *West Germany under*

Construction. Politics, Society and Culture in the Adenauer Era (Ann Arbor, Mich., 1997), pp. 33–53; Elizabeth Heineman, 'The Hour of the Woman: Memories of Germany's "Crisis Years" and West German Identity', *American Historical Review*, vol. 101, no. 2 (1996), pp. 364–74; Andrea Pető, 'Memory and the Narrative of Rape in Budapest and Vienna in 1945', in Richard Bessel and Dirk Schumann (eds), *Life after Death. Approaches to a Cultural and Social History of Europe during the 1940s and 1950s* (Cambridge, 2003), pp. 129–48.

22 Quoted in zur Nieden, *Alltag im Ausnahmezustand*, p. 187.

23 Atina Grossmann, 'Trauma, Memory, and Motherhood. Germans and Jewish Displaced Persons in Post-Nazi Germany, 1945–1949', in Bessel and Schumann (eds), *Life after Death*, pp. 100–1.

24 See Lutz Niethammer, 'Privat-Wirtschaft. Erinnerungsfragmente einer anderen Umerziehung', in Lutz Niethammer (ed.), *'Hinterher merkt man, dass es richtig war, dass es schiefgegangen ist'. Nachkriegs-Erfahrungen im Ruhrgebiet* (Berlin and Bonn, 1983), pp. 22–34.

25 This was made clear by Walter Ulbricht in May 1945. When confronted by Communists asking how doctors were to respond to women who had been raped and were seeking abortions, Ulbricht stated curtly that this was not a theme for discussion. See Wolfgang Leonhard, *Die Revolution entlässt ihre Kinder* (Cologne, 1990), pp. 461–2.

26 Heineman, 'The Hour of the Woman', p. 367.

27 Helene Albers, *Zwischen Hof, Haushalt und Familie. Bäuerinnen in Westfalen-Lippe (1920–1960)* (Paderborn, 2001), p. 380.

28 Michael L. Highes, '"Through No Fault of Our Own": West Germans Remember Their War Losses', *German History*, vol. 18, no. 2 (2000), p. 193.

29 Sabine Behrenbeck, 'Heldenkult oder Friedensmahnung? Kriegerdenkmale nach beiden Weltkriegen', in Gottfried Niedhart and Dieter Riesenberger (eds), *Lernen aus dem Krieg? Deutsche Nachkriegszeiten 1918 und 1945. Beitrage zur historischen Friedensforschung* (Munich, 1992), p. 361.

30 Hughes, '"Through No Fault of Our Own"', p. 194.

31 See Michael L. Hughes, *Shouldering the Burdens of Defeat: West Germany and the Reconstruction of Social Justice* (Chapel Hill, 1999), pp. 151–89.

32 Hughes, '"Through No Fault of Our Own"', p. 211.

33 Quoted in Michael Wildt, *Generation des Unbedingten. Das Führungskorps des Reichssicherheitshauptamtes* (Hamburg, 2002), p. 143.

34 Quoted in Clemens Vollnhals, *Evangelische Kirche und Entnazifizierung 1945–1949. Die Last der nationalsozialistischen Vergangenheit* (Munich, 1989), p. 134.

35 Richard Bessel, 'Polizei zwischen Krieg und Sozialismus. Die Anfänge der Volkspolizei nach dem Zweiten Weltkrieg', in Christian Jansen, Lutz Niethammer and Bernd Weisbrod (eds), *Von der Aufgabe der Freiheit. Politische Verantwortung und bürgerliche Gesellschaft im 19. und 20. Jahrhundert. Festschrift für Hans Mommsen zum 5. November 1995* (Berlin, 1995), pp. 525–6.

36 See Heinemann, *What Difference Does a Husband Make?*, pp. 75–107.

37 Heinemann, *What Difference Does a Husband Make?*, p. 127.

38 Quoted in Grossmann, 'Trauma, Memory and Motherhood', p. 122.

39 See the perceptive observations in Frank Biess, 'Männer des Wiederaufbaus – Wiederaufbau der Männer. Kriegsheimkehrer in Ost- und Westdeutschland, 1945–1955', in Karen Hagemann and Stefanie Schüler Springorum (eds), *Heimat-Front. Militär und Geschlechterverhältnisse im Zeitalter der Weltkriege* (Frankfurt am Main and New York, 2002), pp. 354–6.

40 Steinert, *Hitler's War and the Germans*, pp. 313–14.

41 Klaus-Dietmar Henke, *Die amerikanische Besetzung Deutschlands* (Munich, 1995), p. 943.

42 Uwe Backes and Eckhard Jesse, *Politischer Extremismus in der Bundesrepublik Deutschland* (Cologne, 1989), p. 62.

43 See Backes and Jesse, *Politischer Extremismus*, pp. 63–6.

44 Protocol of the Proceedings at Potsdam, 1 August 1945, II. A. 3 (i). Source: <http://www.cnn.com/SPECIALS/cold.war/episodes/01/documents/potsdam.html>.

45 Holger Afflerbach, 'Das Militär in der deutschen Gesellschaft nach 1945', in Holger Afflerbach and Christoph Cornelissen (eds), *Sieger und Besiegte. Materielle und ideele Neuorientierungen nach 1945* (Tübingen and Basel, 1997), p. 249.

46 Wolfram Wette, 'Die deutsche militärische Führungsschicht in den Nachkriegszeiten', in Niedhart and Riesenberger (eds), *Lernen aus dem Krieg?*, p. 40.

47 Quoted in Afflerbach, 'Das Militär in der deutschen Gesellschaft nach 1945', p. 250.

48 Michael Geyer, 'Cold War Angst. The Case of West-German Opposition to Rearmament and Nuclear Weapons', in Hanna Schissler (ed.), *The Miracle Years. A Cultural History of West Germany, 1949–1968* (Princeton and Oxford, 2001), p. 387.

49 Mecklenburgisches Landeshauptarchiv Schwerin, Kreistag/Rat des Kreises Uekermünde/Pasewalk, Nr. 118, ff. 2–4: Kreisverwaltung Pasewalk, Landrat, Abt. Information, Pasewalk, 14 July 1952.

50 Wette, 'Die deutsche militärische Führungsschicht in den Nach-kriegszeiten', p. 40.

51 According to a poll conducted in July 1952, two thirds (66 per cent) of those asked 'do you have the feeling that we are threatened by Russia or not?' answered that they felt threatened. Quoted in Afflerbach, 'Das Militär in der deutschen Gesellschaft nach 1945', p. 250.

52 In 1958 a mere 2,447, or 0.5 per cent of the 464,418 men called for military service refused; at the peak, in 1991, the proportion had risen to almost two fifths (39.7 per cent). See Afflerbach, 'Das Militär in der deutschen Gesellschaft nach 1945', p. 263.

53 Wette, *Die Wehrmacht. Feindbilder, Vernichtungskrieg, Legenden* (Frankfurt am Main, 2002), pp. 204–5.

54 Erich von Manstein, *Verlorene Siege* (Bonn, 1955).

55 Franz Halder, *Hitler als Feldherr* (Munich, 1949).

56 Johannes Klotz, 'Die Ausstellung "Vernichtungskrieg. Verbrechen der Wehrmacht 1941 bis 1944". Zwischen Geschichtswissenschaft und Ge-schichtspolitik', in Detlev Bald, Johannes Klotz and Wolfram Wette, *Mythos Wehrmacht. Nachkriegsdebatten und Traditionspflege* (Berlin, 2001), pp. 116–76.

57 Norbert Frei, *Vergangenheitspolitik Die Anfänge der Bundesrepublik und die NS-Vergangenheit* (Munich, 1996), p. 77.

58 For example, in a poll conducted in October 1953 well over half (55 per cent) of the people questioned denied that accusations could be levelled against the behaviour of Wehrmacht soldiers in the occupied territories; 21 per cent answered yes, but only in isolated instances; and a mere 6 per cent answered with an unambiguous 'yes'. See Militärgeschichtliches Forschungsamt (ed.), *Anfänge westdeutscher Sicherheitspolitik 1945–1956, Band 2, Die EVG-Phase* (bearbeitet von Lutz Köllner u.a.) (Munich, 1990), p. 487.

59 See Robert G. Moeller, *War Stories. The Search for a Usable Past in the Federal Republic of Germany* (Berkeley, Los Angeles and London, 2001).

60 See the suggestive comments by Sabine Behrenbeck, 'The Transformation of Sacrifice: German Identity between Heroic Narrative and Economic Success', in Paul Betts and Greg Eghigian (eds), *Pain and Prosperity. Reconsidering Twentieth-Century German History* (Stanford, 2003), esp. pp. 134–5.

61 See Klotz, 'Die Ausstellung'.

62 Ulrich Herbert, 'Good Times, Bad Times: Memories of the Third Reich', in Richard Bessel (ed.), *Life in the Third Reich* (2nd edn, Oxford, 2001), pp. 97–110.

63 Statistisches Bundesamt (ed.), *Die deutschen Vertreibungsverluste. Bevöl-kerungsbilanzen für die deutschen Vertreibungsgebiete 1939/50* (Wiesbaden, 1958), p. 33.

64 Protocol of the Proceedings at Potsdam, 1 August 1945, XII. Orderly Transfer of German Populations. Source: <http://www.cnn.com/ SPECIALS/cold.war/episodes/01/documents/potsdam.html>.

65 Statistisches Bundesamt (ed.), *Die deutschen vertreibungsverluste*, p. 37.

66 Naimark, *Fires of Hatred*, pp. 108–38; Norman Davies and Roger Moorhouse, *Microcosm. Portrait of a Central European City* (London, 2003), pp. 417–25.

67 See the series published during the 1950s by the West German Ministry for Refugees and edited by Theodor Schieder, Bundesministerium für Vertriebene (ed.), *Dokumentation der Vertreibung der Deutschen aus Ost-Mitteleuropa* (Bonn, 1957).

68 Götz Aly, *Rasse und Klasse. Nachforschungen zum deutschen Wesen* (Frankfurt am Main, 2003), p. 232.

69 'Vorwort', Bundesministerium für Vertriebene (ed.), (bearbeitet von Theodor Schieder), *Die Vertreibung der deutschen Bevolkerung aus den Gebieten östlich der Oder-Neisse* (Band I/1. *Dokumentation der Vertreibung der Deutschen aus Ost-Mitteleuropa*) (Bonn, 1953), p. I.

70 This was a main reason for the removal by the Soviet Military Administration of Andreas Hermes from the leadership of the Christian Democratic Union in the Soviet Occupation Zone in December 1945. See Stefan Donth, *Vertriebene und Flüchtlinge in Sachsen 1945–1952. Die Politik der Sowjetischen Militäradministration unter der SED* (Cologne, Weimar and Vienna, 2000), pp. 82–92.

71 While roughly half of the political refugees from Nazi Germany returned, at most only about 4 per cent of those who had left for 'racial' reasons did so. Werner Röder and Herbert A. Strauss (eds), *Biographisches Handbuch der deutschsprachigen Emigration nach 1933/International Biographical Dictionary of Central European Emigrés 1933–1945*, Volume II, Part 1 (Munich, 1983), p. xxxxix.

72 Frank Stern, 'The Historic Triangle: Occupiers, Germans and Jews in Postwar Germany', in Robert G. Moeller (ed.), *West Germany under Construction. Politics, Society and Culture in the Adenauer Era* (Ann Arbor, 1997), p. 202.

73 Michael Brenner, 'East European and German Jews in Postwar Germany 1945–50', in Y. Michal Bodemann (ed.), *Jews, Germans, Memory: Reconstructions of Jewish Life in Germany* (Ann Arbor, Mich., 1996), p. 50.

74 See Constantin Goschler, 'The Attitude towards Jews in Bavaria after the

Second World War', in Robert G. Moeller (ed.), *West Germany under Construction*, pp. 231–3.

75 Speech by Major General Gerald Templer, Director of the British Military Government, at a Konferenz der Chefs der Länder und Provinzen der britischen Zone in Detmold, 19./20. November 1945, in *Akten zur Vorgeschichte der Bundesrepublik Deutschland 1945–1949, Band 1, September 1945–Dezember 1946, Teil 1* (Munich, 1989), p. 156.

76 Henke, *Die amerikanische Besetzung Deutschlands*, pp. 847–8; Susanne Schlösser, ' "Was sich in den Weg stellt, mit Vernichtung schlagen". Richard Drauz, NSDAP-Kreisleiter von Heilbronn', in Michael Kissner and Joachim Scholtyseck (eds), *Die Führer der Provinz. NS-Biographien aus Baden und Württemberg* (Konstanz, 1997), p. 157.

77 As of 1 January 1947, the number of those who had been interned in all four zones stood at 249,892 (95,250 in the American Zone, 68,500 in the British, 18,963 in the French, and 67,179 in the Soviet); of these, 93,498 had been released by this date (44,244 in the American Zone, 34,000 in the British, 8040 in the French, and 7214 in the Soviet Zone). See Clemens Vollnhals (ed.), *Entnazifizierung. Politische Säuberung und Rehabilitierung in den vier Besatzungszonen 1945–1949* (Munich, 1991), p. 251.

78 Protocol of the Proceedings at Potsdam, 1 August 1945, II.A.6. Source: <http://www.cnn.com/SPECIALS/cold.war/episodes/01/documents/potsdam. html>.

79 Norbert Frei, 'Hitlers Eliten nach 1945 – eine Bilanz', in Norbert Frei (ed.), *Karrieren im Zwielicht. Hitlers Eliten nach 1945* (2nd edn., Frankfurt am Main and New York, 2002), p. 306.

80 Jeffrey Herf, *Divided Memory. The Nazi Past in the Two Germanys* (Cambridge, Mass., and London, 1997), pp. 335–37.

81 See generally Frei (ed.), *Karrieren im Zwielicht*.

82 Vollnhals (ed.), *Entnazifizierung*, p. 18.

83 Vollnhals (ed.), *Entnazifizierung*, p. 19.

84 See the denazification statistics for the western zones, in Vollnhals (ed.), *Entnazifizierung*, pp. 332–3.

85 See especially Lutz Niethammer, *Die Mitläuferfabrik. Die Entnazifizierung am Beispiel Bayerns* (Bonn and Berlin, 1982).

86 Dieter Stiefel, *Entnazifizierung in Österreich* (Vienna, Munich and Zürich, 1981), pp. 308–9.

87 See Stiefel, *Entnazifizierung in Österreich*, pp. 326–8.

88 Karl Heinrich Knappstein, 'Die versäumte Revolution', *Die Wandlung* (August 1947). Printed in Vollnhals (ed.), *Entnazifizierung*, pp. 310–11.

89 See Vollnhals (ed.), *Entnazifizierung*, p. 61.

90 Regierungserklärung des Bundeskanzlers Konrad Adenauer vom 20. September 1949. Source: <http://www.dhm.de/lemo/html/dokumente/ JahreDesAufbausInOstUndWest_erklaerungAdenauerRegierungserk laerung1949/>.

91 Speech by Major General Gerald Templer, Director of the British Military Government, at a conference of the heads of the Länder and Provinces of the British Zone in Detmold, 19/20 November 1945, in *Akten zur Vorgeschichte der Bundesrepublik Deutschland 1945–1949, Band 1, September 1945–Dezember 1946, Teil 1* (Munich, 1989), p. 157.

92 See Frei, *Vergangenheitspolitik*; Frei (ed.), *Karrieren im Zwielicht*.

93 See van Melis, *Entnazifizierung in Mecklenburg-Vorpommern*; Timothy R. Vogt, *Denazification in Soviet-Occupied Germany. Brandenburg, 1945–1948* (Cambridge, Mass., and London, 2000). For a concise discussion of the denazification in the Soviet Zone, see Vollnhals (ed.), *Entnazifizierung*, pp. 43–55.

94 According to data released by the Soviet Foreign Ministry in July 1990, of the 122,671 people who were interned close to 43,000 died as a consequence of disease; 776 were sentenced to death. See Vollnhals (ed.), *Entnazifizierung*, p. 55.

95 Frei (ed.), *Karrieren im Zwielicht*, p. 129.

96 Hannah Arendt, 'The Aftermath of Nazi Rule. Report from Germany', in *Commentary*, 10 (October 1950), pp. 342–53, here pp. 342–3.

97 Ian Kershaw, *Hitler 1889–1936: Hubris* (London, 1998), p. xxx.

SELECT BIBLIOGRAPHY

Michael Thad Allen, *The Business of Genocide. The SS, Slave Labor, and the Concentration Camps* (Chapel Hill and London, 2002).

William Sheridan Allen, *The Nazi Seizure of Power. The Experience of a Single German Town* (revised edition, London, 1989).

Götz Aly, *'Final Solution'. Nazi Population Policy and the Murder of the European Jews* (London, 1999).

Pierre Aycoberry, *The Nazi Question* (London, 1983).

Omer Bartov, *The Barbarisation of Warfare. German Officers and Soldiers in Combat on the Eastern Front, 1941–1945* (London, 1986).

Omer Bartov, *Hitler's Army. Soldiers, Nazis, and War in the Third Reich* (Oxford, 1991).

Omer Bartov, *Murder in our Midst: the Holocaust, Industrial Killing, and Representation* (New York and Oxford, 1996).

Omer Bartov (ed.), *The Holocaust. Origins, Implementation, Aftermath* (London, 2000).

Richard Bessel, *Political Violence and the Rise of Nazism* (New Haven and London, 1984).

Richard Bessel (ed.), *Fascist Italy and Nazi Germany. Comparisons and Contrasts* (Cambridge, 1996).

Richard Bessel (ed.), *Life in the Third Reich* (revised edition, Oxford, 2001).

Richard Bessel and Dirk Schuman (eds), *Life after Death. Approaches to a Cultural and Social History of Europe during the 1940s and 1950s* (Cambridge, 2003).

Karl Dietrich Bracher, *The German Dictatorship. The Origins, Structure and Effects of National Socialism* (Harmondsworth, 1971).

Richard Breitman, *The Architect of Genocide: Himmler and the Final Solution* (Hanover, NH, 1991).

Renate Bridenthal, et al., *When Biology Became Destiny. Women in Weimar and Nazi Germany* (New York, 1984).

Martin Broszat, *The Hitler State. The Foundation and Development of the Internal Structure of the Third Reich* (London, 1981).

Christopher Browning, *Fateful Months. Essays on the Emergence of the Final Solution* (Cambridge, 1991).

Christopher Browning, *Ordinary Men. Reserve Police Battalion 101 and the Final Solution in Poland* (New York, 1992).

Christopher Browning, *The Path to Genocide. Essays on the Launching of the Final Solution* (Cambridge, 1992).

Christopher Browning, *Nazi Policy, Jewish Labor, German Killers* (Cambridge, 2000).

Evan Burr Bukey, *Hitler's Austria. Popular Sentiment in the Nazi Era, 1938–1945* (Chapel Hill and London, 2000).

Hedley Bull (ed.), *The Challenge of the Third Reich* (Oxford, 1986).

Michael Burleigh (ed.), *Confronting the Nazi Past* (London, 1996).

Michael Burleigh, *The Third Reich. A New History* (London, 2000).

Michael Burleigh and Wolfgang Wippermann, *The Racial State. Germany 1933–1945* (Cambridge, 1991).

Jane Caplan and Thomas Childers (eds), *Reevaluating the Third Reich* (New York, 1993).

William Carr, *Arms, Autarky and Aggression. A Study in German Foreign Policy, 1933–1945* (London, 1972).

William Carr, *Hitler: A Study of Personality in Politics* (London, 1978).

Thomas Childers, *The Nazi Voter. The Social Foundations of Fascism in Germany* (Chapel Hill and London, 1983).

Thomas Childers (ed.), *The Formation of the Nazi Constituency 1918–1933* (London, 1986).

David F. Crew (ed.), *Nazism and German Society 1933–1945* (London, 1994).

Wilhelm Deist, *The Wehrmacht and German Rearmament* (London, 1982).

Richard J. Evans, *The Coming of the Third Reich* (London, 2003).

Conan Fischer, *Stormtroopers. A Social, Economic and Ideological Analysis 1929–1935* (London, 1983).

Norbert Frei, *National Socialist Rule in Germany. The Führer State 1933–1945* (Oxford, 1993).

Henry Friedlander, *The Origins of Nazi Genocide: From Euthanasia to the Final Solution* (Chapel Hill and London, 1995).

Saul Friedländer, *Nazi Germany and the Jews*, vol. i.: *The Years of Persecution 1933–1939* (New York, 1997).

Peter Fritzsche, *Germans into Nazis* (Cambridge, Mass., 1998).

Robert Gellately, *The Gestapo and German Society. Enforcing Racial Policy 1933–1945* (Oxford, 1990).

Robert Gellately, *Backing Hitler. Consent and Coercion in Nazi Germany* (Oxford, 2001).

Robert Gellately and Nathan Stoltzfus (eds), *Social Outsiders in Nazi Germany* (Princeton, 2001).

Michael Geyer and John W. Boyer (eds), *Resistance against the Third Reich, 1933–1990* (Chicago, 1994).

Hermann Graml, *Antisemitism in the Third Reich* (Oxford, 1992).

Richard Grunberger, *A Social History of the Third Reich* (Harmondsworth, 1974).

Elizabeth D. Heineman, *What Difference Does a Husband Make? Women and Marital Status in Nazi and Postwar Germany* (Berkeley, Los Angeles and London, 1999).

Ulrich Herbert, *Hitler's Foreign Workers: Enforced Foreign Labor in Germany under the Third Reich* (Cambridge, 1997).

Ulrich Herbert (ed.), *National Socialist Extermination Policies. Contemporary German Perspectives and Controversies* (New York and Oxford, 2000).

Klaus Hildebrand, *The Third Reich* (London, 1984).

Gerhard Hirschfeld (ed.), *The Politics of Genocide. Jews and Soviet Prisoners of War in Nazi Germany* (London, 1986).

Konrad H. Jarausch and Michael Geyer, *Shattered Past. Reconstructing German Histories* (Princeton and Oxford, 2003).

Eric Johnson, *The Nazi Terror. The Gestapo, Jews and Ordinary Germans* (London, 2000).

Marion Kaplan, *Between Dignity and Despair: Jewish Life in Nazi Germany* (New York, 1998).

Michael Kater, *The Nazi Party. A Social Profile of Members and Leaders, 1919–1945* (Oxford, 1983).

Ian Kershaw, *Popular Opinion and Political Dissent in the Third Reich. Bavaria, 1933–45* (Oxford, 1983).

Ian Kershaw, *The 'Hitler Myth'. Image and Reality in the Third Reich* (Oxford, 1987).

Ian Kershaw (ed.), *Weimar: Why Did German Democracy Fail?* (London, 1990).

Ian Kershaw, *The Nazi Dictatorship. Problems and Perspectives of Interpretation* (fourth edition, London, 2000).

Ian Kershaw, *Hitler, 1889–1936: Hubris* (London, 1998).

Ian Kershaw, *Hitler, 1936–1945: Nemesis* (London, 2000).

Ian Kershaw and Moshe Levin (eds), *Stalinism and Nazism: Dictatorship in Comparison* (Cambridge, 1997).

Martin Kitchen, *Nazi Germany at War* (London, 1995).

MacGregor Knox, *Common Destiny. Dictatorship, Foreign Policy, and War in Fascist Italy and Nazi Germany* (Cambridge, 2000).

David Clay Large (ed.), *Contending with Hitler. Varieties of German Resistance in the Third Reich* (Cambridge, 1991).

Christian Leitz (ed.), *The Third Reich* (Oxford, 1999).

Tim Mason, *Social Policy in the Third Reich. The Working Class and the 'National Community'* (Providence and Oxford, 1993).

Tim Mason, *Nazism, Fascism and the Working Class* (Cambridge, 1996).

Mark Mazower, *Inside Hitler's Greece: The Experience of Occupation 1941–1944* (New Haven, 1993).

Allen Merson, *Communist Resistance in Nazi Germany* (London, 1985).

Robert G. Moeller, *War Stories. The Search for a Usable Past in the Federal Republic of Germany* (Berkeley, Los Angeles and London, 2001).

Hans Mommsen, *From Weimar to Auschwitz. Essays in German History* (Oxford, 1991).

Hans Mommsen, *The Rise and Fall of Weimar Democracy* (Chapel Hill and London, 1996).

George L. Mosse, *Fallen Soldiers. Reshaping the Memory of the World Wars* (New York, 1990).

Klaus-Jürgen Müller, *The Army, Politics, and Society in Germany, 1933–1945: Studies in the Army's Relationship to Nazism* (Manchester, 1987).

Jeremy Noakes (ed.), *Nazism 1919–1945* (4 vols, Exeter, 1983, 1984, 1988, 1998).

R. J. Overy, *War and Economy in the Third Reich* (Oxford, 1994).

R. J. Overy, *The Nazi Economic Recovery, 1932–1938* (second edition, Cambridge, 1996).

Detlev J. K. Peukert, *Inside Nazi Germany. Conformity and Opposition in Everyday Life* (London, 1987).

Detlev J. K. Peukert, *The Weimar Republic. The Crisis of Classical Modernity* (London, 1991).

Lisa Pine, *Nazi Family Policy, 1933–1945* (Oxford, 1997).

Laurence Rees, *The Nazis. A Warning from History* (London, 1998).

Karl A. Schleunes, *The Twisted Road to Auschwitz. Nazi Policy towards German Jews 1933–1939* (Chicago, 1970).

David Schoenbaum, *Hitler's Social Revolution. Class and Status in Nazi Germany, 1933–1939* (New York and London, 1997).

Theo Schulte, *The German Army and Nazi Policies in Occupied Russia* (Providence, 1989).

Peter D. Stachura (ed.), *The Shaping of the Nazi State* (London, 1978).

Peter D. Stachura (ed.), *The Nazi Machtergreifung* (London, 1983).

Marlis Steinert, *Hitler's War and the Germans* (Athens, Ohio, 1977).

Jill Stephenson, *Women in Nazi Germany* (London, 1975).

Henry A. Turner (ed.), *Nazism and the Third Reich* (New York, 1972).

Henry A. Turner, *German Big Business and the Rise of Hitler* (New York and Oxford, 1985).

Henry A. Turner, *Hitler's Thirty Days to Power* (London, 1996).

Nikolaus Wachsmann, *Hitler's Prisons. Legal Terror in Nazi Germany* (New Haven and London, 2004).

Gerhard L. Weinberg, *A World at Arms. A Global History of World War II* (Cambridge, 1994).

David Welch, *The Third Reich: Politics and Propaganda* (London, 1993).

Robert S. Wistrich, *Hitler and the Holocaust* (New York, 2001).

INDEX